THE BATTLE OF THREE RIVERS PART ONE

SKYWARD™

ACTION LAB

7

$2.99

DALE
ROCHELLE
LOVETT
DOWNER
ZAHLER

COMIC GEEK SPEAK
BEST OF 2013
NOMINEE

Skyward - Action Lab - Cover A
www.actionlabcomics.com
7 99475 50681 9 00711

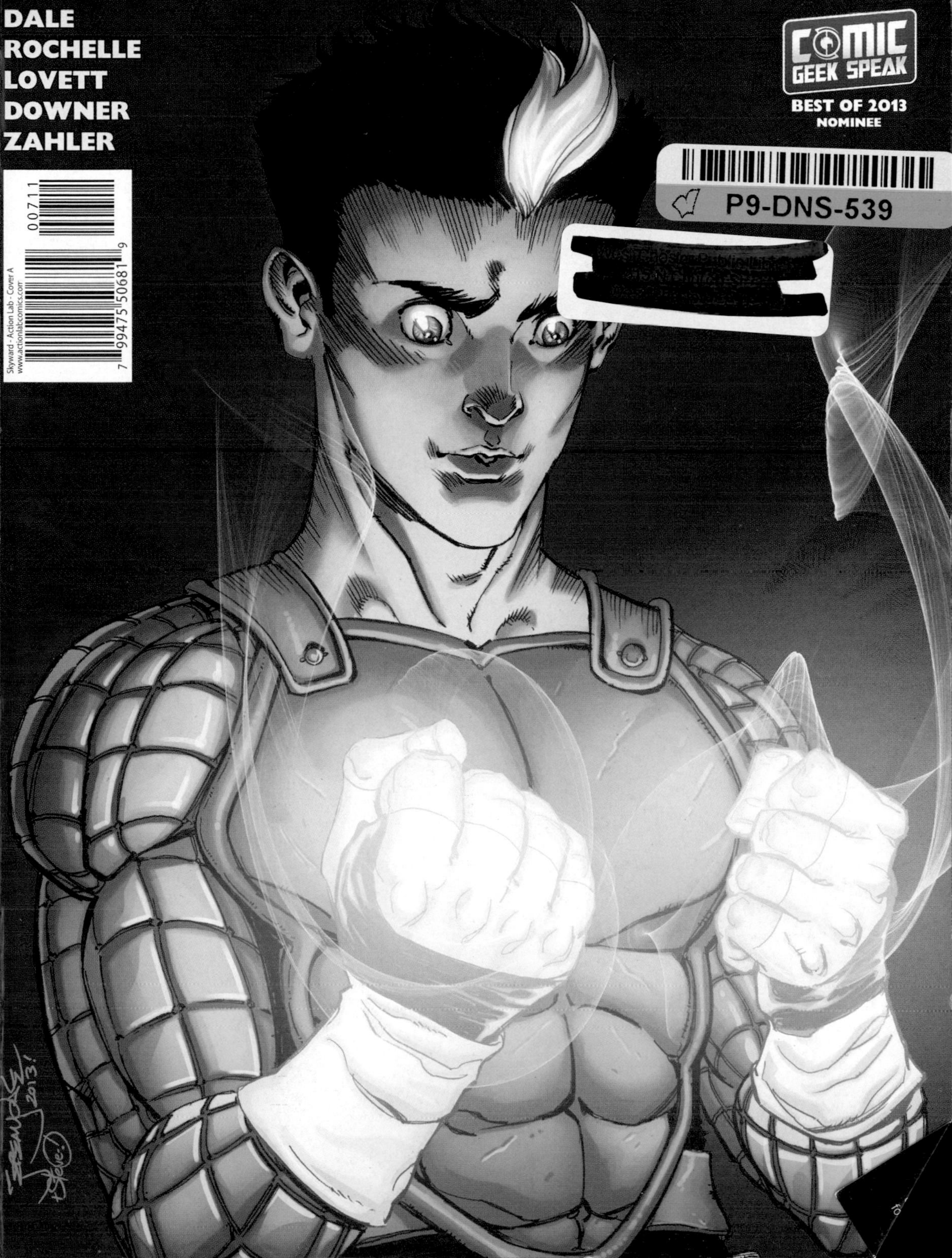

SKYWARD ™

BATTLE OF THREE RIVERS

Jeremy Dale
Creator / Writer / Artist
@jeremydale

Nate Lovett
Colors, interior pages 2-4, 6-8, 12
@natelovett

James Rochelle
Colors, interior pages 1, 5, 9, 11
facebook.com/james.rochelle1

Dash Martin
Colors, interior page 10
@dashmartin

Thom Zahler
Letters
@loveandcapes

Hoyt Silva
Color Flats
@hoytsilva

Covers by
Jeremy Dale
@jeremydale

and

Phil Noto
@philnoto

Previously:

Prince Dom of Three Rivers and his lifelong friend, Mia, are hopelessly lost in the woods, trying to track down the city's elite guards, The River Riders-- who are in turn seeking out signs of an invading army at their doorsteps.

So far, no luck on all ends.

Meanwhile, Jon has helped the Rabites end Skerrigan's brutal attack on the camp-- Do ya think Abigail saw?

Was she, um-- impressed?

Dude, you gotta tell me.

For more visit
www.skywardcomic.com

FOR ACTION LAB ENTERTAINMENT
Kevin Freeman - **President**
Bryan Seaton - **Chief Financial Officer**
Shawn Pryor - **VP Digital Media**
Dave Dwonch - **Creative Director**
Shawn Gabborin - **Editor In Chief**
Jason Martin - **Editor**
Kelly Dale & Jamal Igle - **Directors of Marketing**
Jim Dietz - **Social Media Director**
Jeremy Whitley - **Education Outreach Director**
Chad Cicconi & Colleen Boyd - **Associate Editors**
WWW.ACTIONLABCOMICS.COM

jeremy-dale.com

JEREMY DALE - the talent

KELLY DALE - project editor

KIRBY THE DOG - canine relations

WWW.JEREMY-DALE.COM

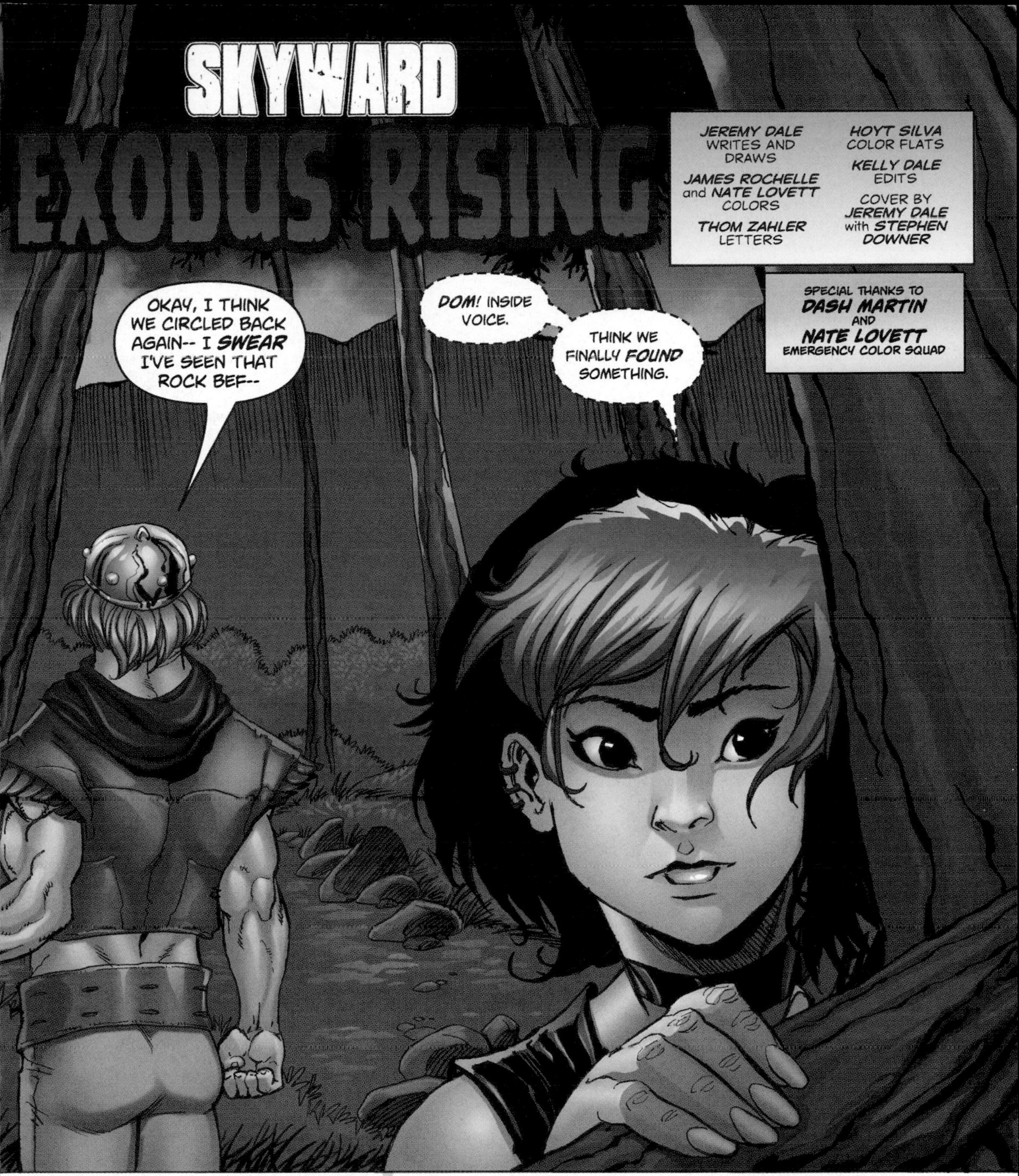
SKYWARD
EXODUS RISING
JEREMY DALE WRITES AND DRAWS
JAMES ROCHELLE and NATE LOVETT COLORS
THOM ZAHLER LETTERS
HOYT SILVA COLOR FLATS
KELLY DALE EDITS
COVER BY JEREMY DALE with STEPHEN DOWNER
SPECIAL THANKS TO DASH MARTIN AND NATE LOVETT EMERGENCY COLOR SQUAD
OKAY, I THINK WE CIRCLED BACK AGAIN-- I SWEAR I'VE SEEN THAT ROCK BEF--
DOM! INSIDE VOICE.
THINK WE FINALLY FOUND SOMETHING.

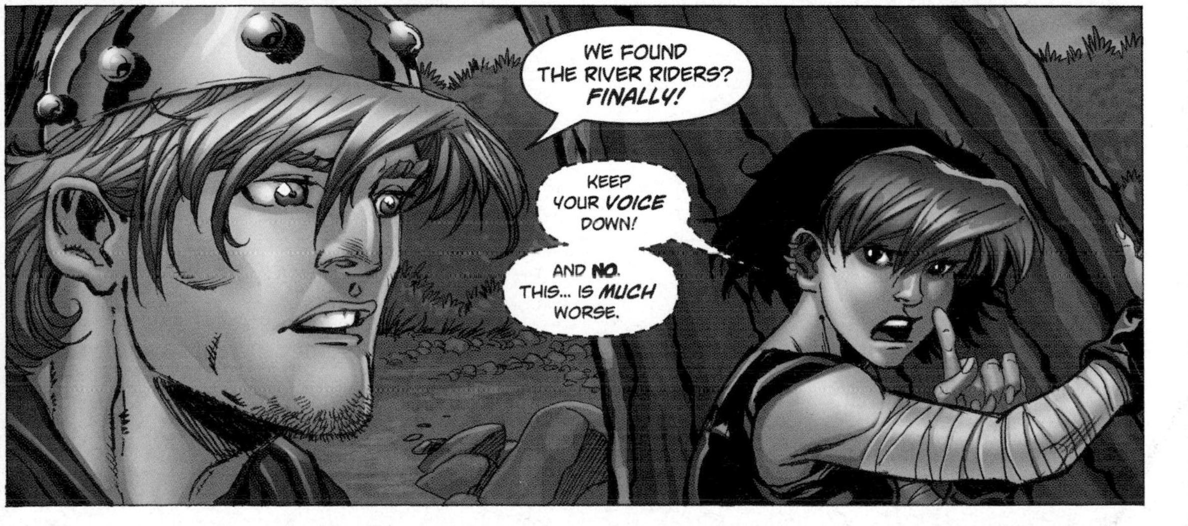
WE FOUND THE RIVER RIDERS? FINALLY!
KEEP YOUR VOICE DOWN!
AND NO. THIS... IS MUCH WORSE.

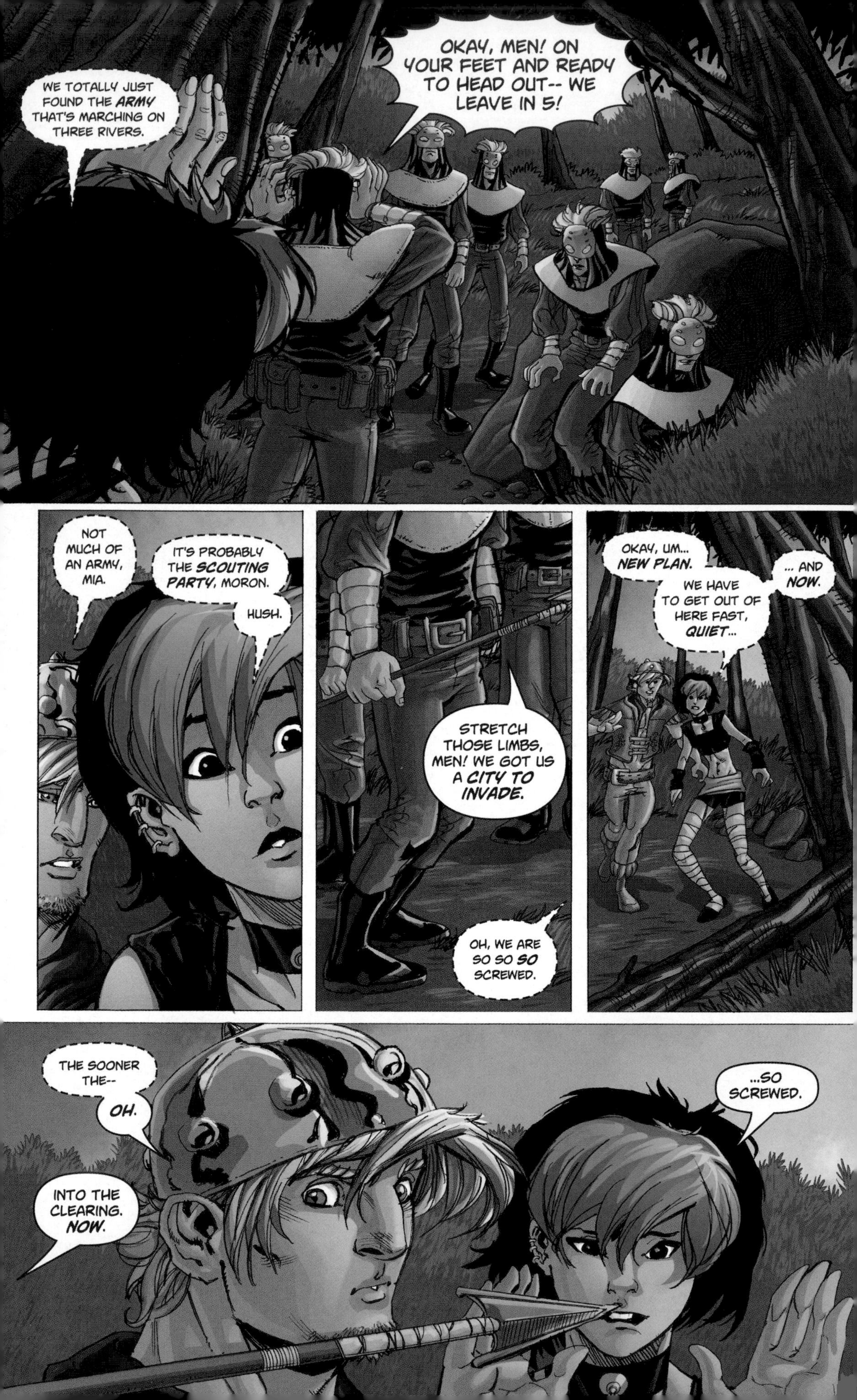
WE TOTALLY JUST FOUND THE ARMY THAT'S MARCHING ON THREE RIVERS.
OKAY, MEN! ON YOUR FEET AND READY TO HEAD OUT-- WE LEAVE IN 5!
NOT MUCH OF AN ARMY, MIA.
IT'S PROBABLY THE SCOUTING PARTY, MORON.
HUSH.
STRETCH THOSE LIMBS, MEN! WE GOT US A CITY TO INVADE.
OH, WE ARE SO SO SO SCREWED.
OKAY, UM... NEW PLAN.
WE HAVE TO GET OUT OF HERE FAST, QUIET...
... AND NOW.
THE SOONER THE--
OH.
INTO THE CLEARING. NOW.
...SO SCREWED.

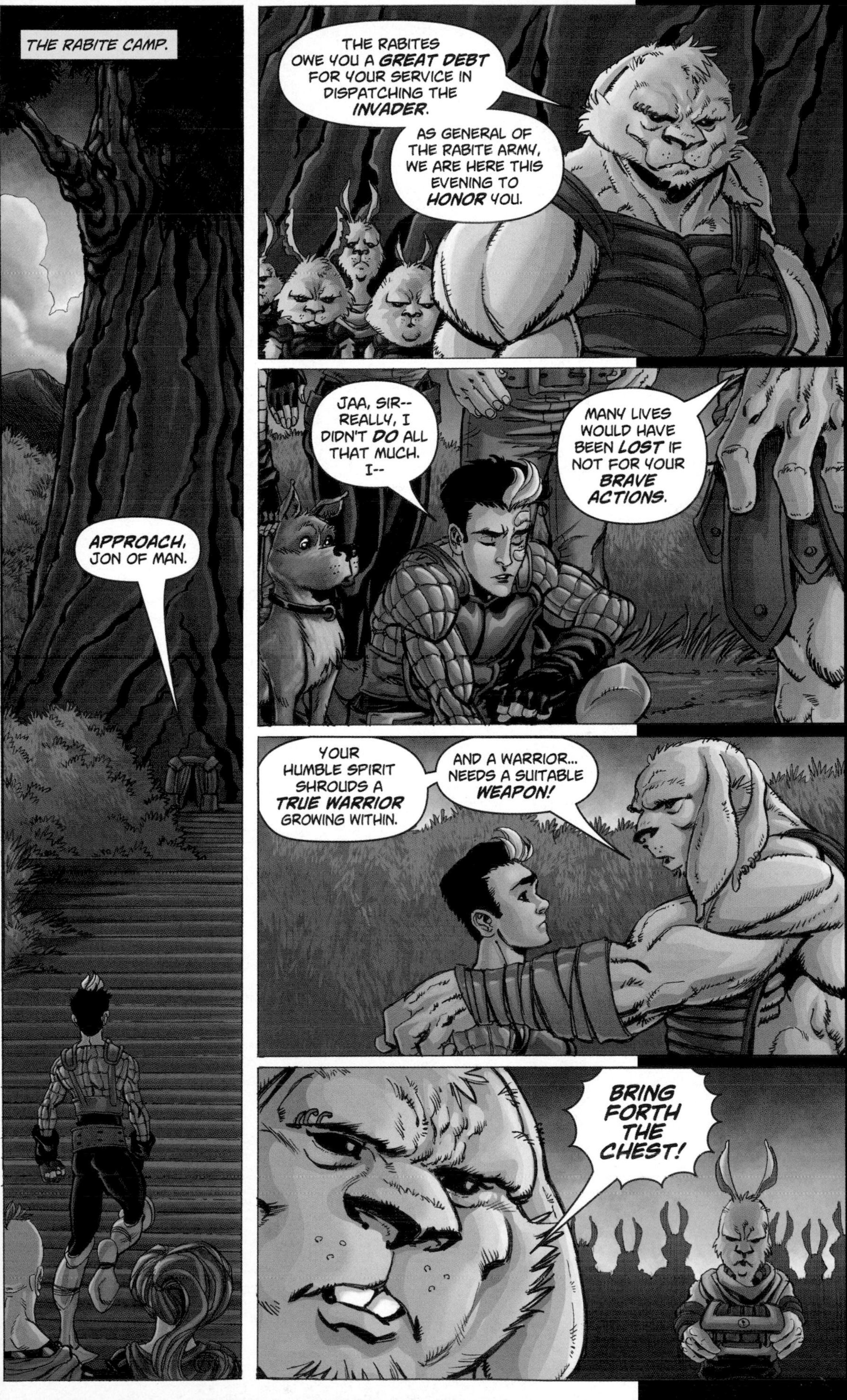
THE RABITE CAMP.
APPROACH, JON OF MAN.
THE RABITES OWE YOU A GREAT DEBT FOR YOUR SERVICE IN DISPATCHING THE INVADER.
AS GENERAL OF THE RABITE ARMY, WE ARE HERE THIS EVENING TO HONOR YOU.
JAA, SIR-- REALLY, I DIDN'T DO ALL THAT MUCH. I--
MANY LIVES WOULD HAVE BEEN LOST IF NOT FOR YOUR BRAVE ACTIONS.
YOUR HUMBLE SPIRIT SHROUDS A TRUE WARRIOR GROWING WITHIN.
AND A WARRIOR... NEEDS A SUITABLE WEAPON!
BRING FORTH THE CHEST!

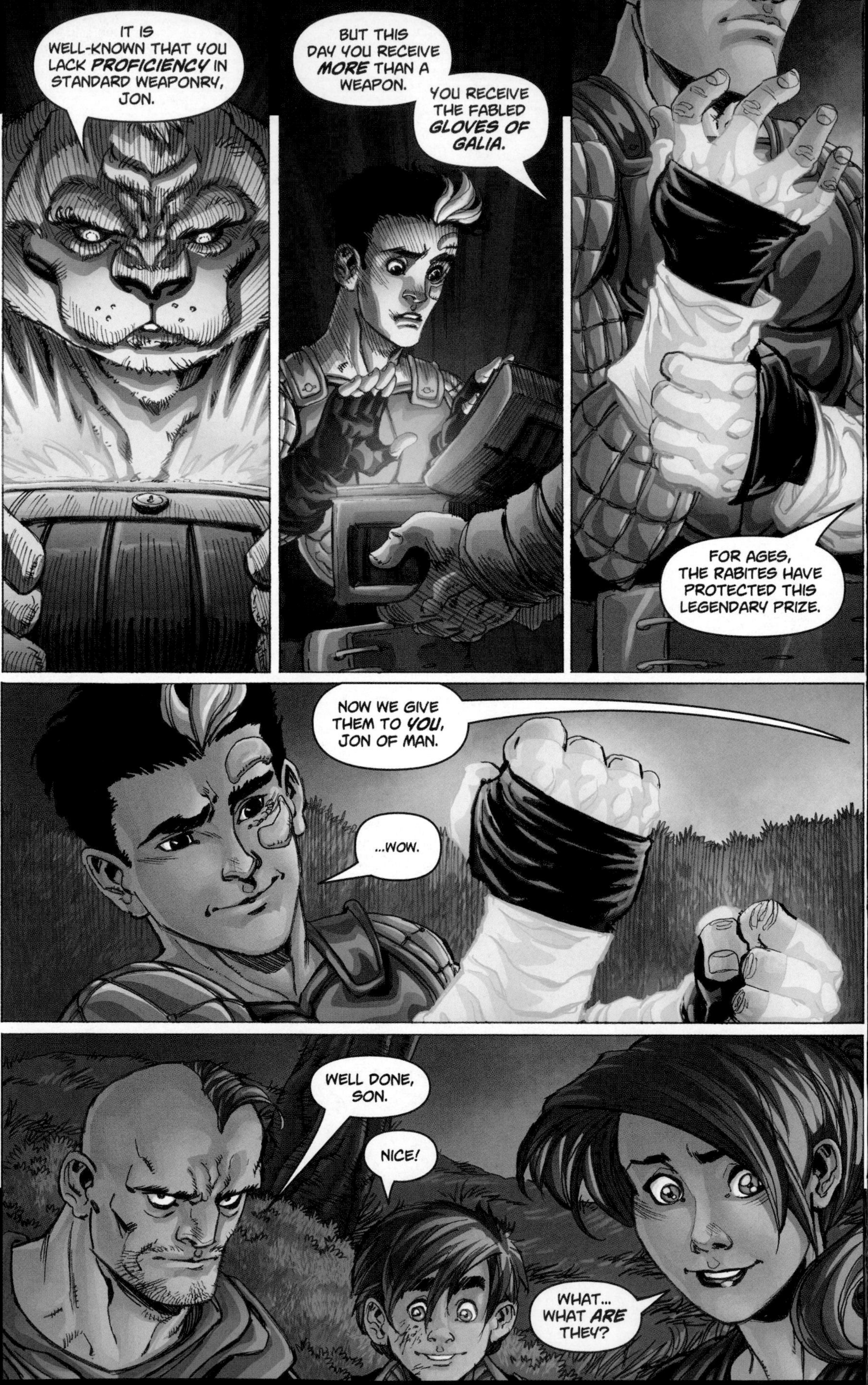
IT IS WELL-KNOWN THAT YOU LACK PROFICIENCY IN STANDARD WEAPONRY, JON.
BUT THIS DAY YOU RECEIVE MORE THAN A WEAPON.
YOU RECEIVE THE FABLED GLOVES OF GALIA.
FOR AGES, THE RABITES HAVE PROTECTED THIS LEGENDARY PRIZE.
NOW WE GIVE THEM TO YOU, JON OF MAN.
...WOW.
WELL DONE, SON.
NICE!
WHAT... WHAT ARE THEY?

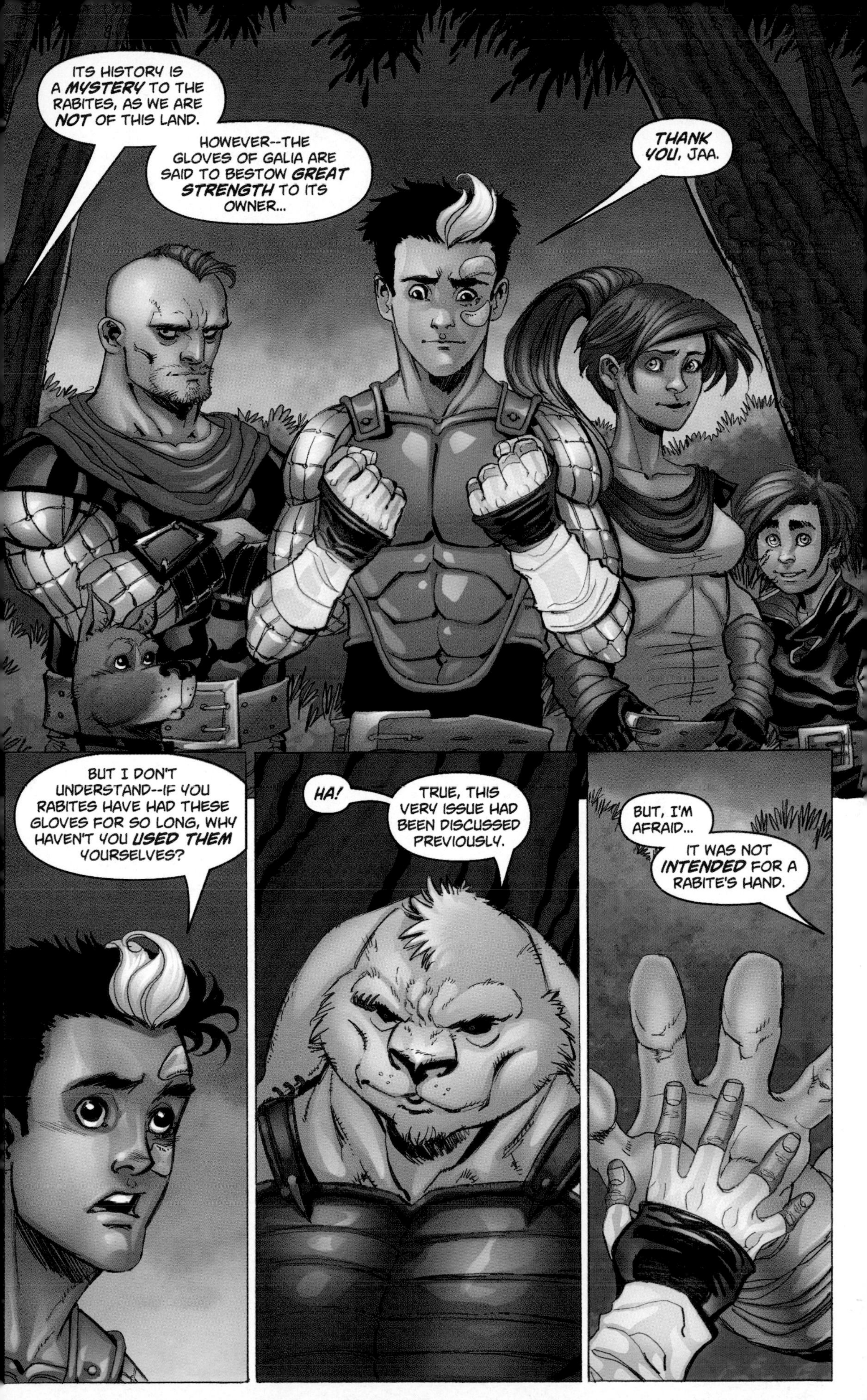
ITS HISTORY IS A MYSTERY TO THE RABITES, AS WE ARE NOT OF THIS LAND.
HOWEVER--THE GLOVES OF GALIA ARE SAID TO BESTOW GREAT STRENGTH TO ITS OWNER...
THANK YOU, JAA.
BUT I DON'T UNDERSTAND--IF YOU RABITES HAVE HAD THESE GLOVES FOR SO LONG, WHY HAVEN'T YOU USED THEM YOURSELVES?
HA!
TRUE, THIS VERY ISSUE HAD BEEN DISCUSSED PREVIOUSLY.
BUT, I'M AFRAID...
IT WAS NOT INTENDED FOR A RABITE'S HAND.

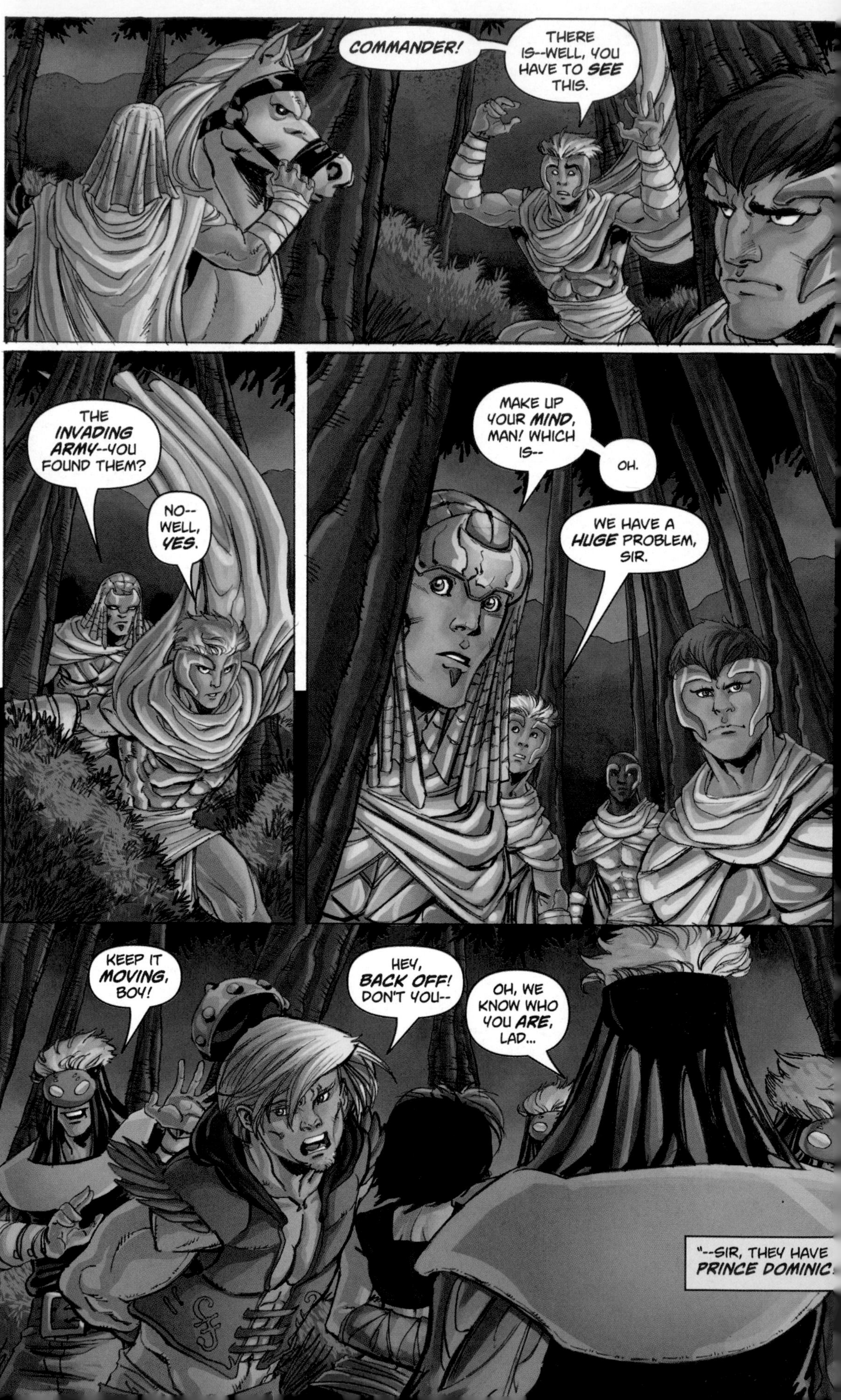
COMMANDER!
THERE IS--WELL, YOU HAVE TO SEE THIS.
THE INVADING ARMY--YOU FOUND THEM?
NO--WELL, YES.
MAKE UP YOUR MIND, MAN! WHICH IS--
OH.
WE HAVE A HUGE PROBLEM, SIR.
KEEP IT MOVING, BOY!
HEY, BACK OFF! DON'T YOU--
OH, WE KNOW WHO YOU ARE, LAD...
"--SIR, THEY HAVE PRINCE DOMINIC."

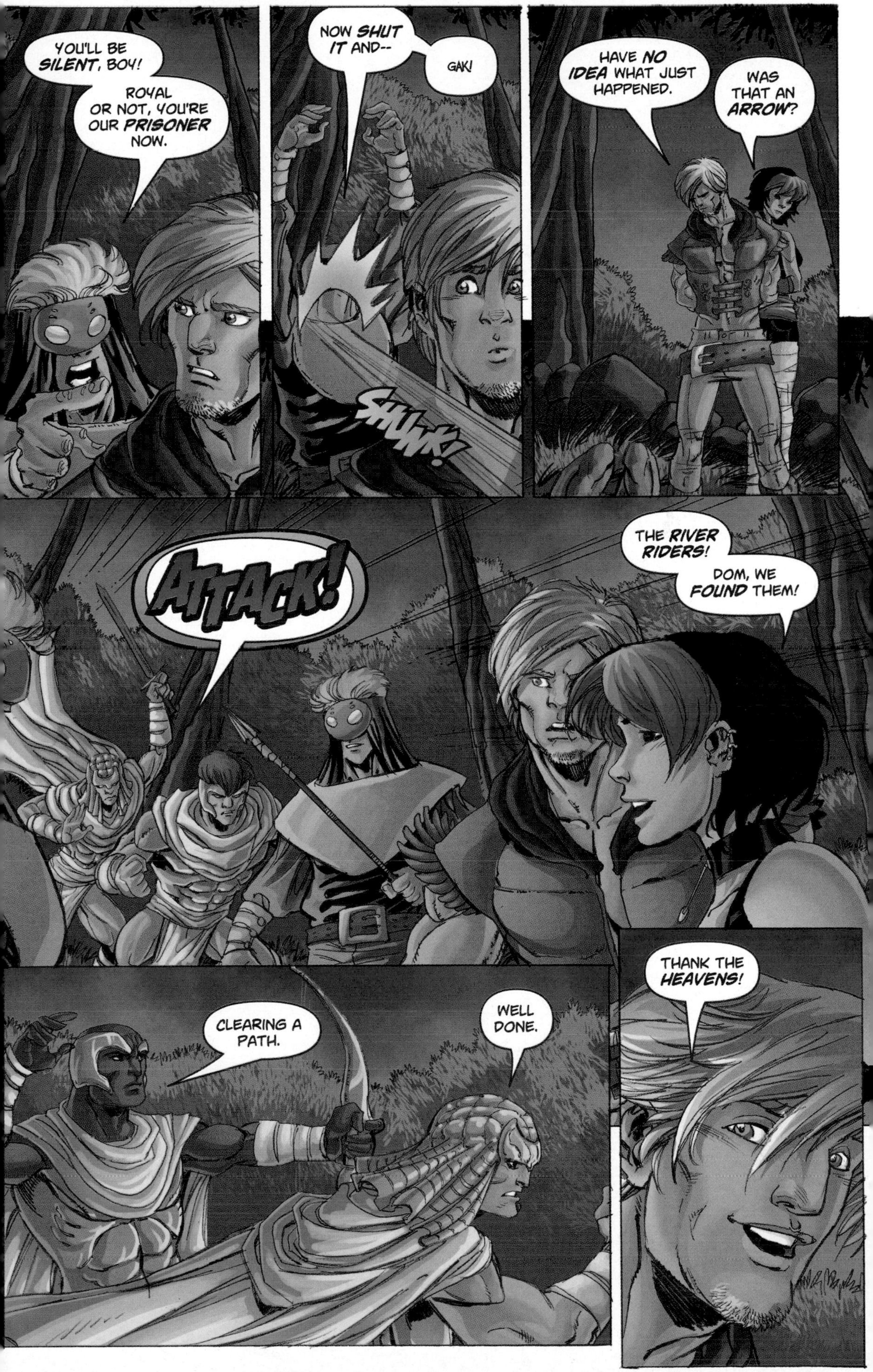
YOU'LL BE SILENT, BOY!
ROYAL OR NOT, YOU'RE OUR PRISONER NOW.
NOW SHUT IT AND--
GAK!
SHUNK!
HAVE NO IDEA WHAT JUST HAPPENED.
WAS THAT AN ARROW?
ATTACK!
THE RIVER RIDERS!
DOM, WE FOUND THEM!
CLEARING A PATH.
WELL DONE.
THANK THE HEAVENS!

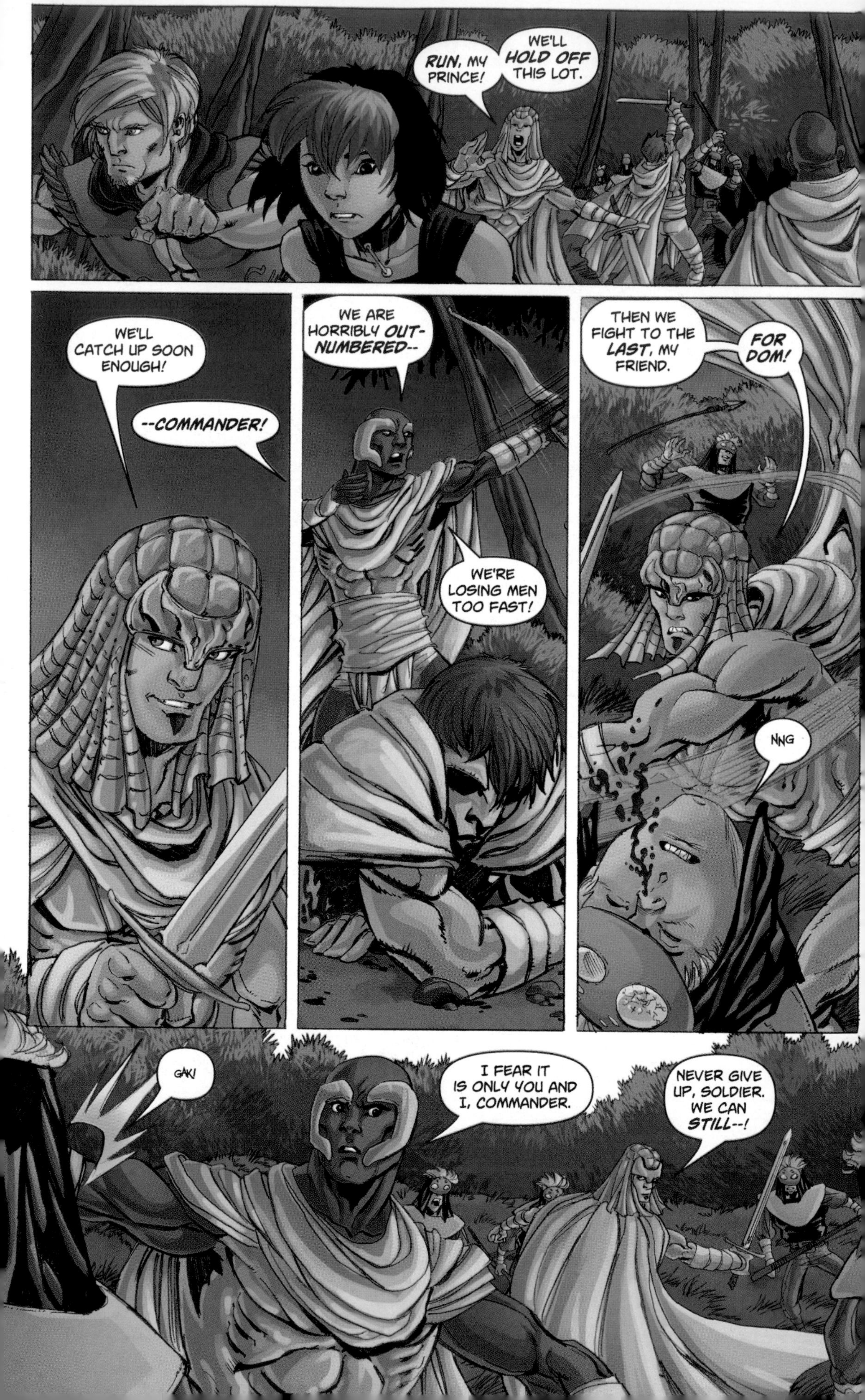
RUN, MY PRINCE!
WE'LL HOLD OFF THIS LOT.
WE'LL CATCH UP SOON ENOUGH!
--COMMANDER!
WE ARE HORRIBLY OUT-NUMBERED--
WE'RE LOSING MEN TOO FAST!
THEN WE FIGHT TO THE LAST, MY FRIEND.
FOR DOM!
NNG
GAK!
I FEAR IT IS ONLY YOU AND I, COMMANDER.
NEVER GIVE UP, SOLDIER. WE CAN STILL--!

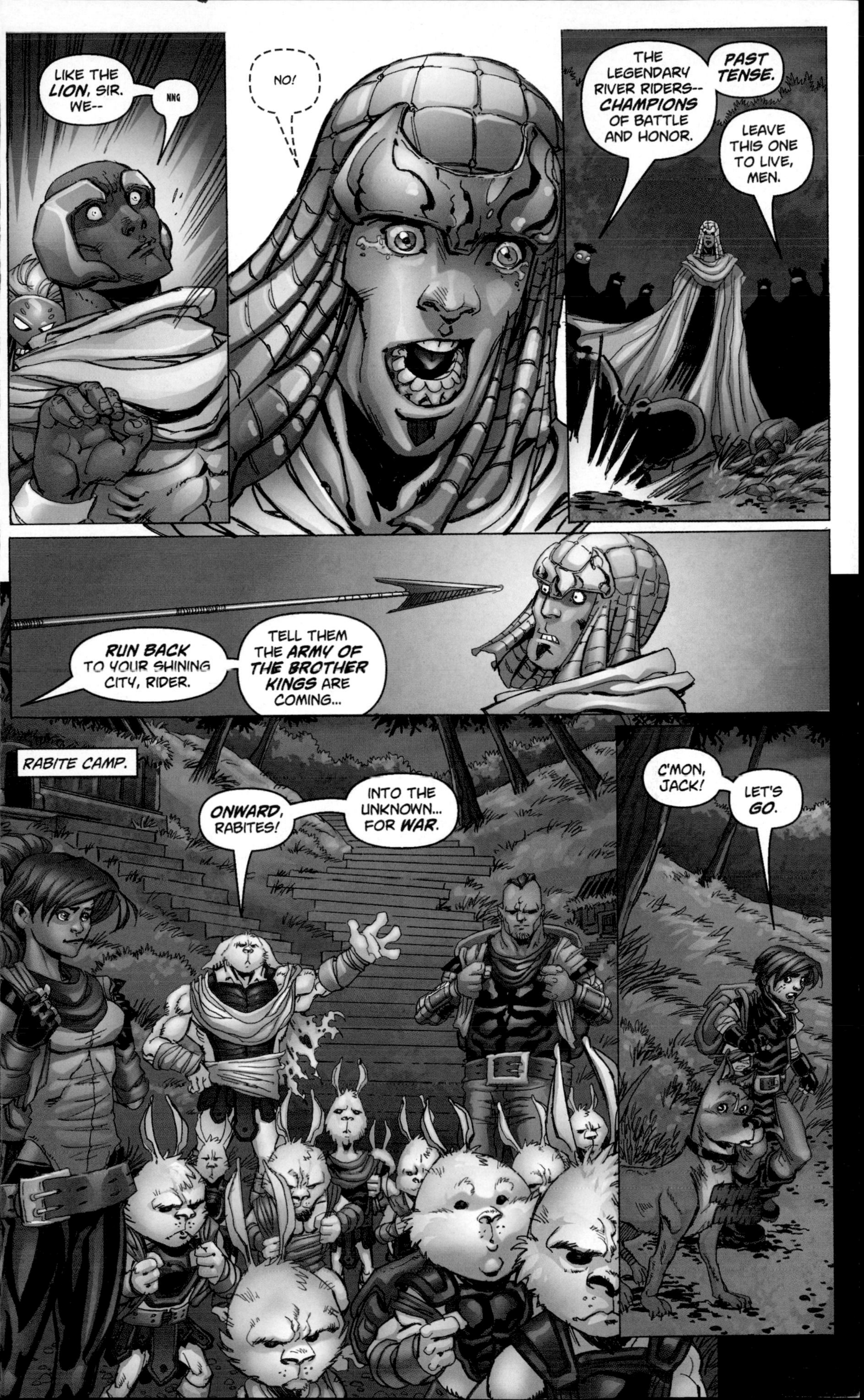
LIKE THE LION, SIR. WE--
NNG
NO!
THE LEGENDARY RIVER RIDERS-- CHAMPIONS OF BATTLE AND HONOR.
PAST TENSE.
LEAVE THIS ONE TO LIVE, MEN.
RUN BACK TO YOUR SHINING CITY, RIDER.
TELL THEM THE ARMY OF THE BROTHER KINGS ARE COMING...
RABITE CAMP.
ONWARD, RABITES!
INTO THE UNKNOWN... FOR WAR.
C'MON, JACK!
LET'S GO.

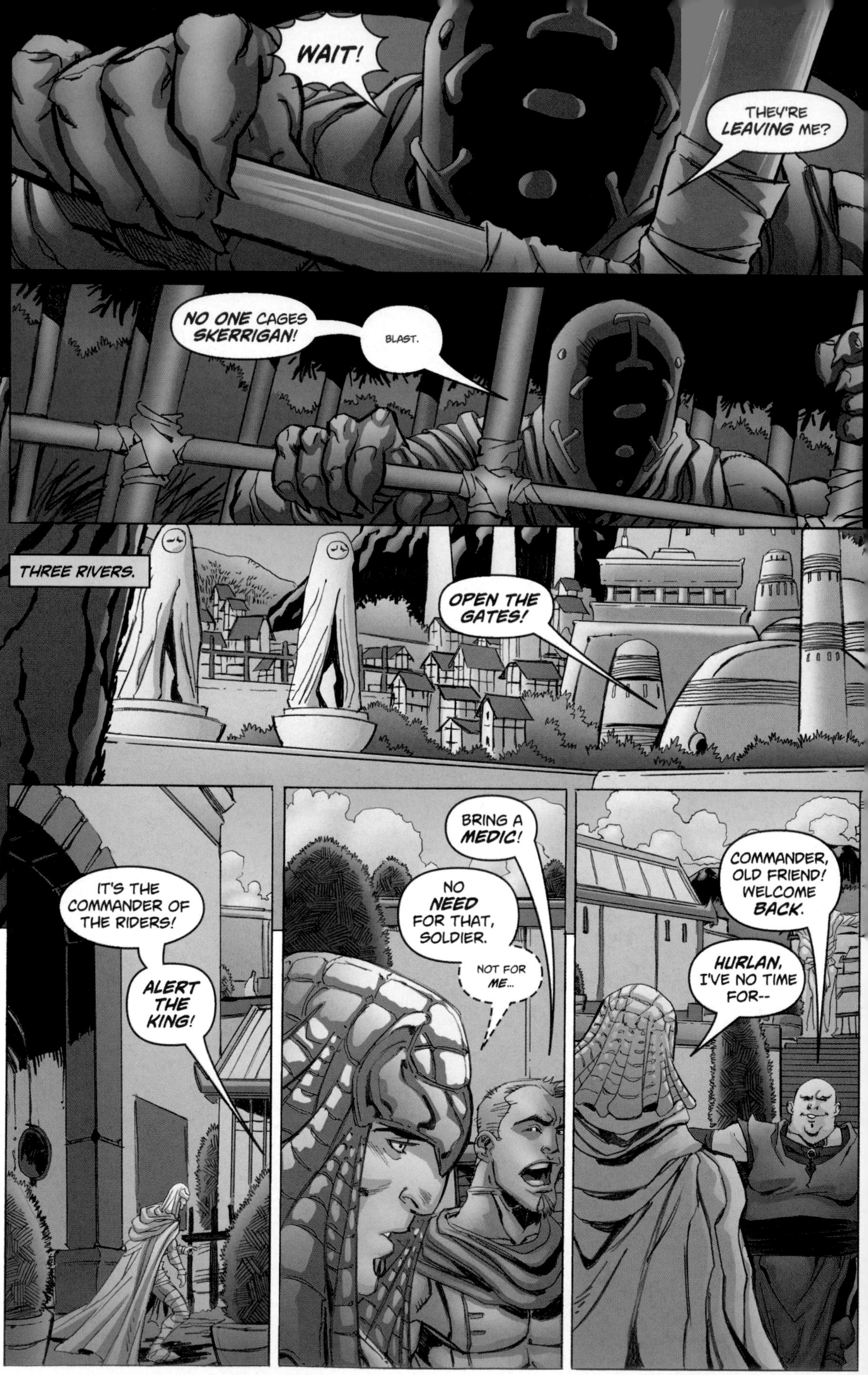
WAIT!
THEY'RE LEAVING ME?
NO ONE CAGES SKERRIGAN!
BLAST.
THREE RIVERS.
OPEN THE GATES!
IT'S THE COMMANDER OF THE RIDERS!
ALERT THE KING!
BRING A MEDIC!
NO NEED FOR THAT, SOLDIER.
NOT FOR ME...
COMMANDER, OLD FRIEND! WELCOME BACK.
HURLAN, I'VE NO TIME FOR--

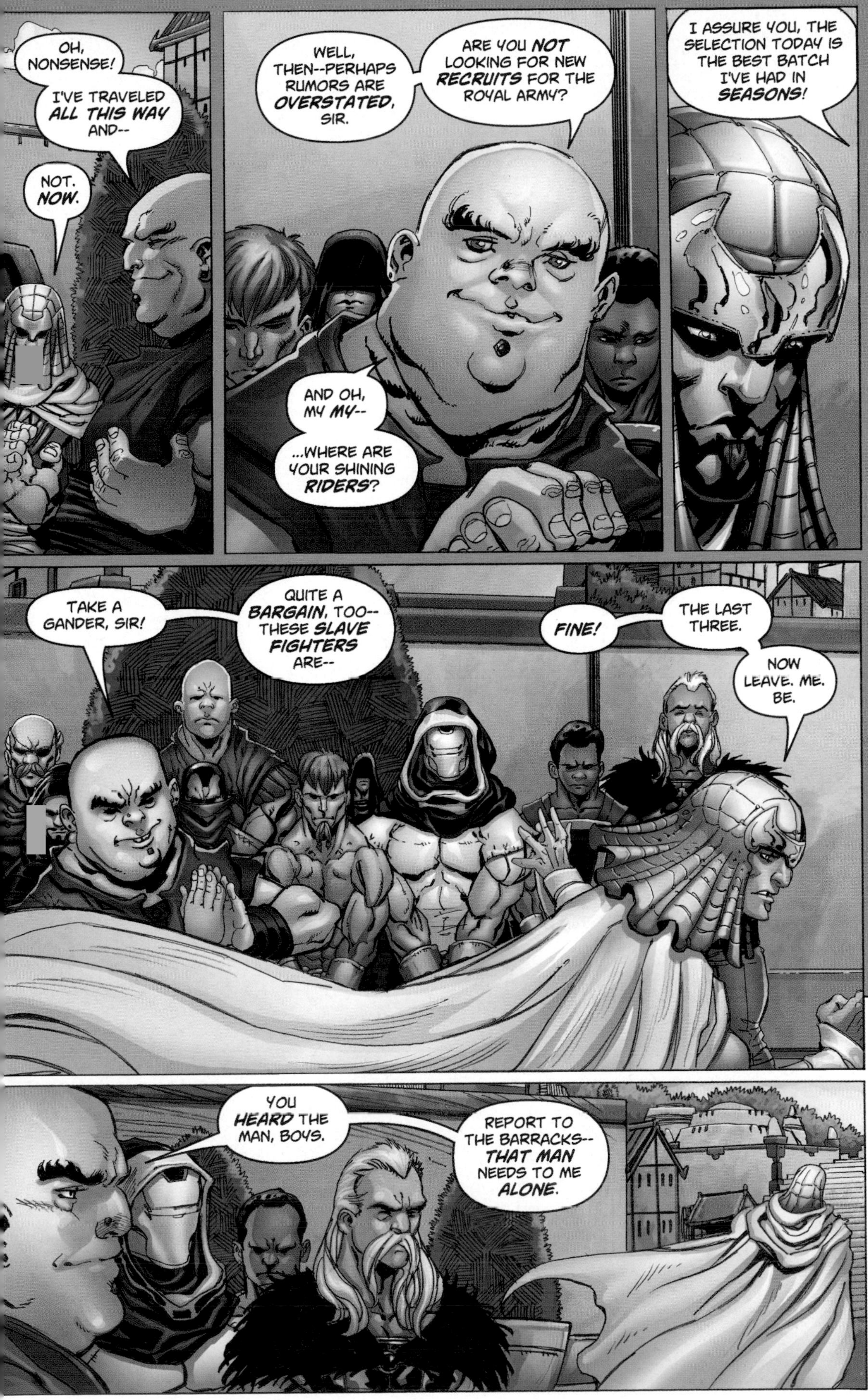
OH, NONSENSE!
I'VE TRAVELED ALL THIS WAY AND--
NOT. NOW.
WELL, THEN--PERHAPS RUMORS ARE OVERSTATED, SIR.
ARE YOU NOT LOOKING FOR NEW RECRUITS FOR THE ROYAL ARMY?
AND OH, MY MY--
...WHERE ARE YOUR SHINING RIDERS?
I ASSURE YOU, THE SELECTION TODAY IS THE BEST BATCH I'VE HAD IN SEASONS!
TAKE A GANDER, SIR!
QUITE A BARGAIN, TOO-- THESE SLAVE FIGHTERS ARE--
FINE!
THE LAST THREE.
NOW LEAVE. ME. BE.
YOU HEARD THE MAN, BOYS.
REPORT TO THE BARRACKS-- THAT MAN NEEDS TO ME ALONE.

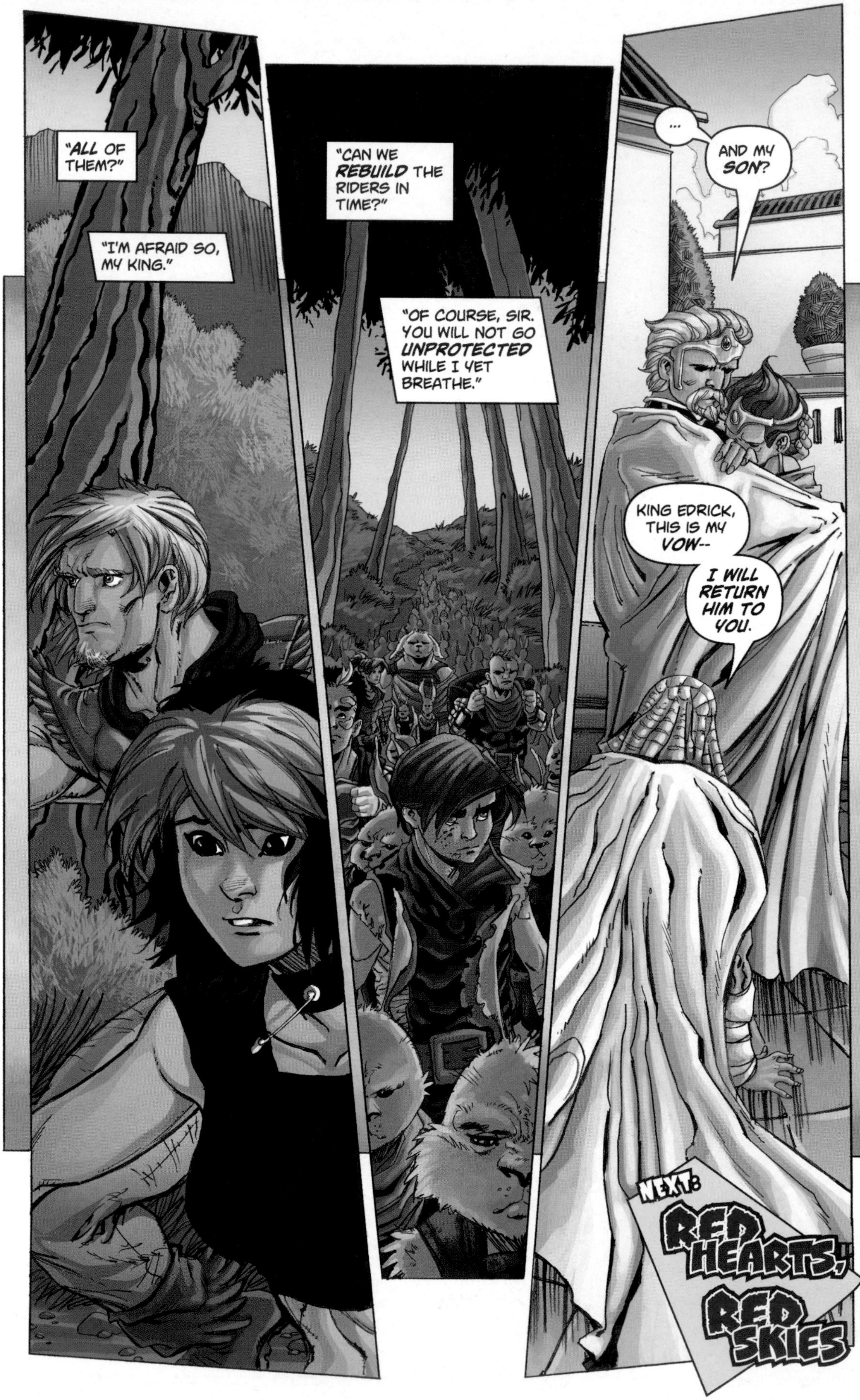
"ALL OF THEM?"
"I'M AFRAID SO, MY KING."
"CAN WE REBUILD THE RIDERS IN TIME?"
"OF COURSE, SIR. YOU WILL NOT GO UNPROTECTED WHILE I YET BREATHE."
...
AND MY SON?
KING EDRICK, THIS IS MY VOW--
I WILL RETURN HIM TO YOU.
NEXT:
RED HEARTS, RED SKIES

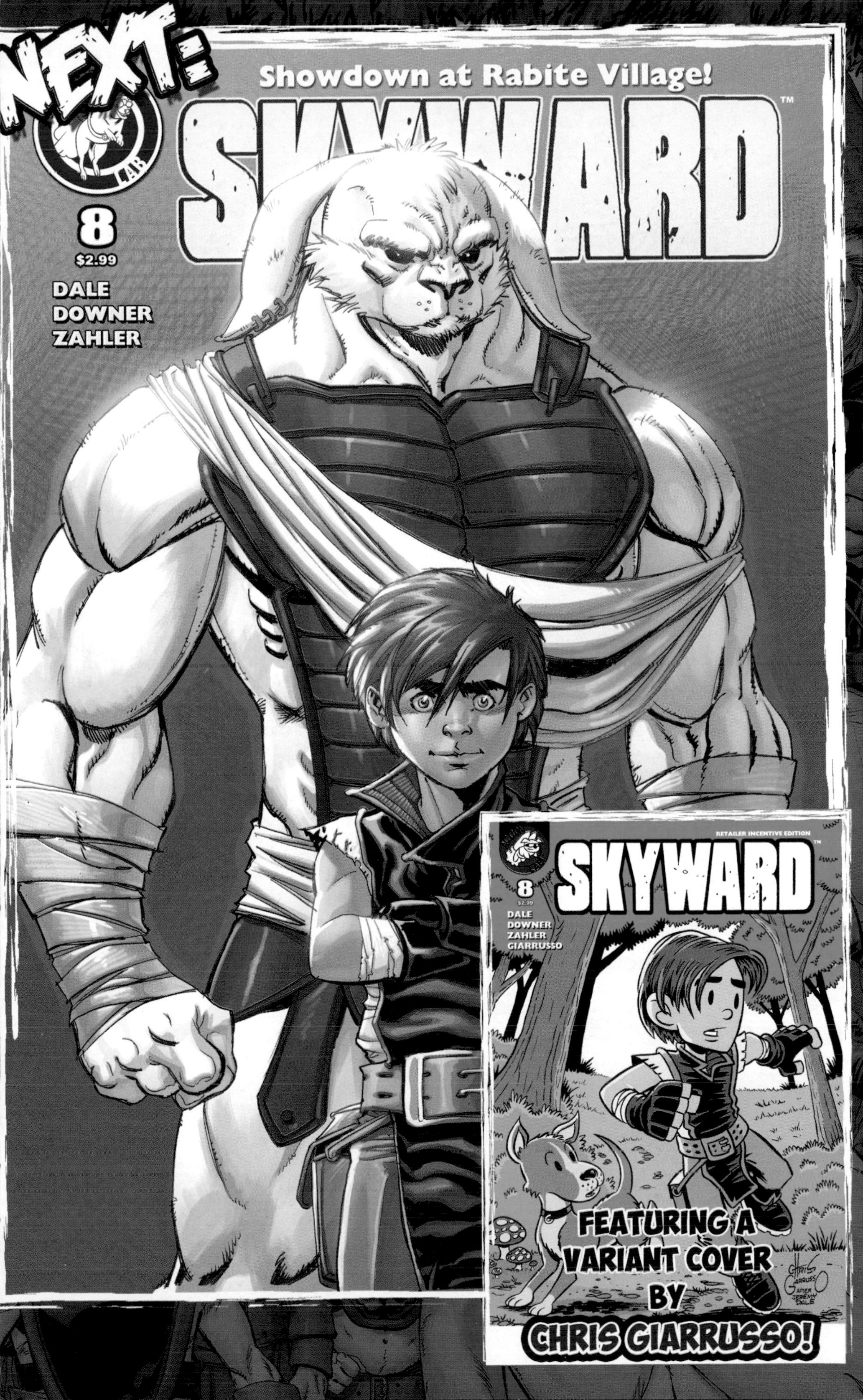
NEXT:
Showdown at Rabite Village!
SKYWARD™
8
$2.99
DALE
DOWNER
ZAHLER
RETAILER INCENTIVE EDITION
SKYWARD™
8
$2.99
DALE
DOWNER
ZAHLER
GIARRUSSO
FEATURING A
VARIANT COVER
BY
CHRIS GIARRUSSO!

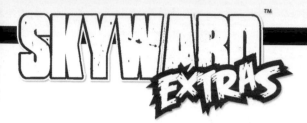

SKYWARD™ EXTRAS

Miss out on our special Halloween ComicFest 2013 story?

You're not alone-- we have received numerous emails and comments from fans asking that we run it again. Hey now-- we aim to please!

The Battle of Three Rivers begins here!

Enjoy. :)

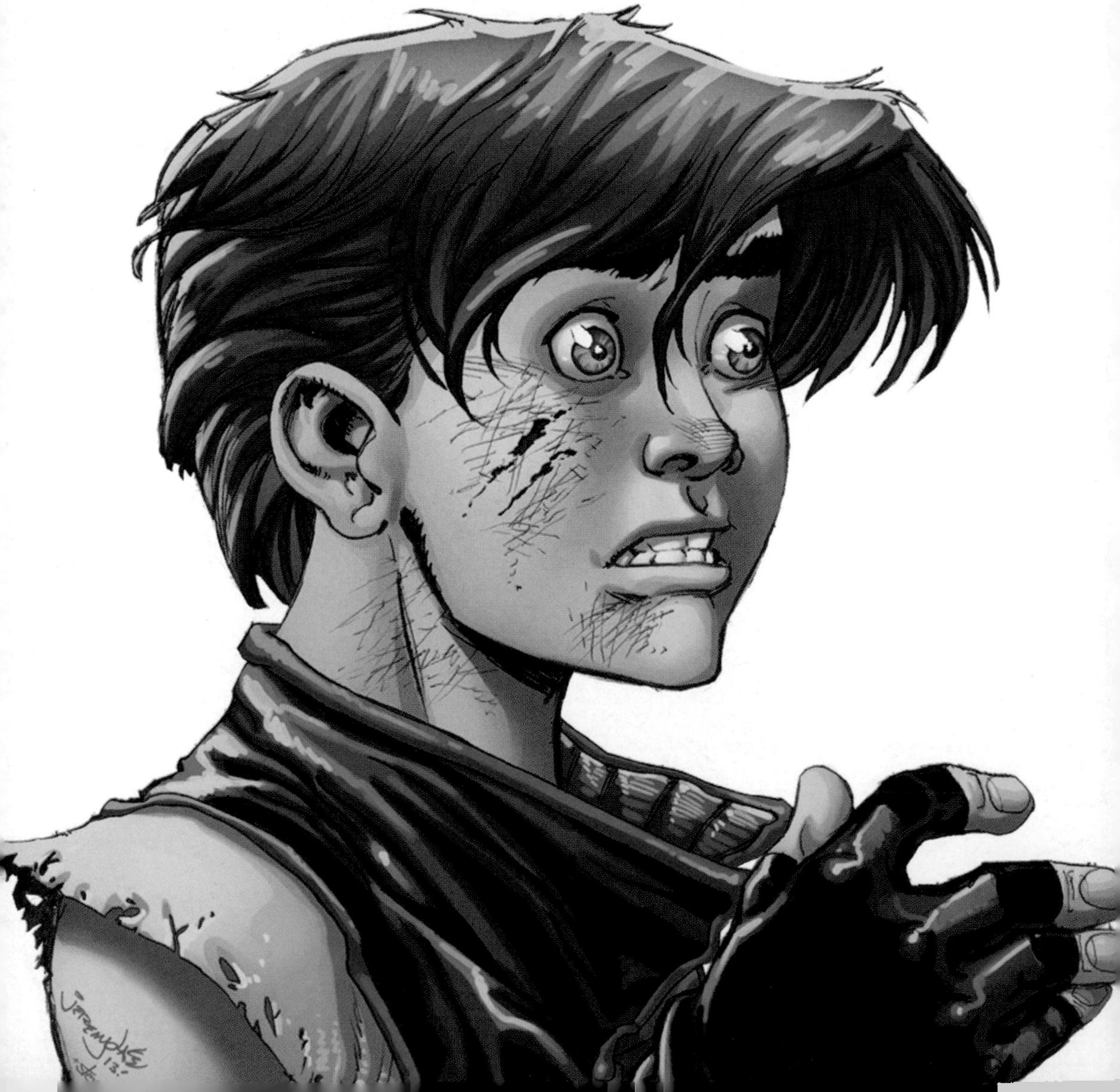

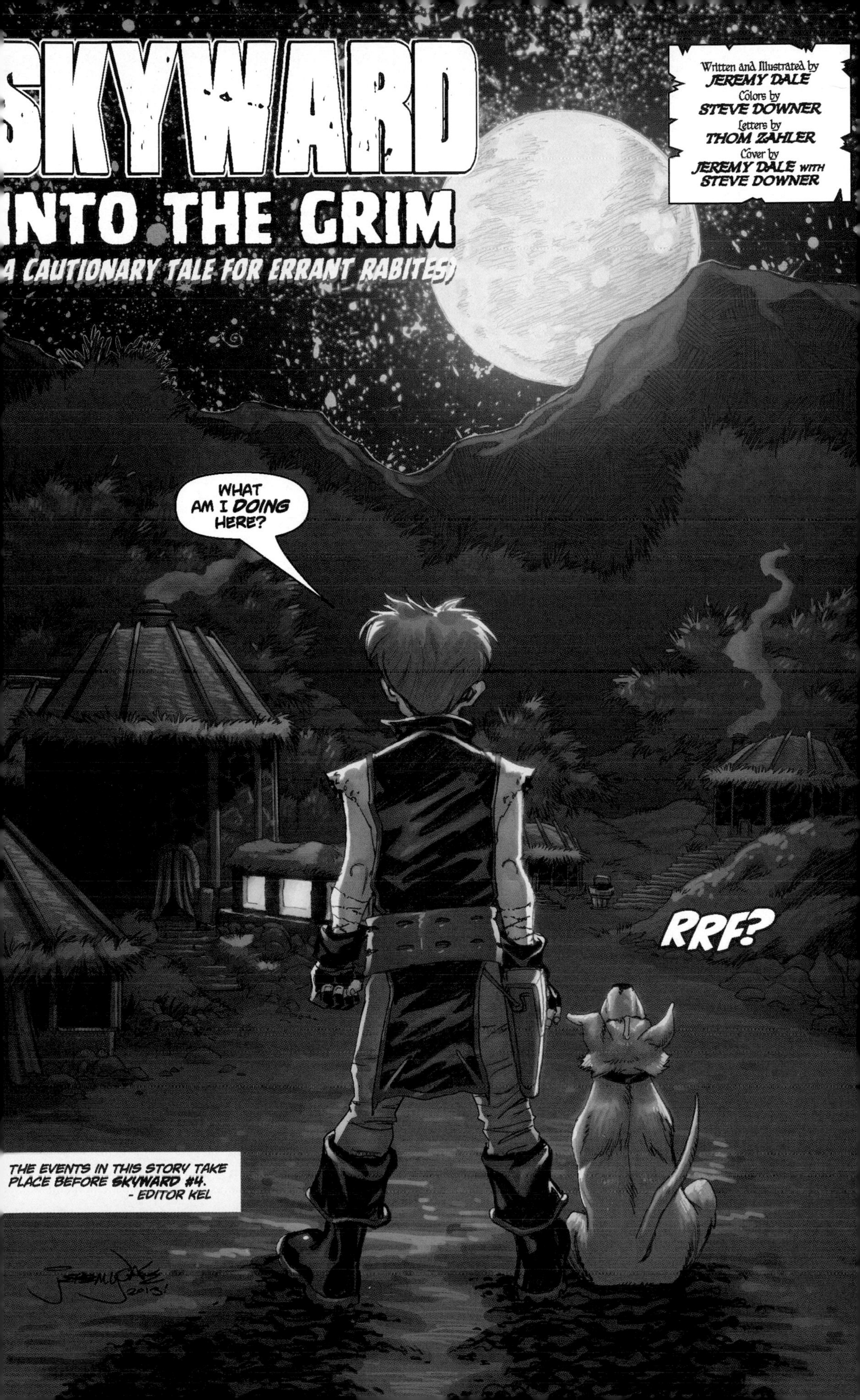
SKYWARD
INTO THE GRIM
(A CAUTIONARY TALE FOR ERRANT RABITES)
Written and Illustrated by
JEREMY DALE
Colors by
STEVE DOWNER
Letters by
THOM ZAHLER
Cover by
JEREMY DALE WITH
STEVE DOWNER
WHAT AM I DOING HERE?
RRF?
THE EVENTS IN THIS STORY TAKE PLACE BEFORE SKYWARD #4.
- EDITOR KEL

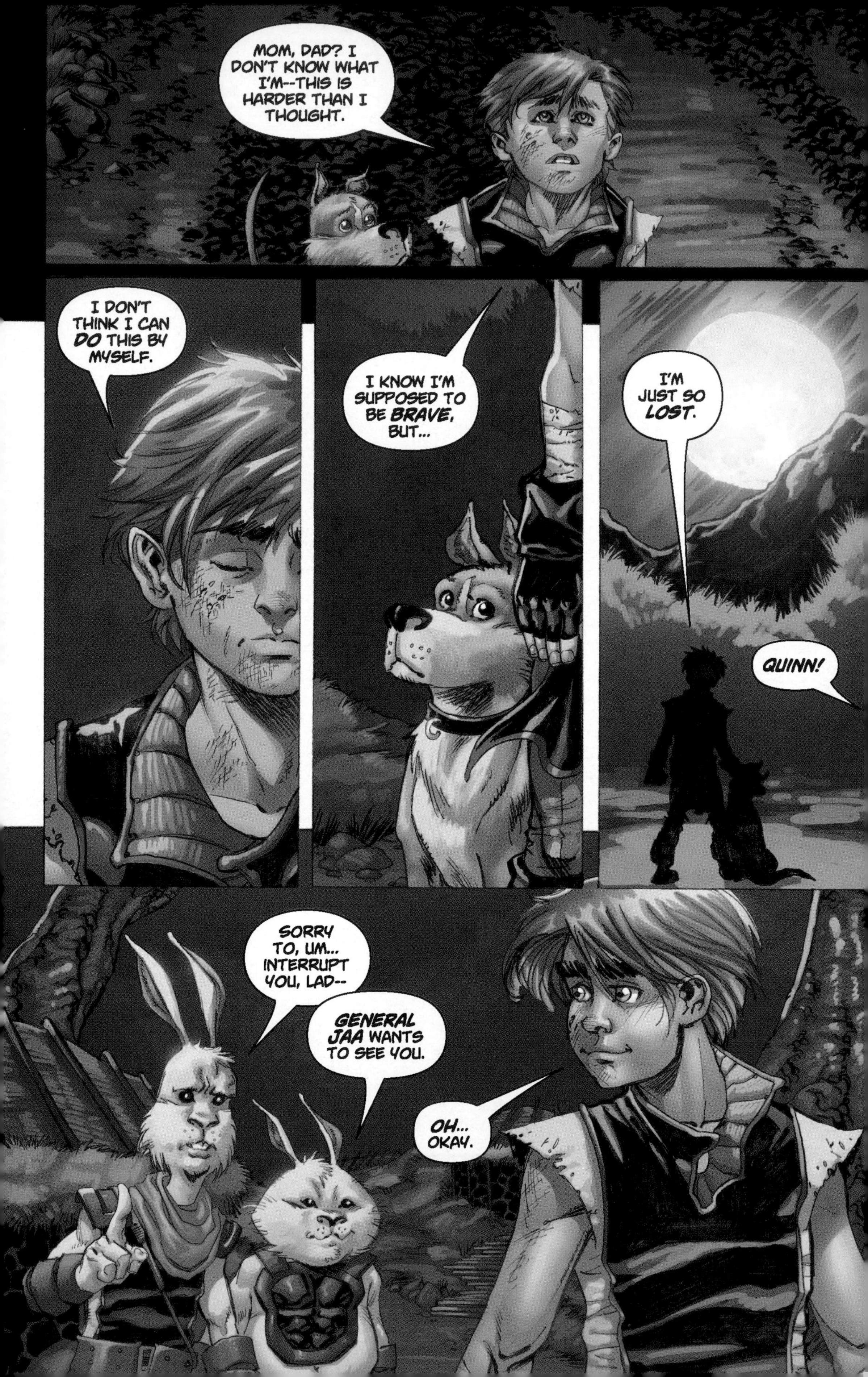
MOM, DAD? I DON'T KNOW WHAT I'M--THIS IS HARDER THAN I THOUGHT.
I DON'T THINK I CAN DO THIS BY MYSELF.
I KNOW I'M SUPPOSED TO BE BRAVE, BUT...
I'M JUST SO LOST.
QUINN!
SORRY TO, UM... INTERRUPT YOU, LAD--
GENERAL JAA WANTS TO SEE YOU.
OH... OKAY.

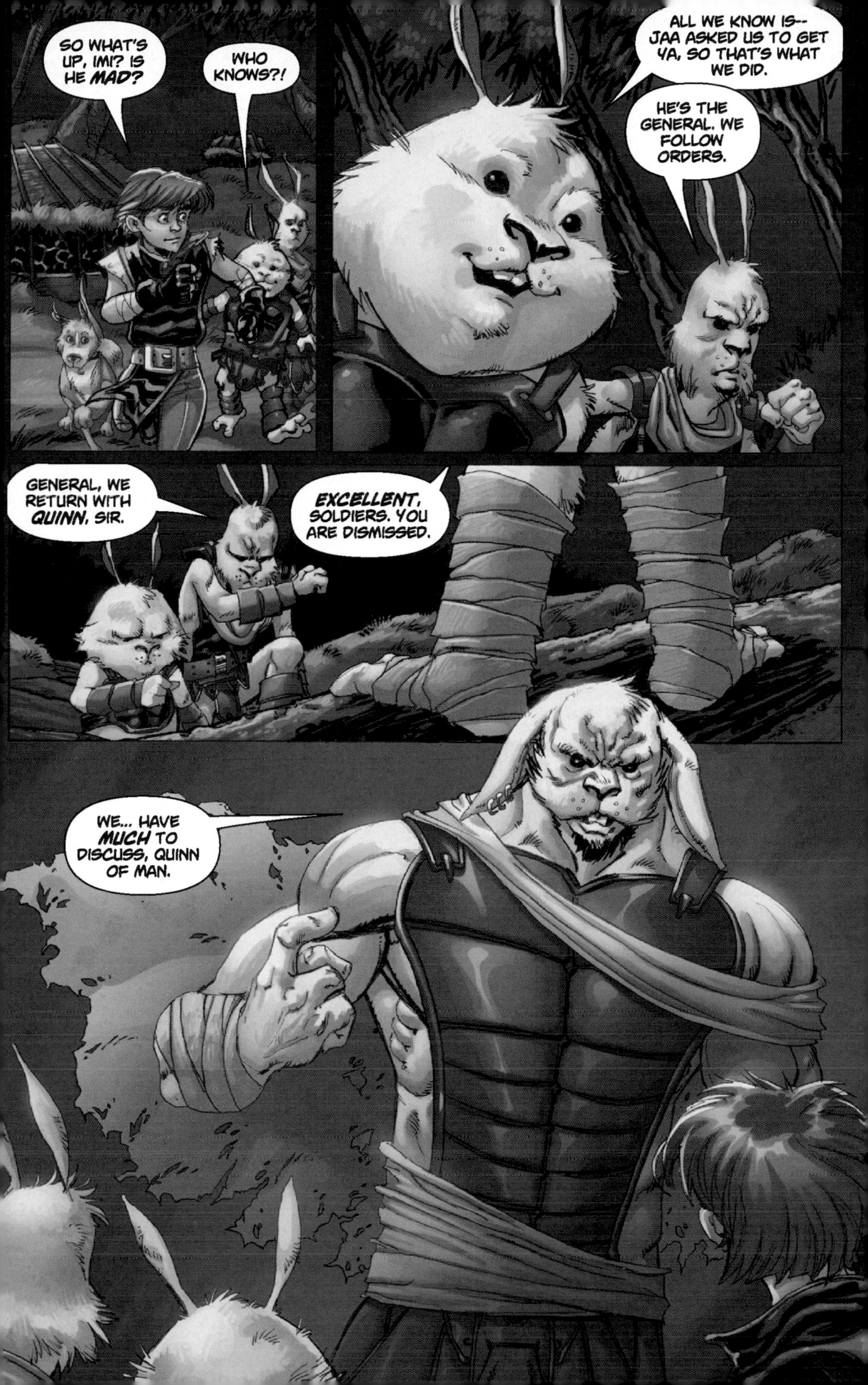

SO WHAT'S UP, IMI? IS HE *MAD?*
WHO KNOWS?!
ALL WE KNOW IS-- JAA ASKED US TO GET YA, SO THAT'S WHAT WE DID.
HE'S THE GENERAL. WE FOLLOW ORDERS.
GENERAL, WE RETURN WITH *QUINN*, SIR.
EXCELLENT, SOLDIERS. YOU ARE DISMISSED.
WE... HAVE *MUCH* TO DISCUSS, QUINN OF MAN.

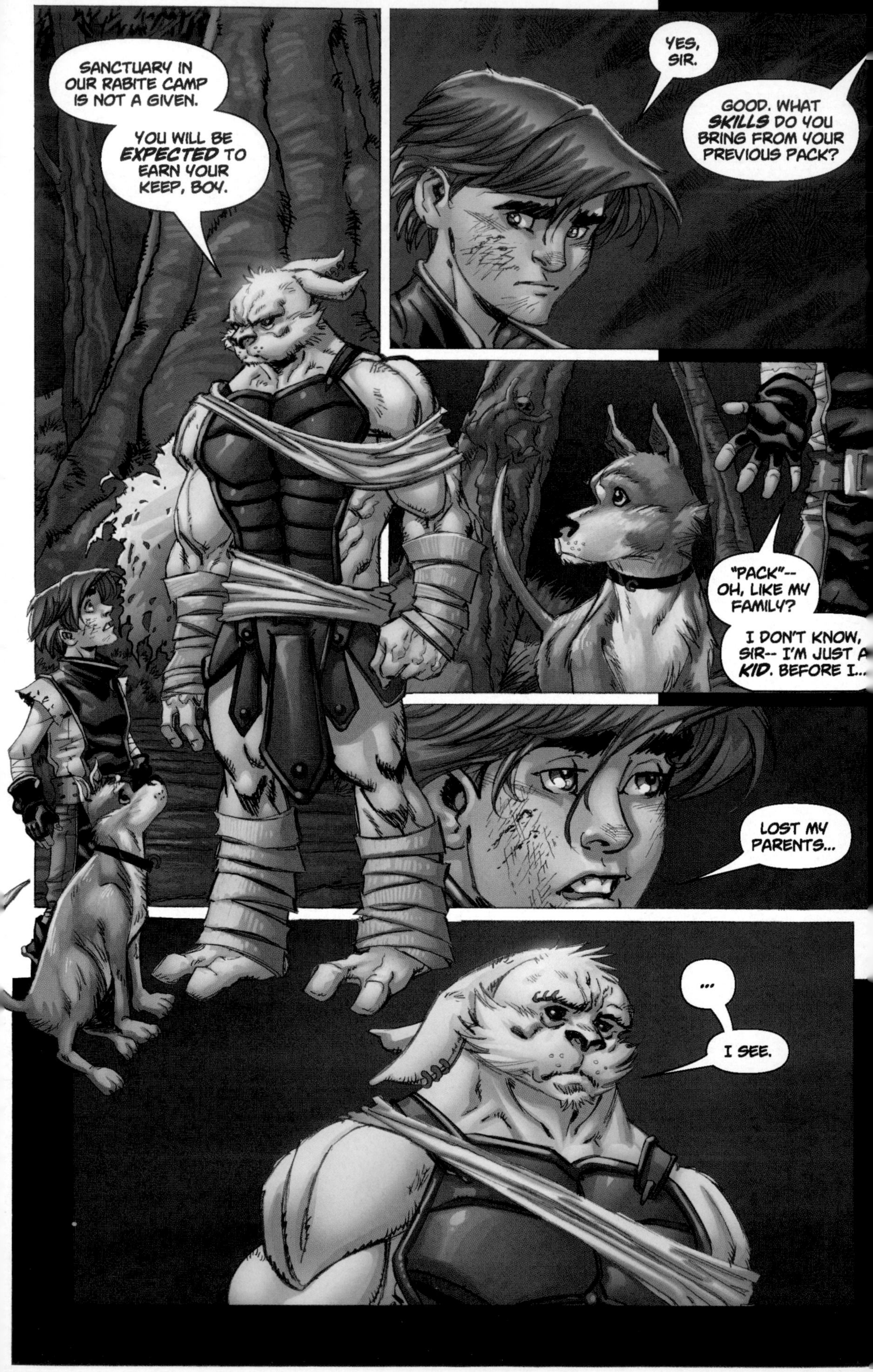
SANCTUARY IN OUR RABITE CAMP IS NOT A GIVEN.
YOU WILL BE EXPECTED TO EARN YOUR KEEP, BOY.
YES, SIR.
GOOD. WHAT SKILLS DO YOU BRING FROM YOUR PREVIOUS PACK?
"PACK"-- OH, LIKE MY FAMILY?
I DON'T KNOW, SIR-- I'M JUST A KID. BEFORE I...
LOST MY PARENTS...
...
I SEE.

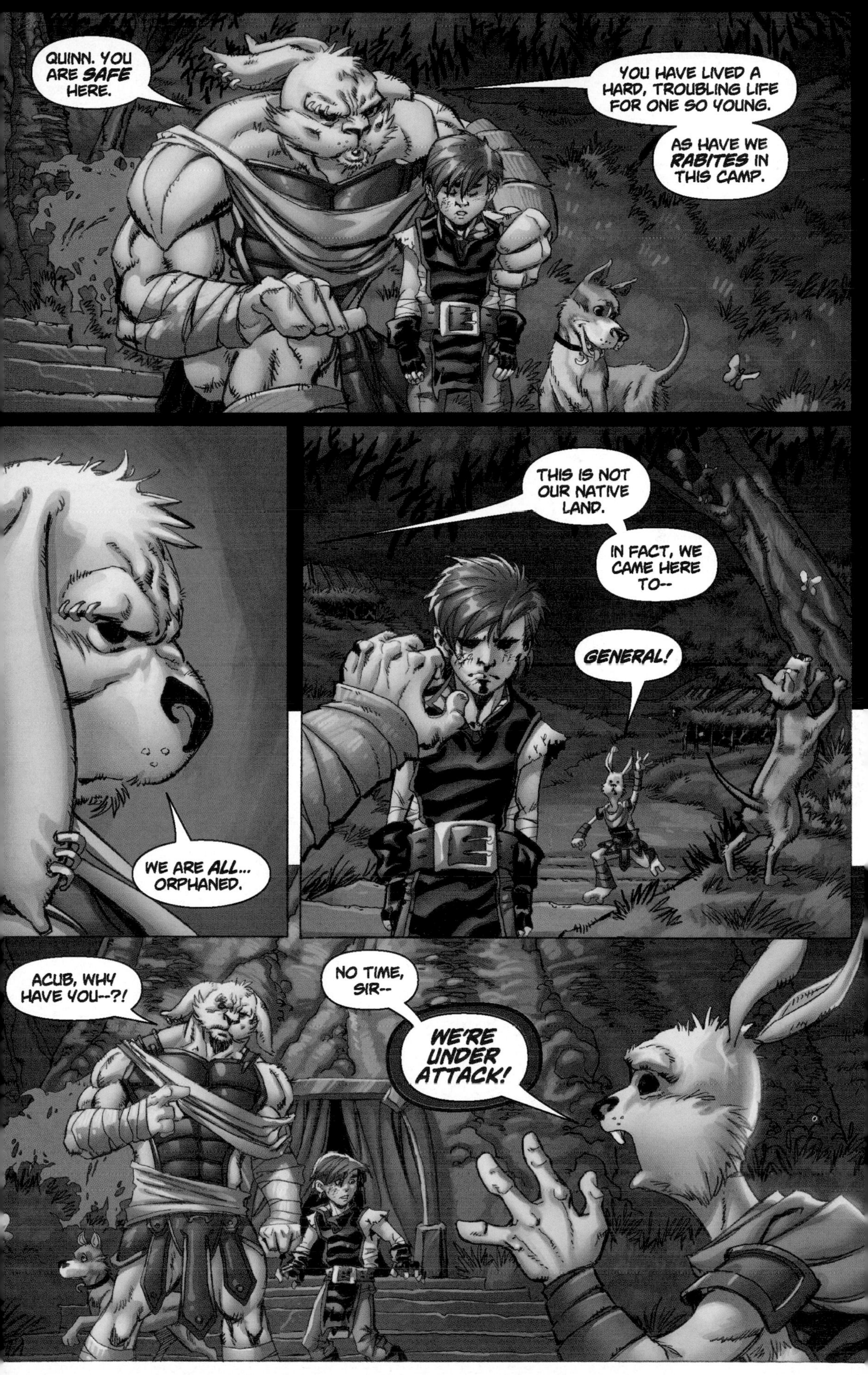
QUINN. YOU ARE SAFE HERE.
YOU HAVE LIVED A HARD, TROUBLING LIFE FOR ONE SO YOUNG.
AS HAVE WE RABITES IN THIS CAMP.
WE ARE ALL... ORPHANED.
THIS IS NOT OUR NATIVE LAND.
IN FACT, WE CAME HERE TO--
GENERAL!
ACUB, WHY HAVE YOU--?!
NO TIME, SIR--
WE'RE UNDER ATTACK!

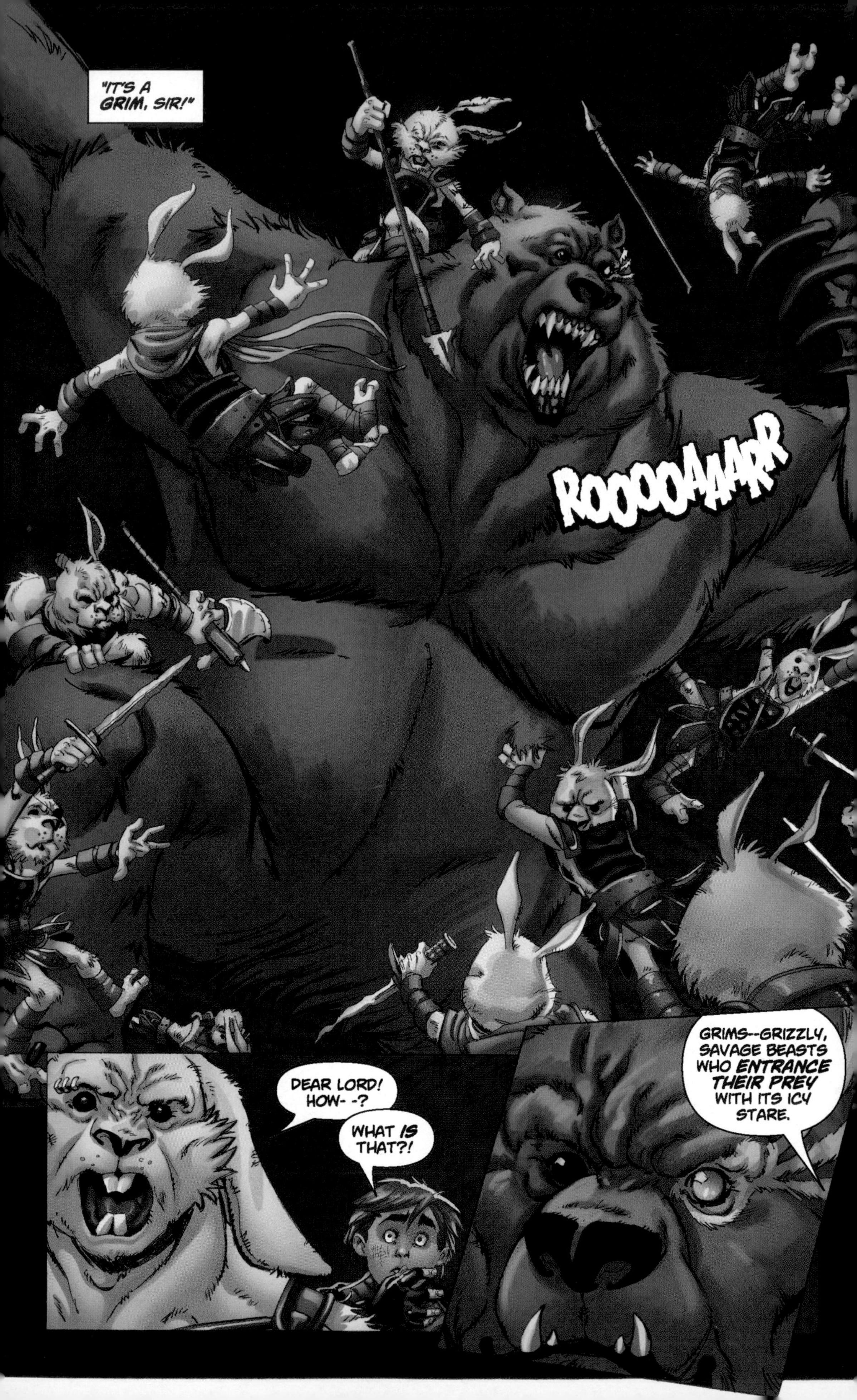
"IT'S A GRIM, SIR!"
ROOOOAAARR
DEAR LORD! HOW- -?
WHAT IS THAT?!
GRIMS--GRIZZLY, SAVAGE BEASTS WHO ENTRANCE THEIR PREY WITH ITS ICY STARE.

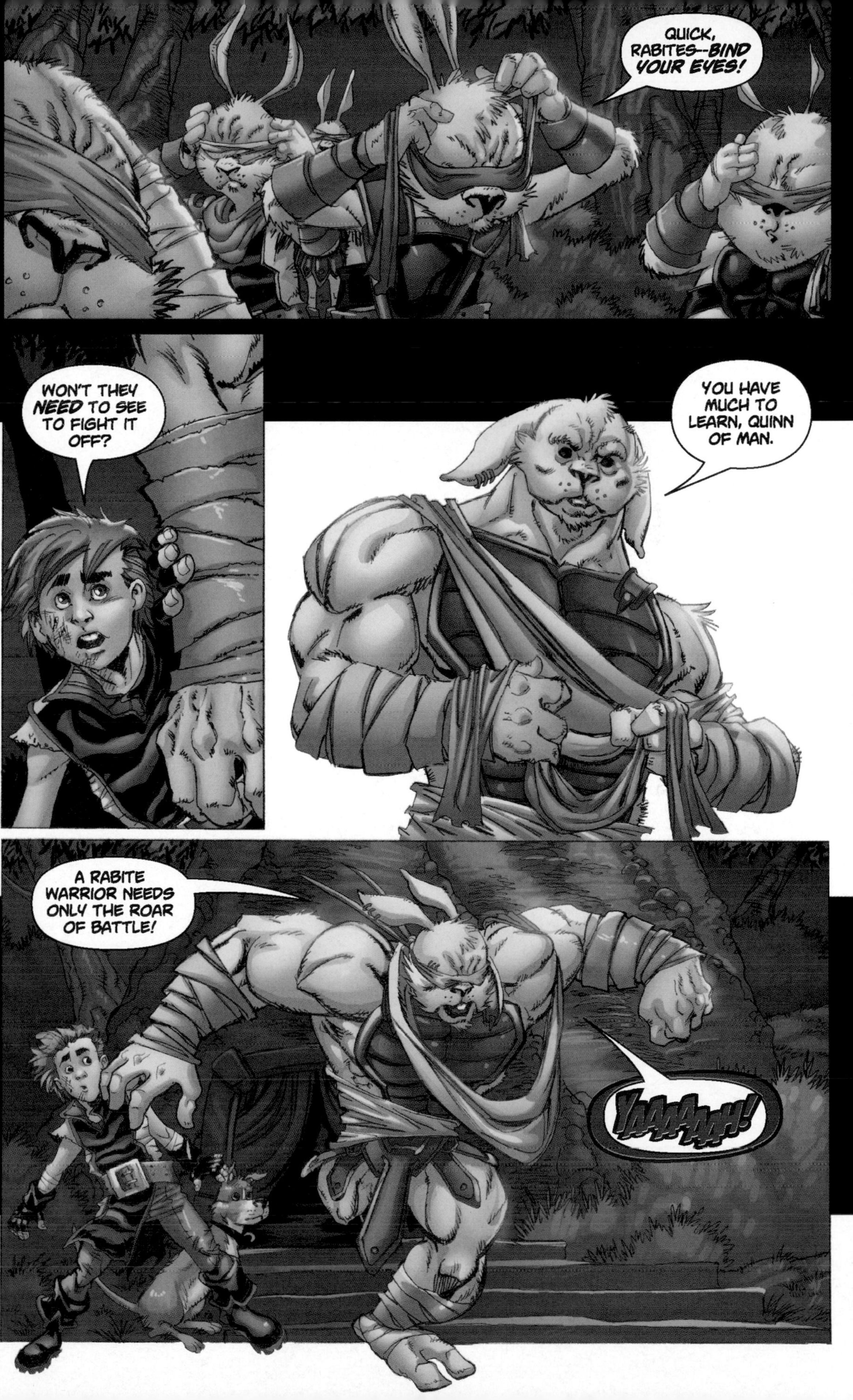
QUICK, RABITES--BIND YOUR EYES!
WON'T THEY NEED TO SEE TO FIGHT IT OFF?
YOU HAVE MUCH TO LEARN, QUINN OF MAN.
A RABITE WARRIOR NEEDS ONLY THE ROAR OF BATTLE!
YAAAAAAH!

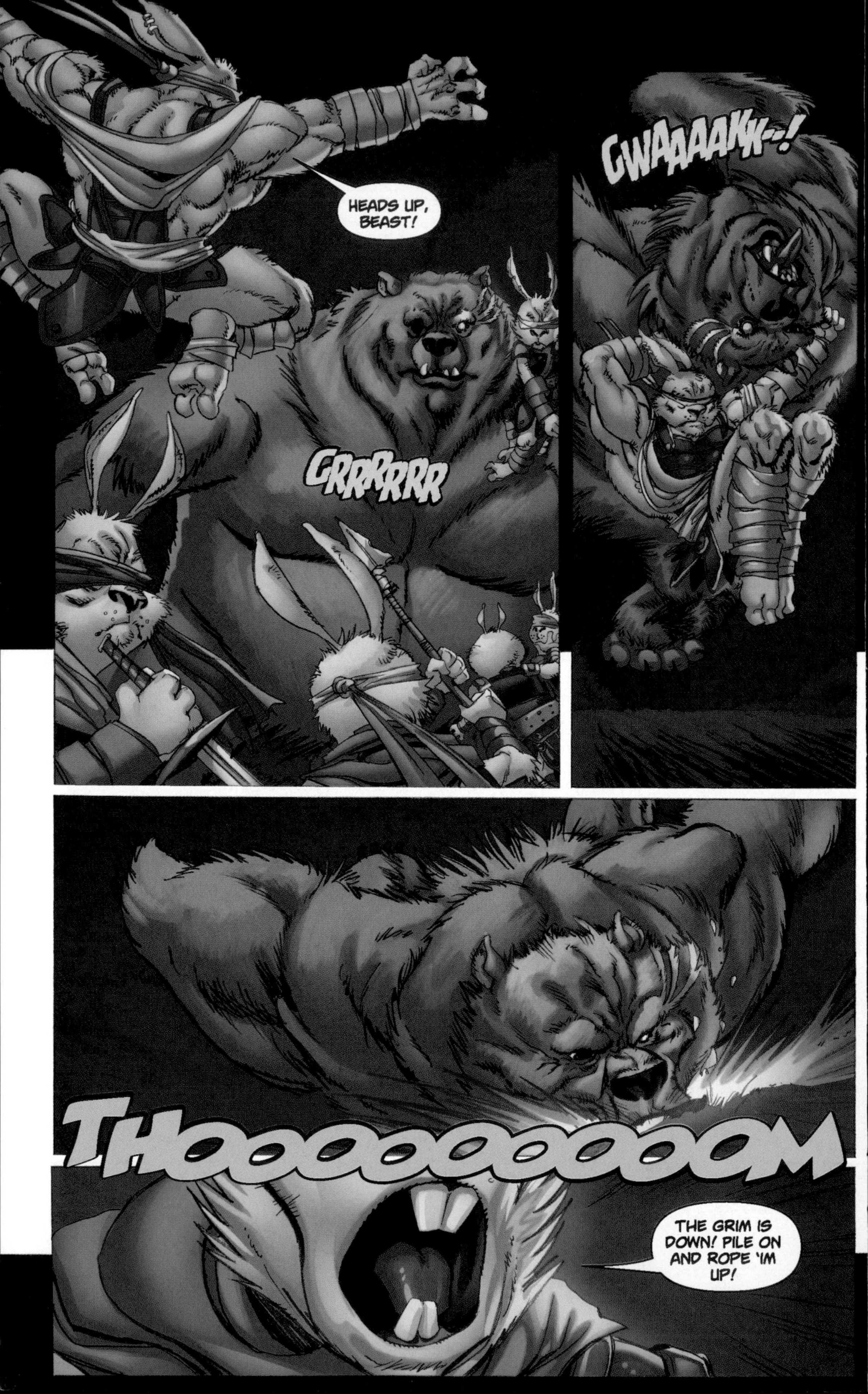
HEADS UP, BEAST!
GRRRRRR
GWAAAAKK--!
THOOOOOOOOOM
THE GRIM IS DOWN! PILE ON AND ROPE 'IM UP!

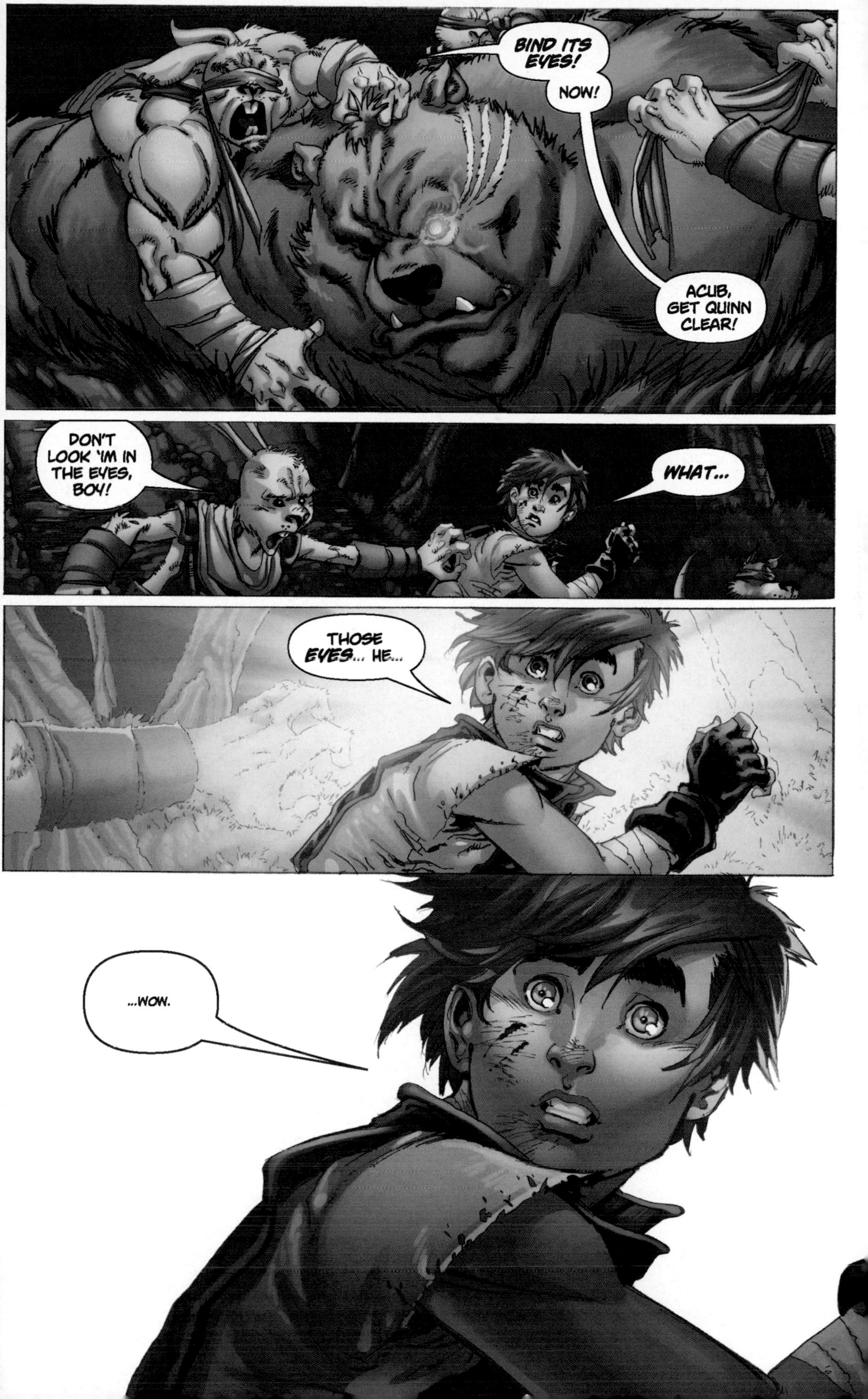
BIND ITS EYES!
NOW!
ACUB, GET QUINN CLEAR!
DON'T LOOK 'IM IN THE EYES, BOY!
WHAT...
THOSE EYES... HE...
...WOW.

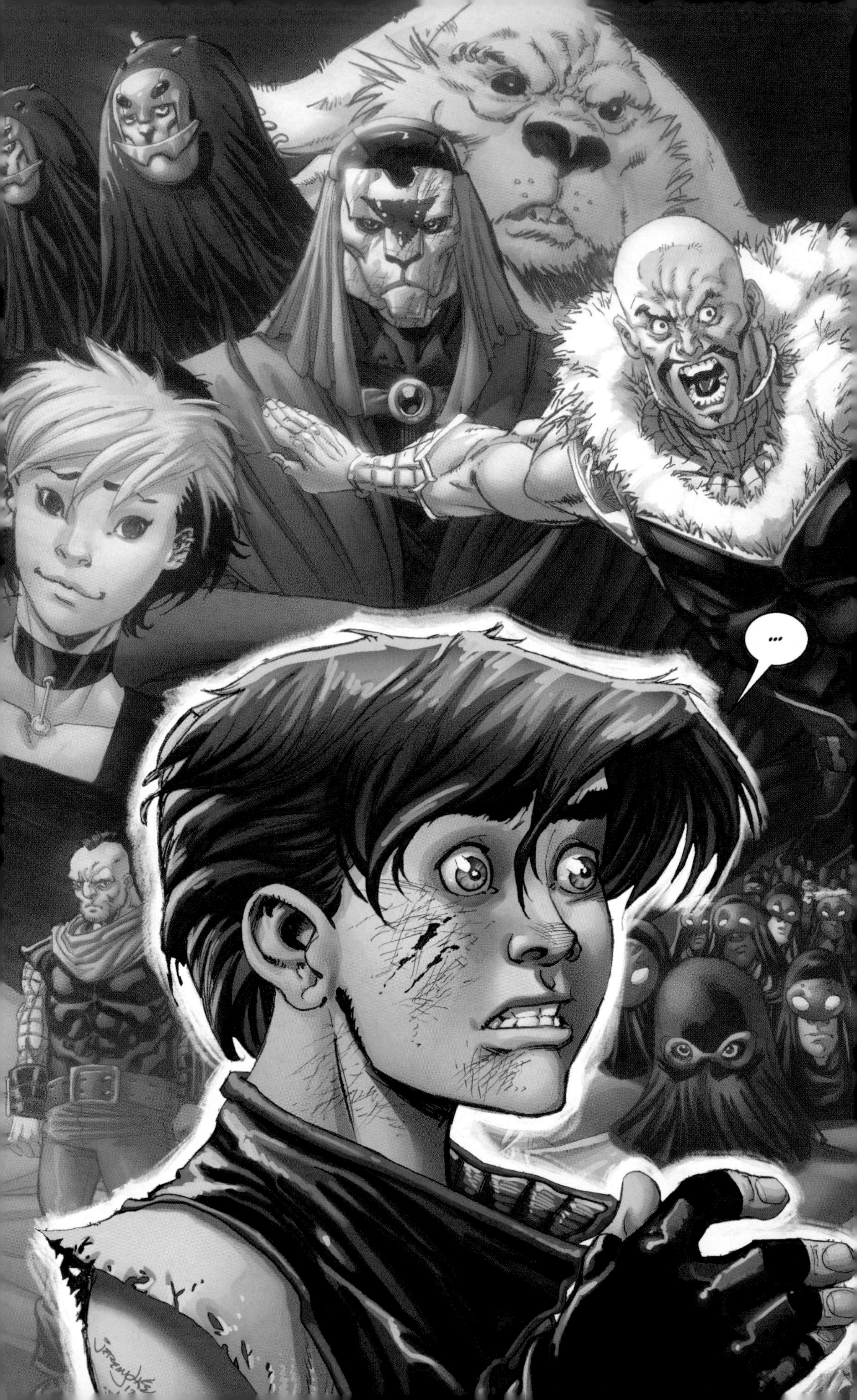
...

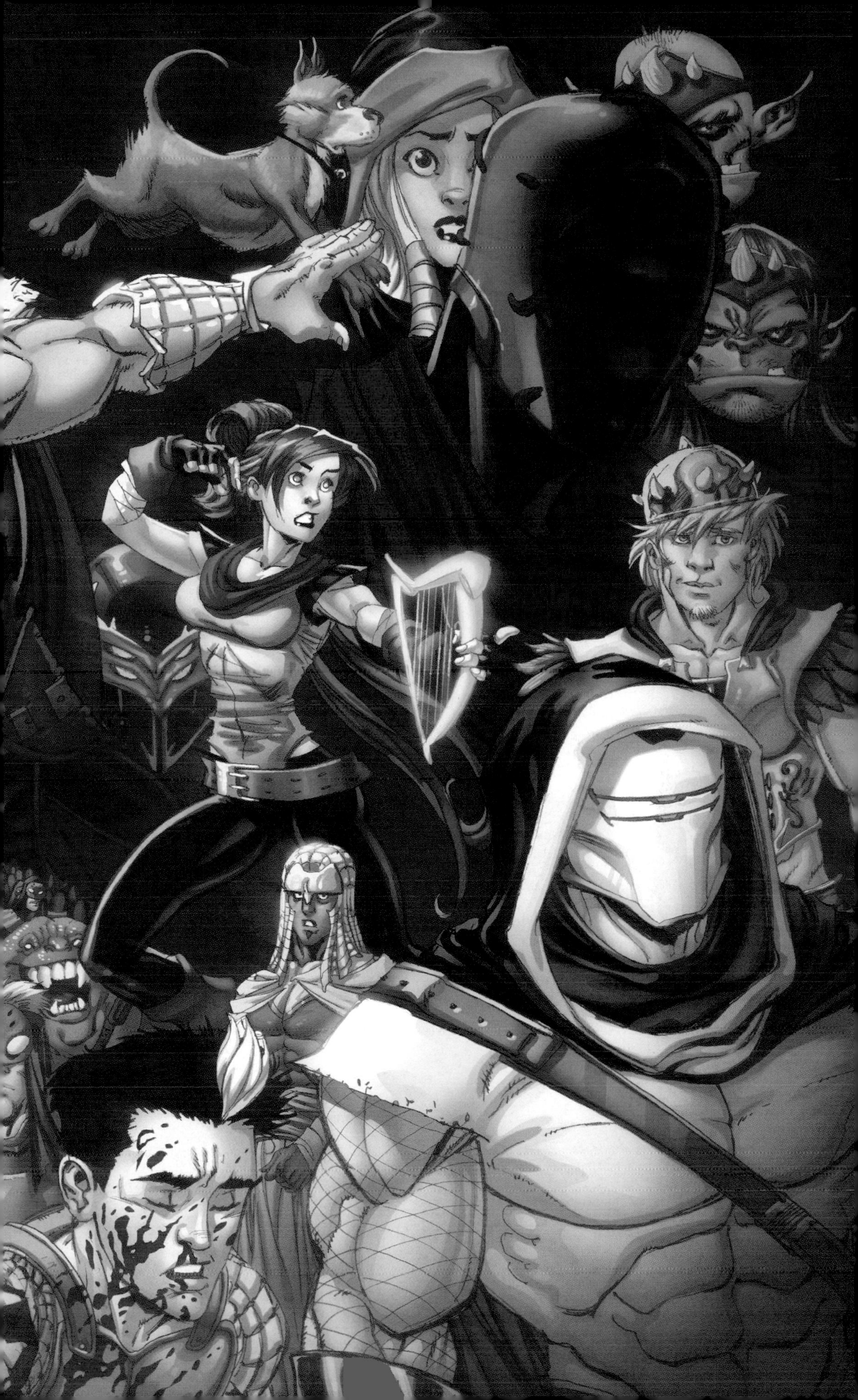

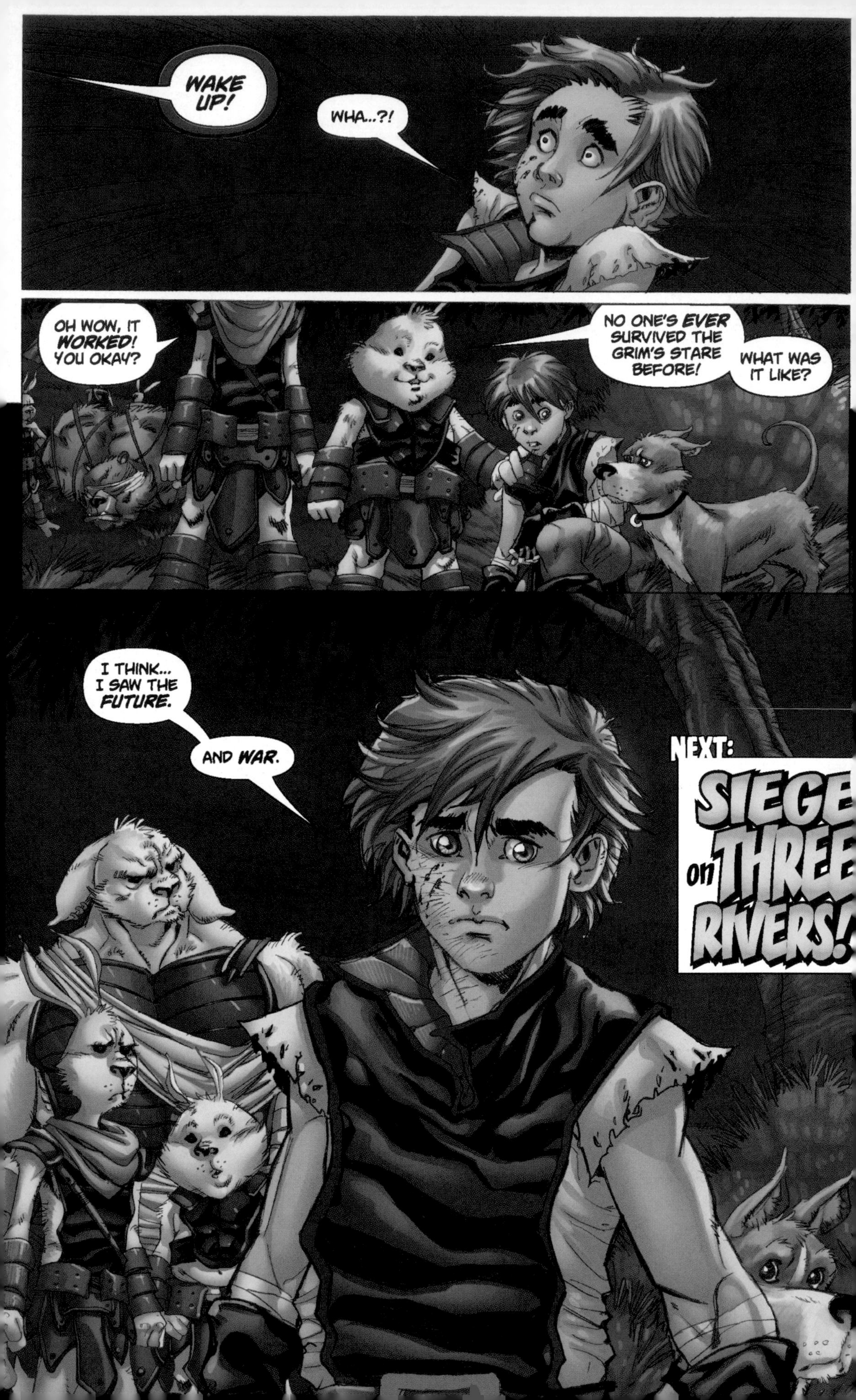
WAKE UP!
WHA...?!
OH WOW, IT WORKED! YOU OKAY?
NO ONE'S EVER SURVIVED THE GRIM'S STARE BEFORE!
WHAT WAS IT LIKE?
I THINK... I SAW THE FUTURE.
AND WAR.
NEXT:
SIEGE on THREE RIVERS!

ACTION LAB: NEW IN 2014

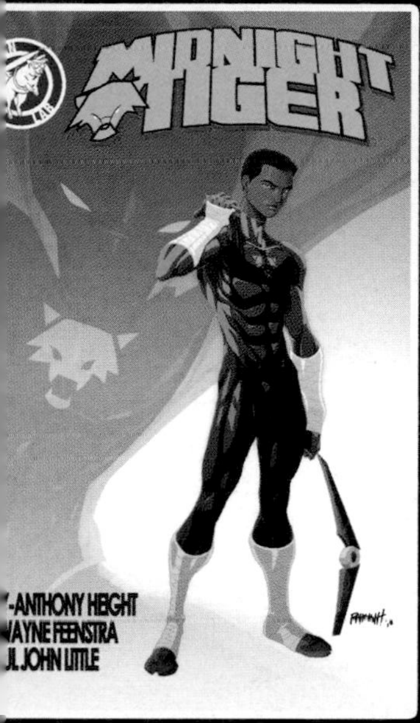
MIDNIGHT TIGER
-ANTHONY HEIGHT
AYNE FEENSTRA
L JOHN LITTLE

MIDNIGHT TIGER
Written by DeWayne Feenstra
Art and Plots by Ray-Anthony Height

From Marvel Comics artist Ray-Anthony Height!
Springing from this year's ALE Free Comic Book Day Issue

Gavin Shaw, a disillusioned highschool senior living in the crime infested city of Apollo Bay, has lost faith in the heroes he admired growing up. After attempting to save the life of a gravely injured hero known as Lionsblood, Gavin finds himself waking up in a hospital bed days later with amazing new super human abilities and smack dab in the middle of a 15 year old secret that could unravel the fabric of the superhero community. Gavin becomes Midnight Tiger, a young hero that's determined not to let that secret destroy his city.

4 ISSUES - SPRING 2014

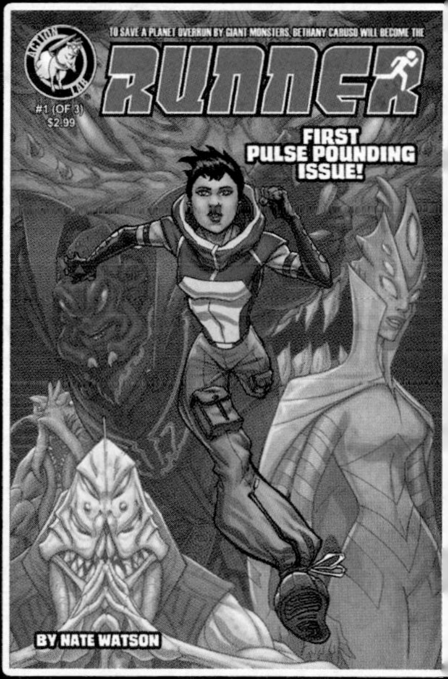
TO SAVE A PLANET OVERRUN BY GIANT MONSTERS, BETHANY CARUSO WILL BECOME THE
RUNNER
#1 (OF 3)
$2.99
FIRST PULSE POUNDING ISSUE!
BY NATE WATSON

RUNNER
Written & Drawn by Nate Watson

From Lucasfilm Animation artist Nate Wason!

As our world is infiltrated by otherworldly zealots and eir army of gigantic monsters, teenage hothead Bethany Caruso is recruited into the XB3 Project, and together with her artificially enhanced team of "Hyper Brawlers" is charged with leading the aliens away from major cities... and into combat!

Parkour meets Kaiju in the most kinetic comic in history!

3 ISSUES - SUMMER 2014

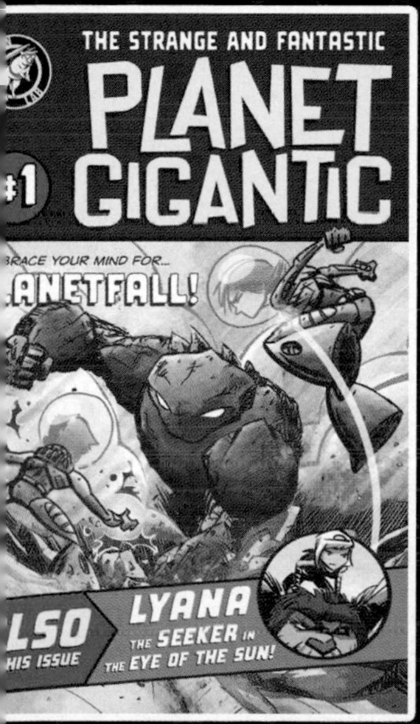
THE STRANGE AND FANTASTIC
PLANET GIGANTIC
#1
BRACE YOUR MIND FOR...
ANETFALL!
LSO
HIS ISSUE
LYANA
THE SEEKER IN THE EYE OF THE SUN!

PLANET GIGANTIC
Written by Eric Grissom
Art by David Halvorson

In the distant future, the Wunderkind Corporation is the leading developer of space exploration technology That technology is children. These genetically engineered human clones have enhanced abilities that range from gravity manipulation to electromagnetic energy generation and are designed to travel hundreds of light years from Earth. Their purpose is to identify potential targets for large scale harvest and mining operations. When two such teenage clones and their robot caretaker MOTHER crash land on a strange planet, they must learn to rely on themselves and their still developing powers as they brave the unforgiving planet.

4 ISSUES - WINTER 2014

THE FUTURE IS NOW!

ACTION LAB: NEW IN 2014

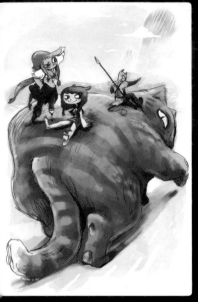

MISHKA AND THE SEA DEVIL
Written and Drawn by Xenia Pamfil

11 Days trapped on an island. 11 different art styles. 1 incredible artist!

Fisherman Mishka is left stranded on a mysterious islanc after an encounter at sea with an equally mysterious bea To get off the island she must unlock the secrets of the monster that trapped her there. Threats come from every direction, but thanks to a colorful cast of characters including Admiral Ghost and Captain Furball, she may just have a fighting chance!

OVERSIZED HARDCOVER - SUMMER 2014

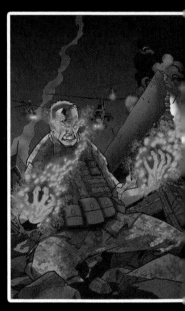

F1RST HERO
Written by Anthony Ruttgaizer
Art by Phillip Sevy
Covers by Lee Moder

What if everyone who had ever developed superpowers had gone insane and become a threat to society? What if ONE man manifested powers but also kept his sanity? Faced with a society that fears superhumans, a government that hunts them down and growing numbers of crazed supervillains all around him, Jacob Roth must decide to either put himself at risk by using his powers to help people or do nothing and remain safe while innocent people get hurt.

4 ISSUES - FALL 2014

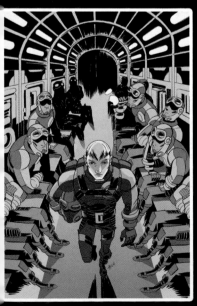

JETPACK B@$T@RD$
Written by James Patrick
Art by Carlos Trigo

From the award winning writer of Batman & Star Tre

After Earth is attacked by a superior alien force, it must resort to guerrilla tactics for its survival. Enter the Jetpack Brigades, who fly like madmen into ener ships, and blow them to hell. Cameron Spinx is a sta pilot who's just been promoted to the elite *Team Scorpion*. But Team Scorpion has a secret which jus might get him killed.

4 ISSUES - WINTER 2014

THE FUTURE IS NOW

ARE YOU A **LEGO® *STAR WARS*®** EXPERT?

Test your knowledge with the questions below!
Find tons of information and facts about your favorite LEGO® sets and minifigures in *LEGO® Star Wars®: The Visual Dictionary: Updated and Expanded*. It even includes an exclusive Luke Skywalker minifigure!

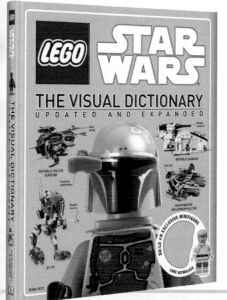

1 **What two LEGO elements were repurposed for the glowing eye and armored shell of a droideka?**

2 **When did the LEGO Group release its first *Star Wars* sets?**

3 **Which LEGO minifigure, complete with brown Jedi cape, came with the Palpatine's Arrest LEGO set?**

4 **What is the name of the fast-moving varactyl that Obi-Wan uses to chase General Grievous on Utapau?**

5 **After surviving the great Jedi purge at the end of the Clone Wars, where does Yoda live in exile?**

6 **Which LEGO minifigure came exclusively with the 2011 edition of the *LEGO Star Wars: Character Encyclopedia*?**

7 **Which LEGO Technic® self-destructs when its "belly-button" socket is pressed?**

LEGO
STAR WARS
THE VISUAL DICTIONARY
UPDATED AND EXPANDED
BUILD AN EXCLUSIVE MINIFIGURE
LUKE SKYWALKER
REPUBLIC POLICE GUNSHIP
AT-RT
BOBA FETT
REPUBLIC GUNSHIP
MICROFIGHTER MILLENNIUM FALCON

8 **From 1999-2014, how many Luke Skywalker minifigures have been created?**

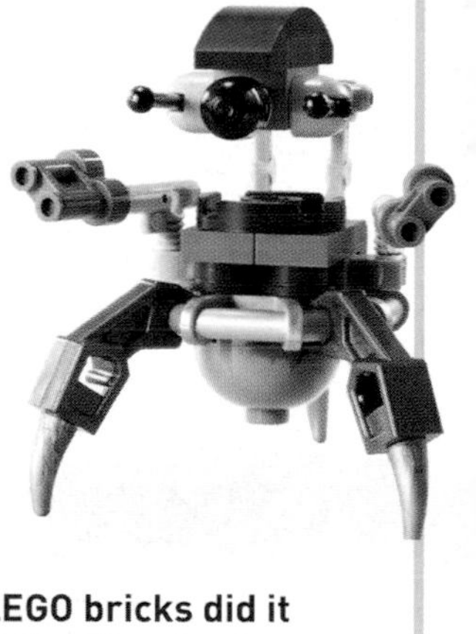

9 **Which LEGO Ultimate Collector Set weighs nearly 9 lbs?**

10 **How many LEGO bricks did it take to build the life-sized X-wing that was featured in Times Square in May 2013?**

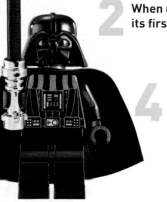

Answers: 1 - Cupcake and Frosting, 2 - 1999, 3 - Anakin, 4 - Boga, 5 - Dagobah, 6 - (Han) Celebration Han, 7 - C-3PO, 8 - 28, 9 - Darth Maul, 10 - 5,335,200

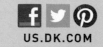

SKYWARD™
BATTLE OF THREE RIVERS

Jeremy Dale
Creator / Writer / Artist
@jeremydale

Kathryn Layno
Colors
@denimcatfish

Thom Zahler
Letters
@loveandcapes

Hoyt Silva
Color Flats
@hoytsilva

Covers by

Jeremy Dale
@jeremydale

and

Chris Giarrusso
@Chris_Giarrusso

For more visit
www.skywardcomic.com

Previously:

So much stuff happened, you guys! Okay, so Jon was given the mysterious Gloves of Galia by the Rabites as a reward for helping them rid their home of Skerrigan, Herod's assassin. They glow pretty.

Prince Dom of Three Rivers & friend Mia stumbled into Herod's scouting party-- luckily, the River Riders rescued them!

Sadly, it cost the Riders their lives. Only their commander returned to the city-- and bumped into slave warrior trader Hurlan, who sold some men to the commander for the upcoming battle.

Yeesh.

FOR ACTION LAB ENTERTAINMENT
Kevin Freeman - President
Bryan Seaton - Chief Financial Officer
Shawn Pryor - VP Digital Media
Dave Dwonch - Creative Director
Shawn Gabborin - Editor In Chief
Jason Martin - Editor
Kelly Dale & Jamal Igle - Directors of Marketing
Jim Dietz - Social Media Director
Jeremy Whitley - Education Outreach Director
Chad Cicconi & Colleen Boyd - Associate Editors
WWW.ACTIONLABCOMICS.COM

jeremy-dale.com

JEREMY DALE - the talent

KELLY DALE - project editor

KIRBY THE DOG - canine relations

WWW.JEREMY-DALE.COM

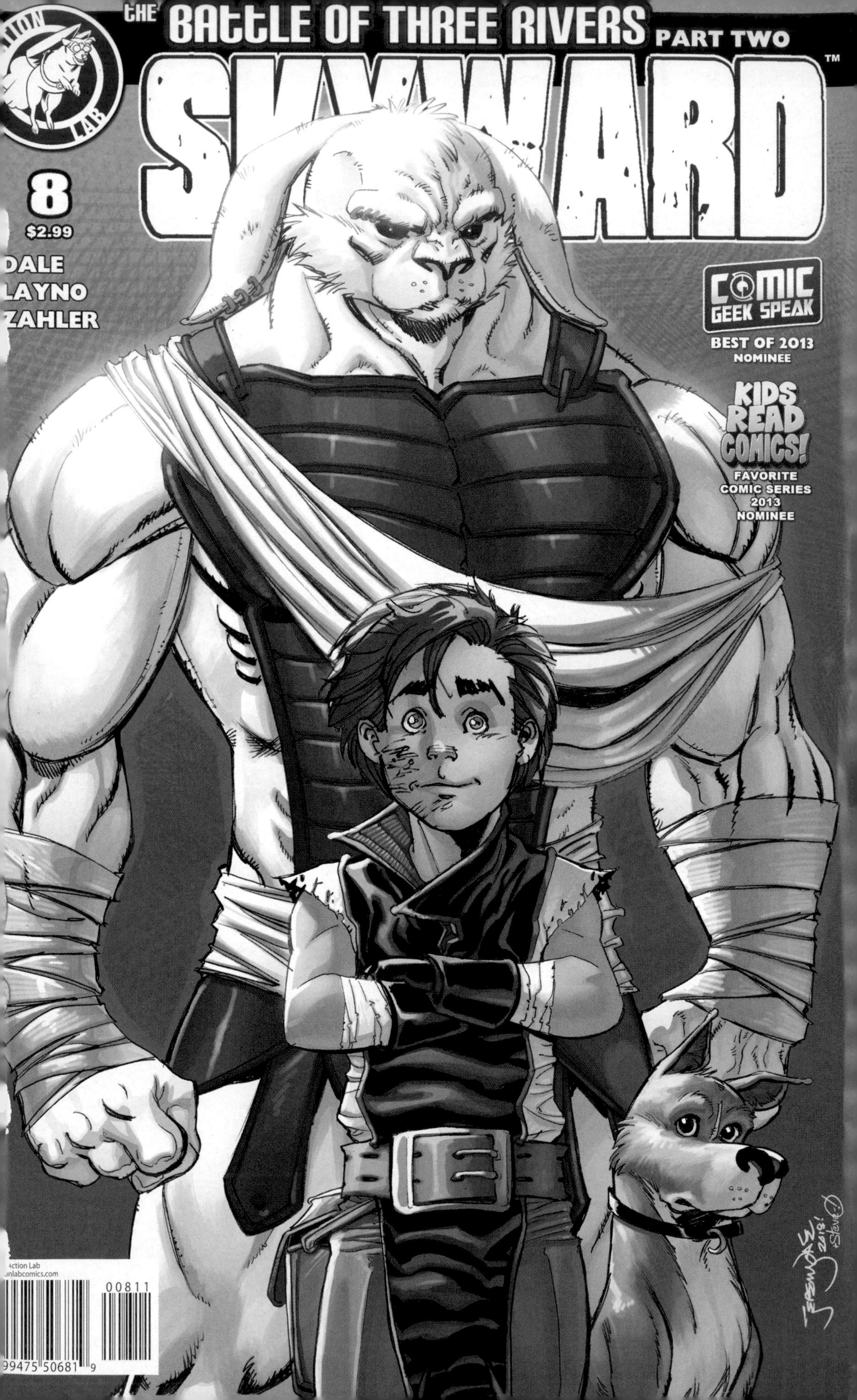
THE BATTLE OF THREE RIVERS PART TWO
SKYWARD™
8
$2.99
DALE
LAYNO
ZAHLER
COMIC GEEK SPEAK
BEST OF 2013
NOMINEE
KIDS READ COMICS!
FAVORITE
COMIC SERIES
2013
NOMINEE

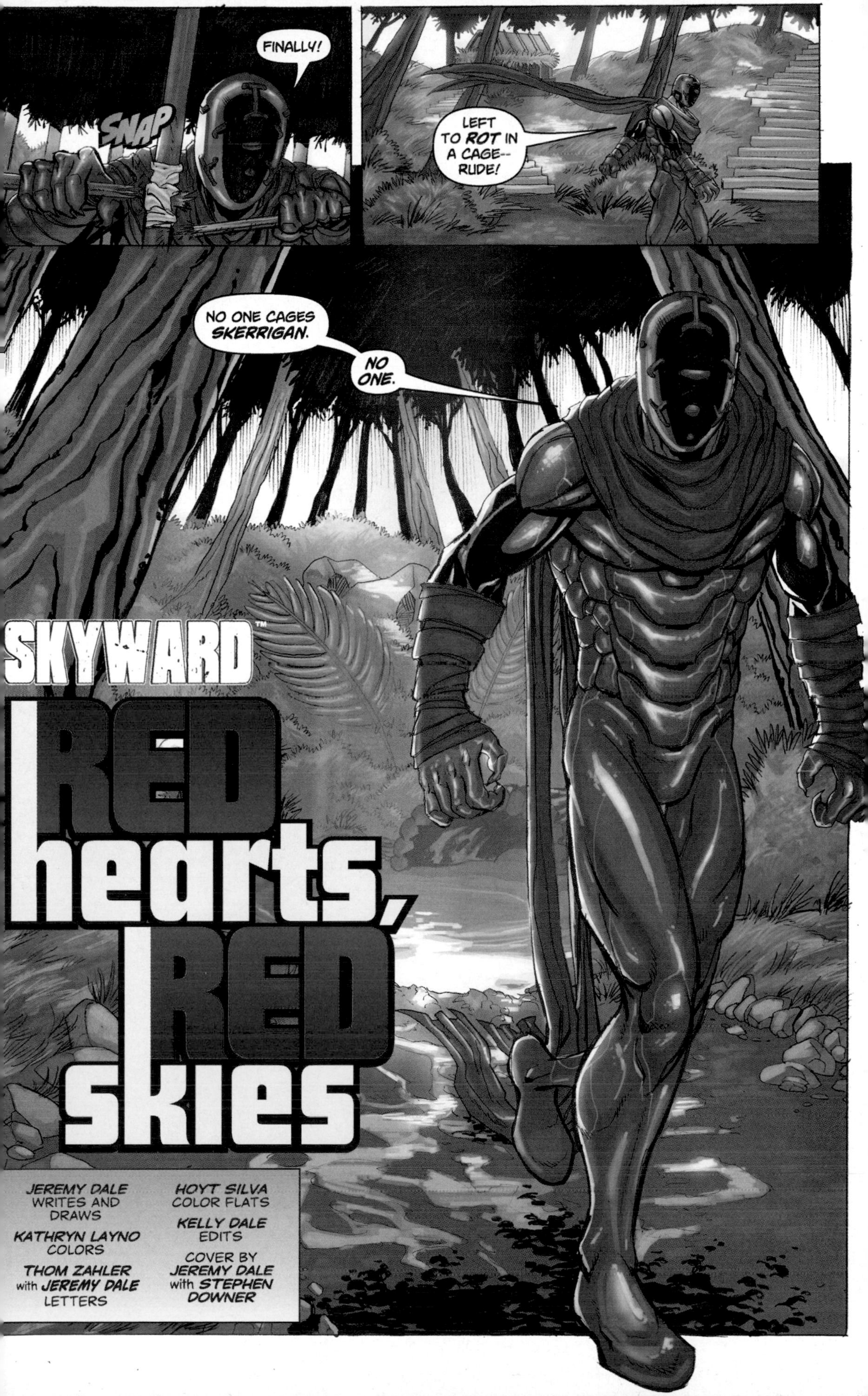
FINALLY!
SNAP
LEFT TO ROT IN A CAGE-- RUDE!
NO ONE CAGES SKERRIGAN.
NO ONE.
SKYWARD™
RED hearts, RED skies
JEREMY DALE WRITES AND DRAWS
KATHRYN LAYNO COLORS
THOM ZAHLER with JEREMY DALE LETTERS
HOYT SILVA COLOR FLATS
KELLY DALE EDITS
COVER BY JEREMY DALE with STEPHEN DOWNER

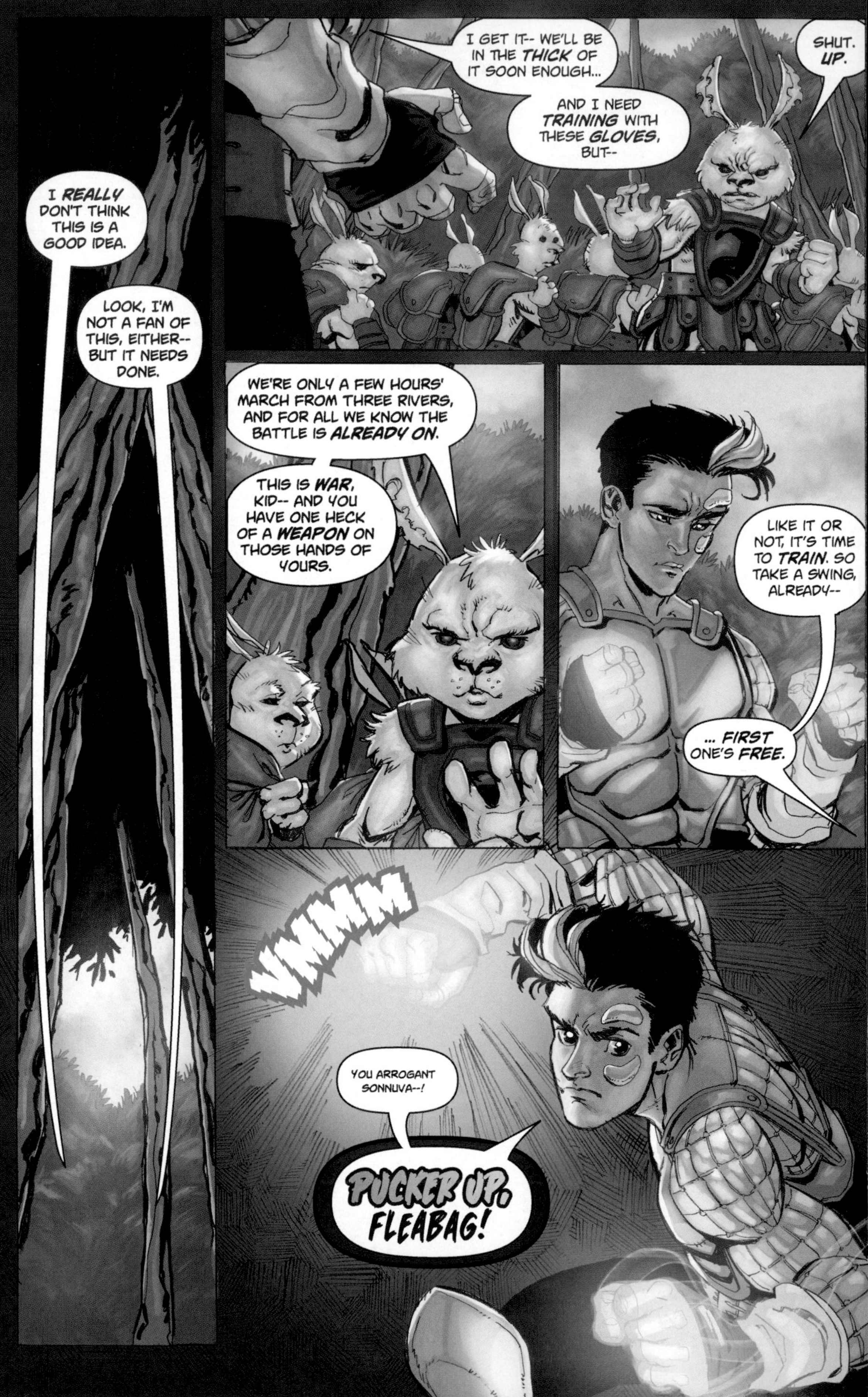
I REALLY DON'T THINK THIS IS A GOOD IDEA.
LOOK, I'M NOT A FAN OF THIS, EITHER-- BUT IT NEEDS DONE.
I GET IT-- WE'LL BE IN THE THICK OF IT SOON ENOUGH...
AND I NEED TRAINING WITH THESE GLOVES, BUT--
SHUT. UP.
WE'RE ONLY A FEW HOURS' MARCH FROM THREE RIVERS, AND FOR ALL WE KNOW THE BATTLE IS ALREADY ON.
THIS IS WAR, KID-- AND YOU HAVE ONE HECK OF A WEAPON ON THOSE HANDS OF YOURS.
LIKE IT OR NOT, IT'S TIME TO TRAIN. SO TAKE A SWING, ALREADY--
... FIRST ONE'S FREE.
VMMM
YOU ARROGANT SONNUVA--!
PUCKER UP, FLEABAG!

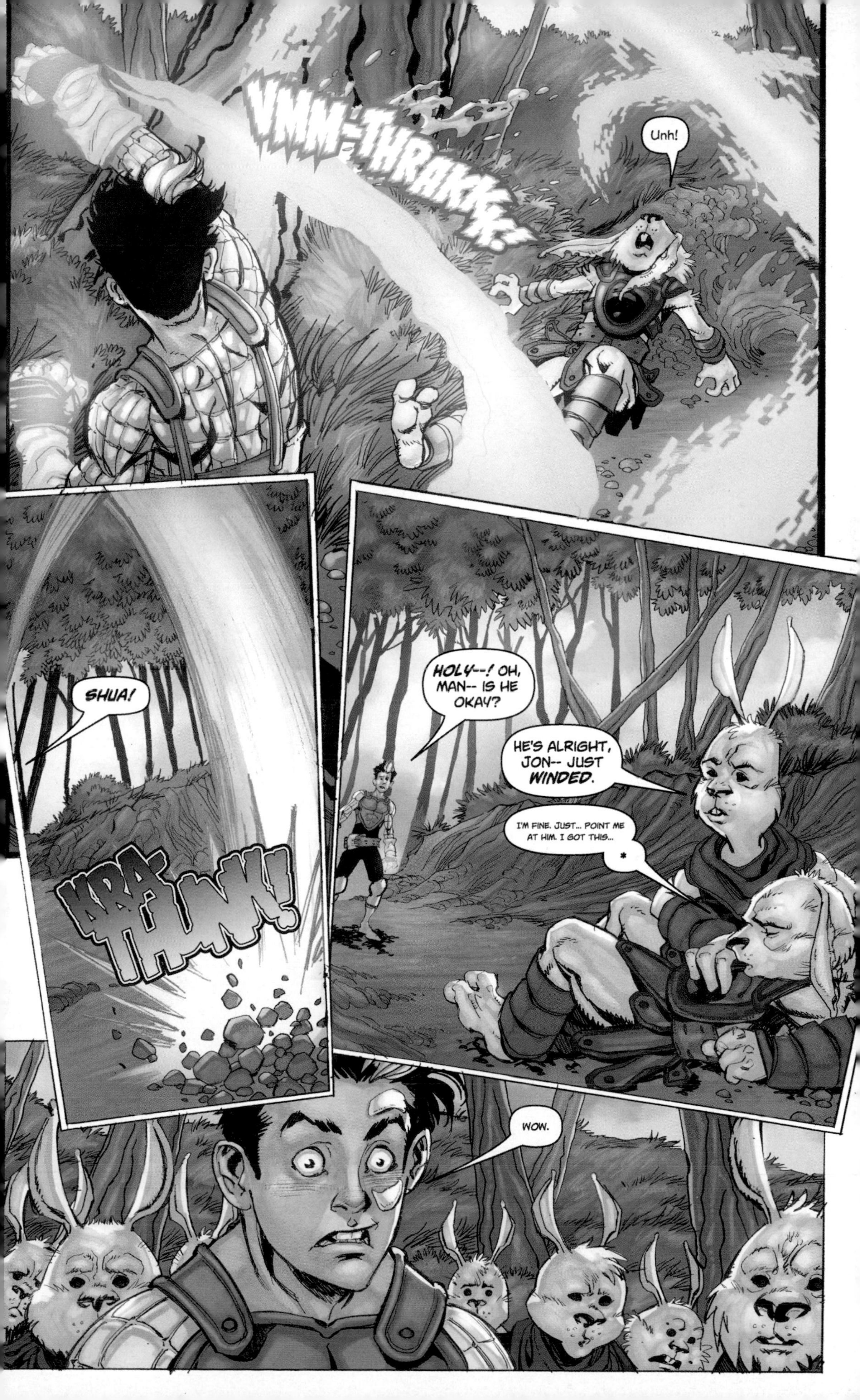
VMM-THRAKKK!
Unh!
SHUA!
KRA-THUNK!
HOLY--! OH, MAN-- IS HE OKAY?
HE'S ALRIGHT, JON-- JUST WINDED.
I'M FINE. JUST... POINT ME AT HIM. I GOT THIS...
*
WOW.

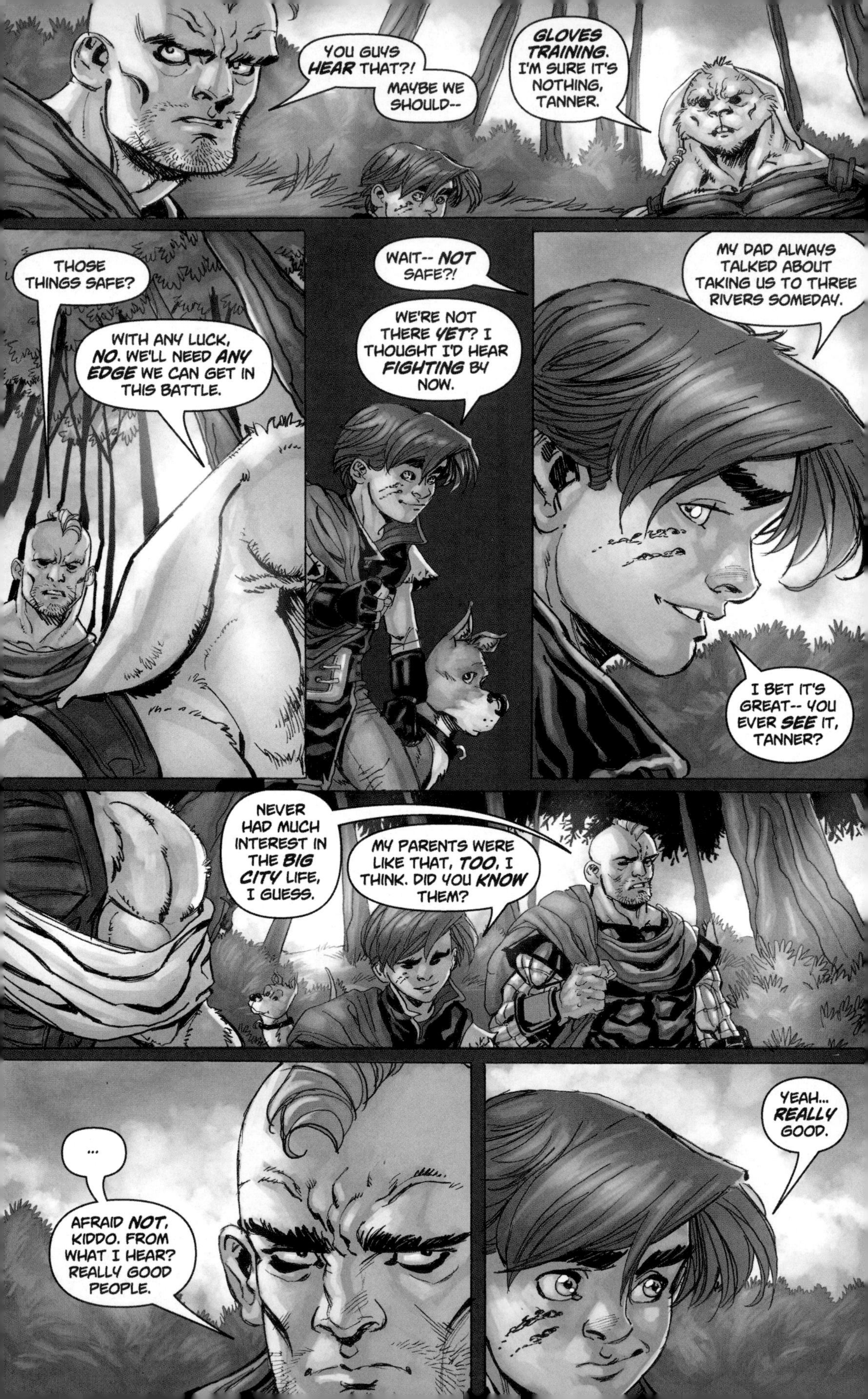

YOU GUYS HEAR THAT?!
MAYBE WE SHOULD--
GLOVES TRAINING. I'M SURE IT'S NOTHING, TANNER.
THOSE THINGS SAFE?
WITH ANY LUCK, NO. WE'LL NEED ANY EDGE WE CAN GET IN THIS BATTLE.
WAIT-- NOT SAFE?!
WE'RE NOT THERE YET? I THOUGHT I'D HEAR FIGHTING BY NOW.
MY DAD ALWAYS TALKED ABOUT TAKING US TO THREE RIVERS SOMEDAY.
I BET IT'S GREAT-- YOU EVER SEE IT, TANNER?
NEVER HAD MUCH INTEREST IN THE BIG CITY LIFE, I GUESS.
MY PARENTS WERE LIKE THAT, TOO, I THINK. DID YOU KNOW THEM?
...
AFRAID NOT, KIDDO. FROM WHAT I HEAR? REALLY GOOD PEOPLE.
YEAH... REALLY GOOD.

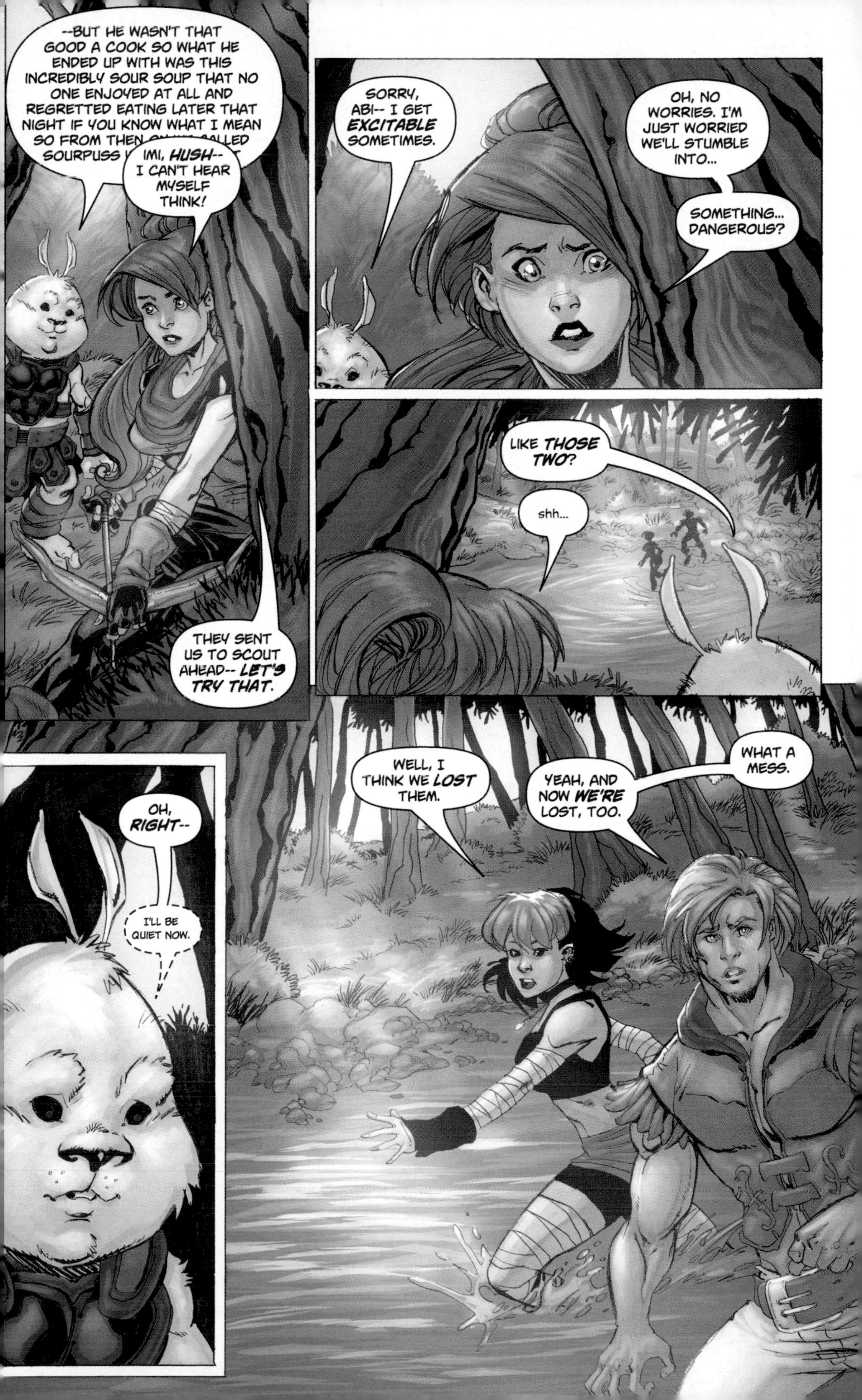
--BUT HE WASN'T THAT GOOD A COOK SO WHAT HE ENDED UP WITH WAS THIS INCREDIBLY SOUR SOUP THAT NO ONE ENJOYED AT ALL AND REGRETTED EATING LATER THAT NIGHT IF YOU KNOW WHAT I MEAN SO FROM THEN SOURPUSS
IMI, HUSH-- I CAN'T HEAR MYSELF THINK!
THEY SENT US TO SCOUT AHEAD-- LET'S TRY THAT.
SORRY, ABI-- I GET EXCITABLE SOMETIMES.
OH, NO WORRIES. I'M JUST WORRIED WE'LL STUMBLE INTO...
SOMETHING... DANGEROUS?
LIKE THOSE TWO?
shh...
OH, RIGHT--
I'LL BE QUIET NOW.
WELL, I THINK WE LOST THEM.
YEAH, AND NOW WE'RE LOST, TOO.
WHAT A MESS.

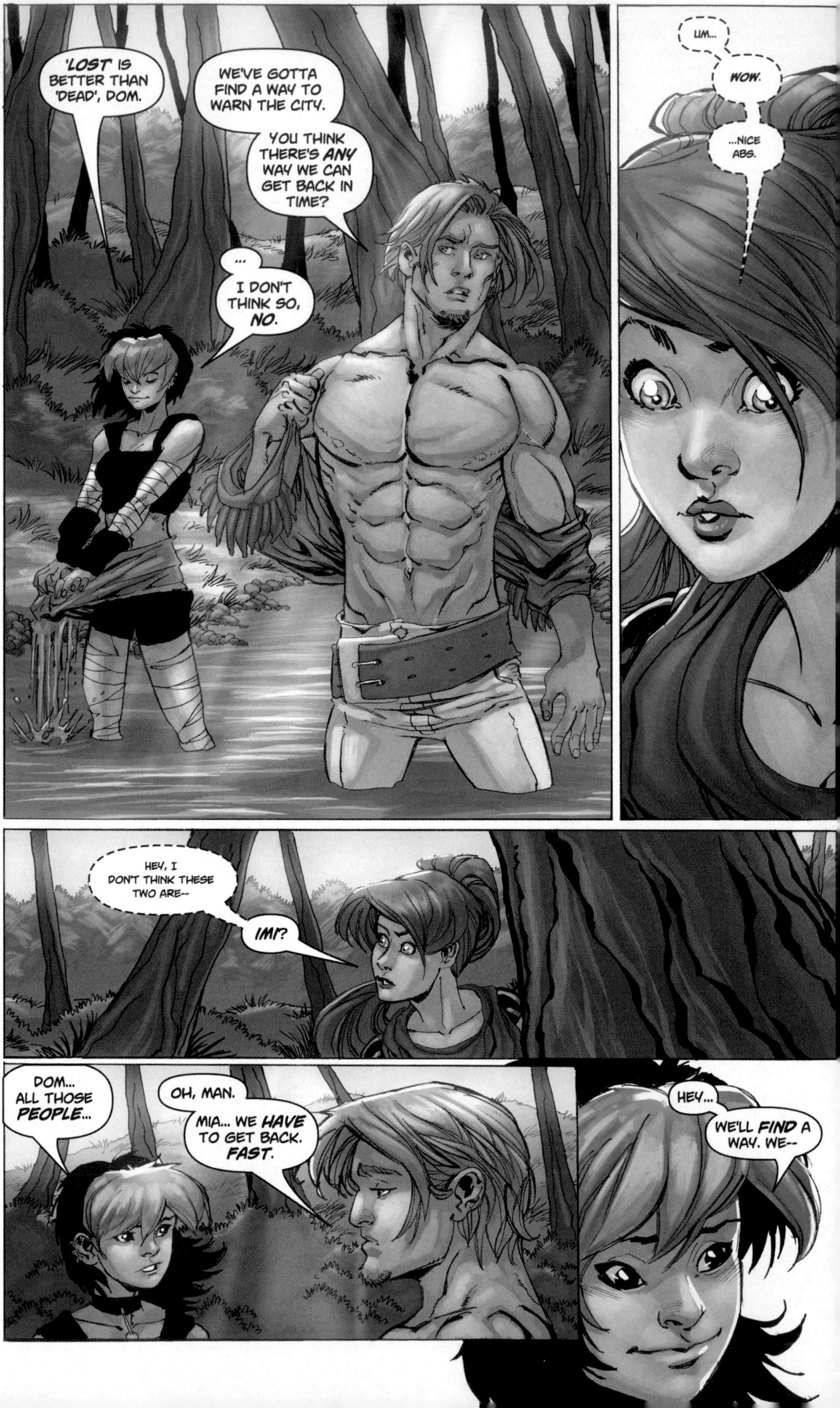
'LOST' IS BETTER THAN 'DEAD', DOM.
WE'VE GOTTA FIND A WAY TO WARN THE CITY.
YOU THINK THERE'S ANY WAY WE CAN GET BACK IN TIME?
...
I DON'T THINK SO, NO.
UM...
WOW.
...NICE ABS.
HEY, I DON'T THINK THESE TWO ARE--
IMI?
DOM... ALL THOSE PEOPLE...
OH, MAN.
MIA... WE HAVE TO GET BACK. FAST.
HEY...
WE'LL FIND A WAY. WE--

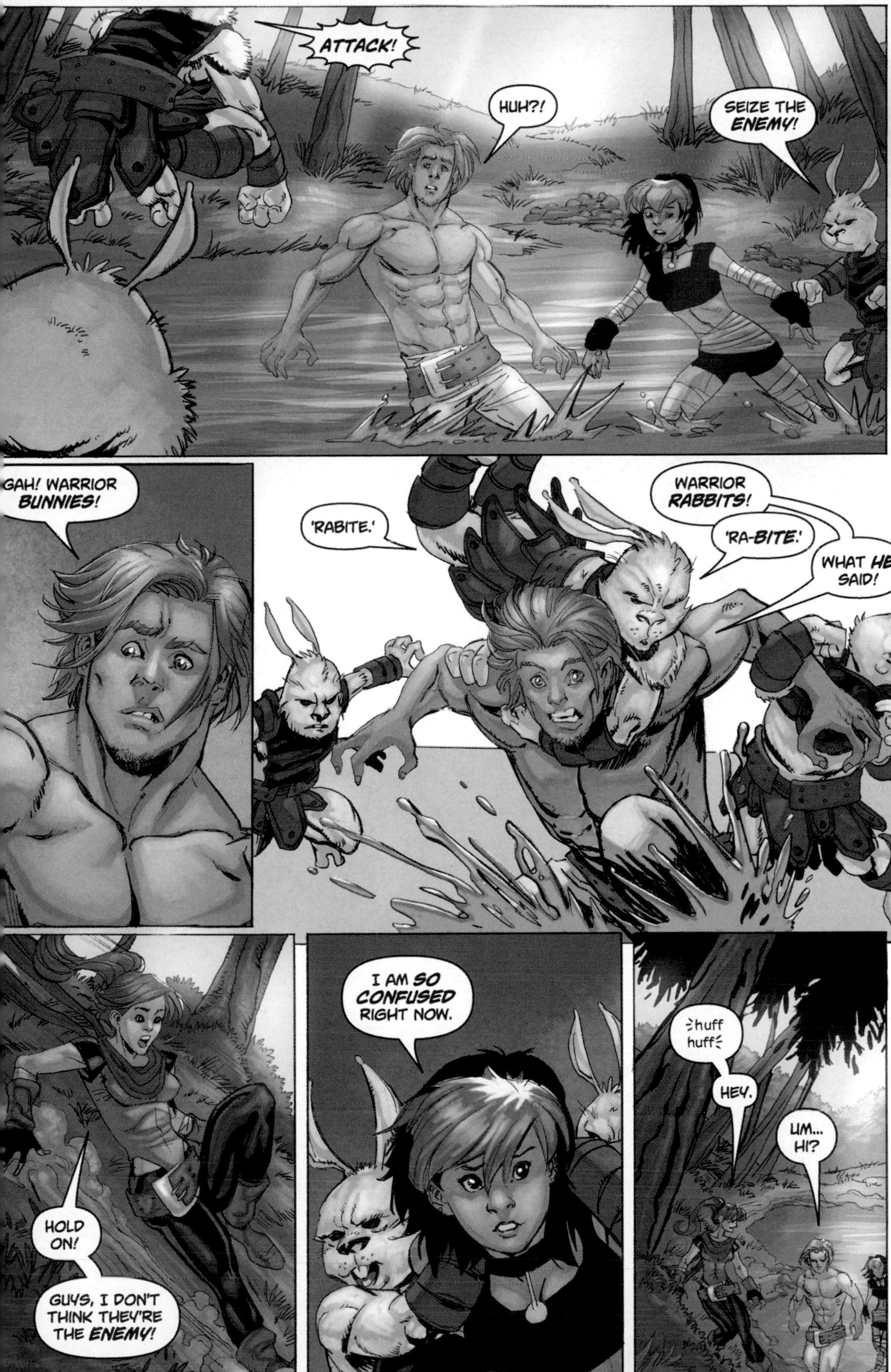
ATTACK!
HUH?!
SEIZE THE ENEMY!
GAH! WARRIOR BUNNIES!
'RABITE.'
WARRIOR RABBITS!
'RA-BITE.'
WHAT HE SAID!
HOLD ON!
GUYS, I DON'T THINK THEY'RE THE ENEMY!
I AM SO CONFUSED RIGHT NOW.
huff huff
HEY.
UM... HI?

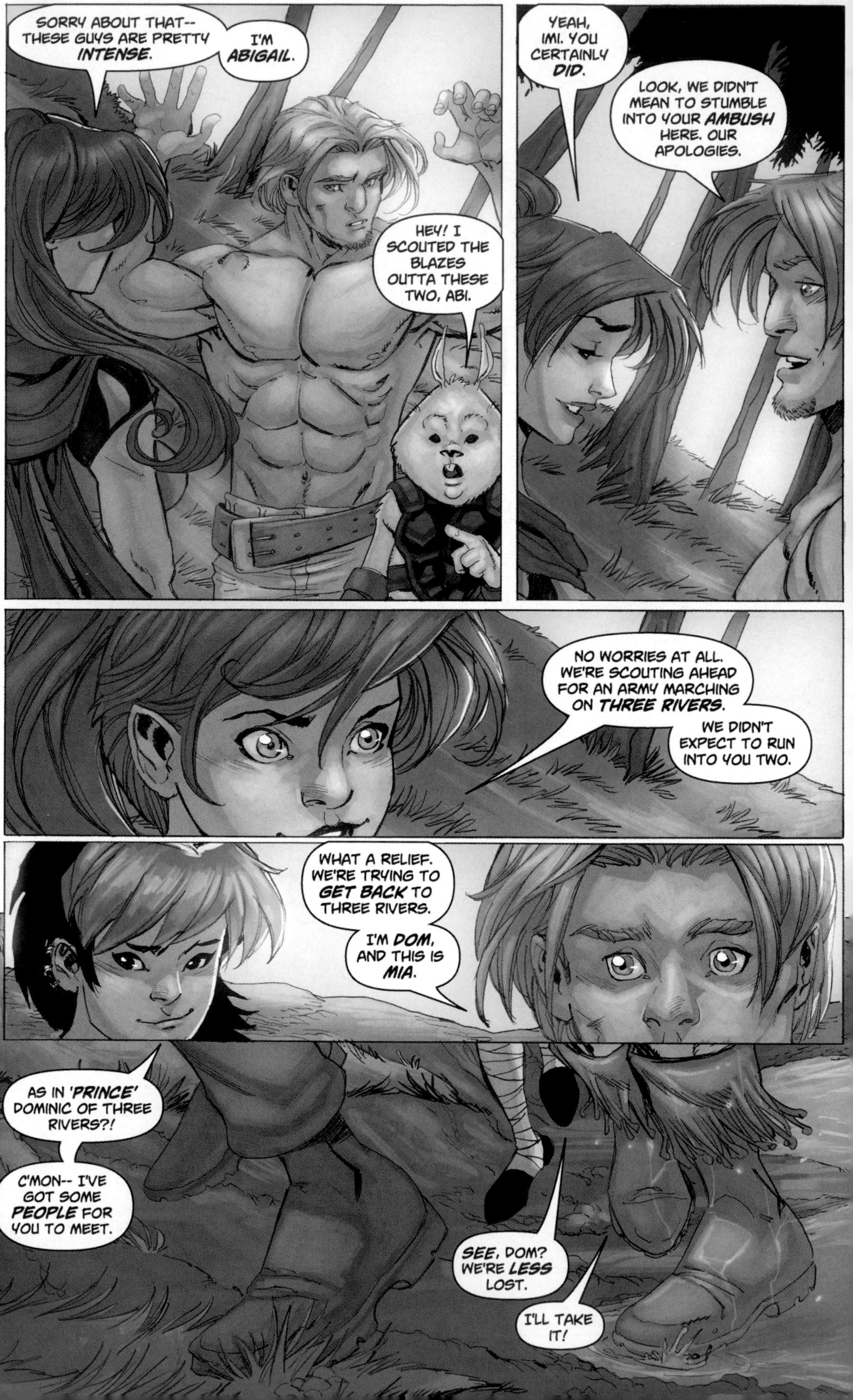
SORRY ABOUT THAT-- THESE GUYS ARE PRETTY INTENSE.
I'M ABIGAIL.
HEY! I SCOUTED THE BLAZES OUTTA THESE TWO, ABI.
YEAH, IMI. YOU CERTAINLY DID.
LOOK, WE DIDN'T MEAN TO STUMBLE INTO YOUR AMBUSH HERE. OUR APOLOGIES.
NO WORRIES AT ALL. WE'RE SCOUTING AHEAD FOR AN ARMY MARCHING ON THREE RIVERS.
WE DIDN'T EXPECT TO RUN INTO YOU TWO.
WHAT A RELIEF. WE'RE TRYING TO GET BACK TO THREE RIVERS.
I'M DOM, AND THIS IS MIA.
AS IN 'PRINCE' DOMINIC OF THREE RIVERS?!
C'MON-- I'VE GOT SOME PEOPLE FOR YOU TO MEET.
SEE, DOM? WE'RE LESS LOST.
I'LL TAKE IT!

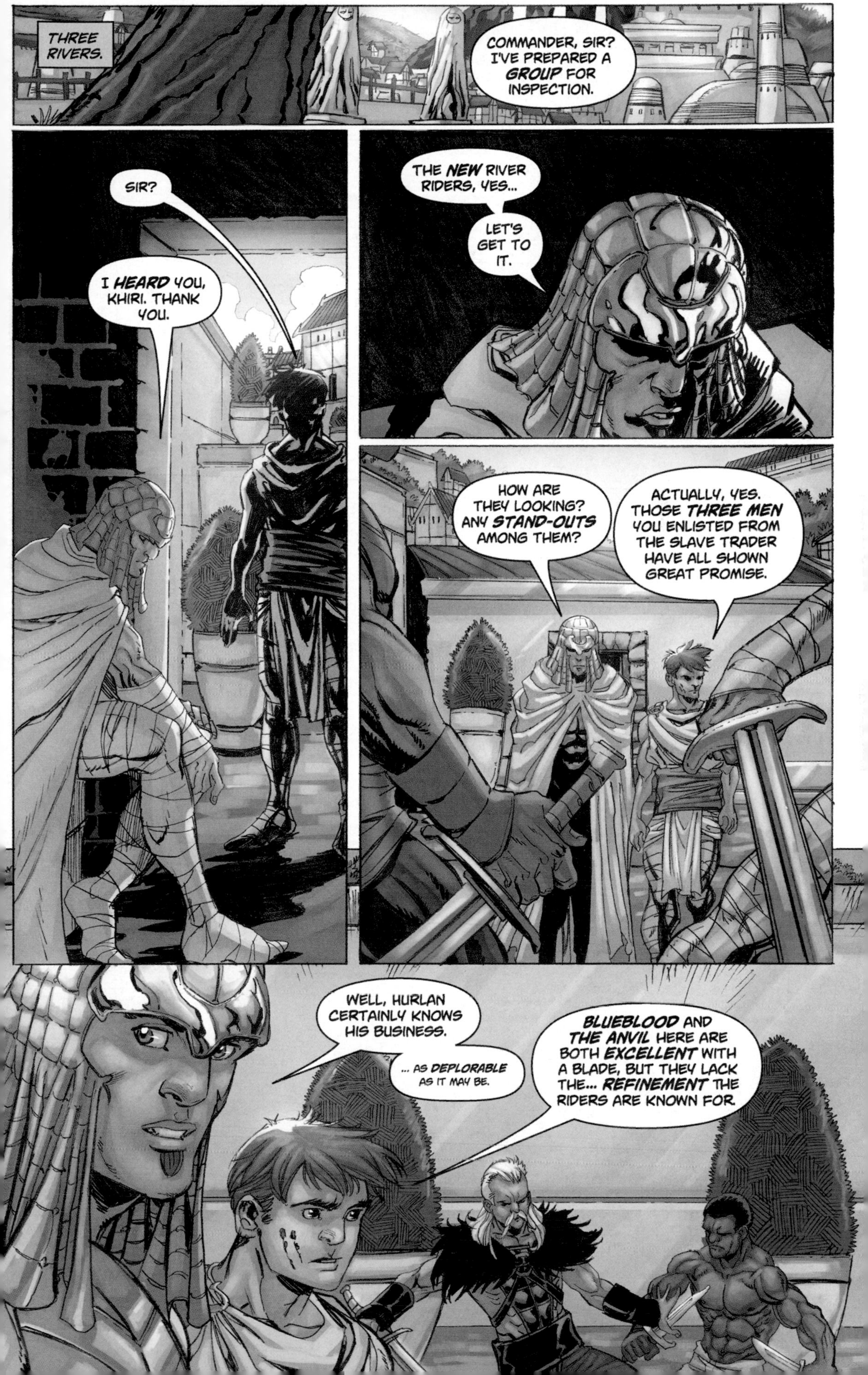
THREE RIVERS.
COMMANDER, SIR? I'VE PREPARED A GROUP FOR INSPECTION.
SIR?
I HEARD YOU, KHIRI. THANK YOU.
THE NEW RIVER RIDERS, YES...
LET'S GET TO IT.
HOW ARE THEY LOOKING? ANY STAND-OUTS AMONG THEM?
ACTUALLY, YES. THOSE THREE MEN YOU ENLISTED FROM THE SLAVE TRADER HAVE ALL SHOWN GREAT PROMISE.
WELL, HURLAN CERTAINLY KNOWS HIS BUSINESS.
... AS DEPLORABLE AS IT MAY BE.
BLUEBLOOD AND THE ANVIL HERE ARE BOTH EXCELLENT WITH A BLADE, BUT THEY LACK THE... REFINEMENT THE RIDERS ARE KNOWN FOR.

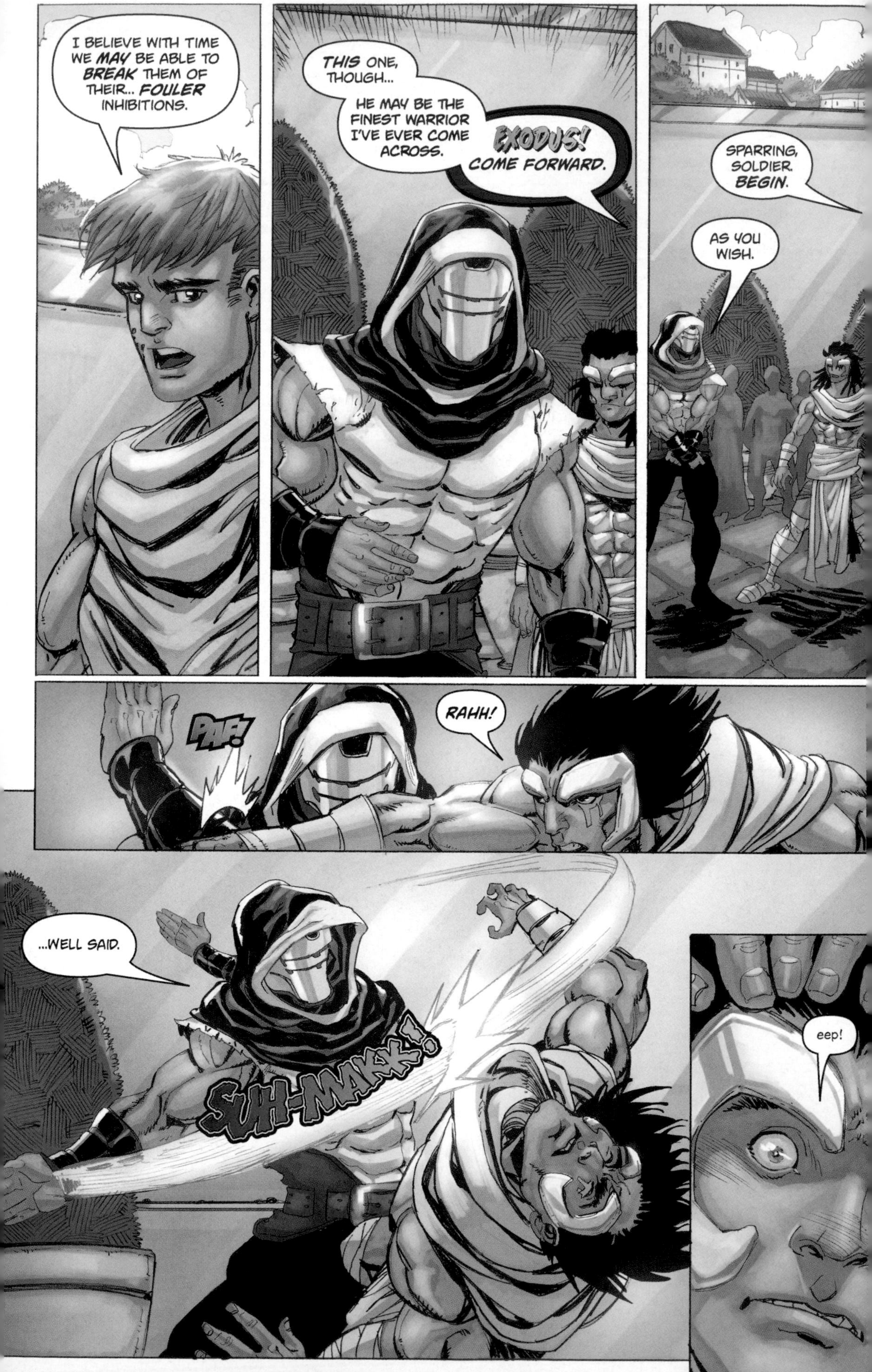
I BELIEVE WITH TIME WE MAY BE ABLE TO BREAK THEM OF THEIR... FOULER INHIBITIONS.
THIS ONE, THOUGH...
HE MAY BE THE FINEST WARRIOR I'VE EVER COME ACROSS.
EXODUS! COME FORWARD.
SPARRING, SOLDIER. BEGIN.
AS YOU WISH.
PAF!
RAHH!
...WELL SAID.
SUH-MAKK!
eep!

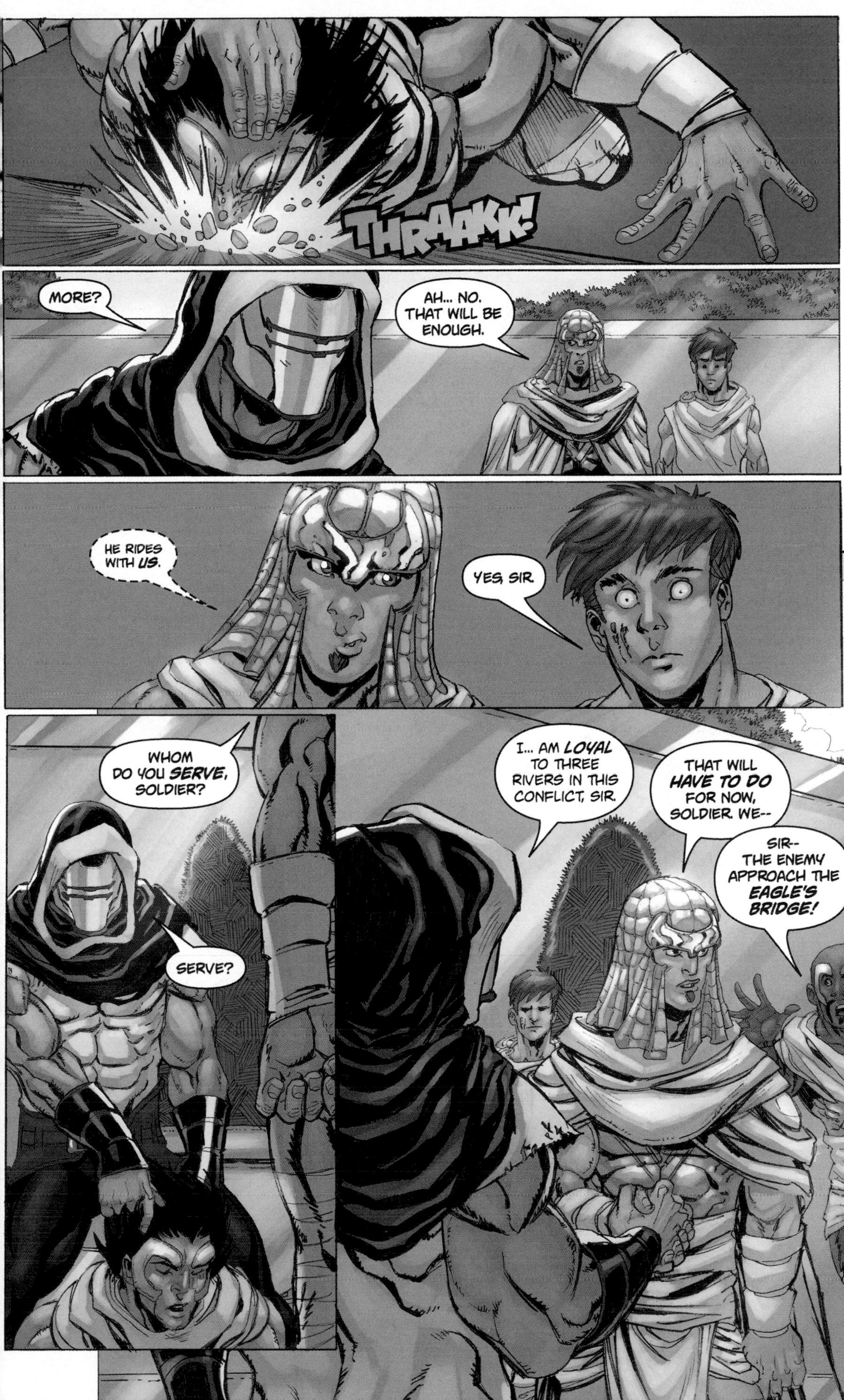
THRAAKK!
MORE?
AH... NO. THAT WILL BE ENOUGH.
HE RIDES WITH *US*.
YES, SIR.
WHOM DO YOU *SERVE*, SOLDIER?
SERVE?
I... AM *LOYAL* TO THREE RIVERS IN THIS CONFLICT, SIR.
THAT WILL *HAVE TO DO* FOR NOW, SOLDIER. WE--
SIR-- THE ENEMY APPROACH THE *EAGLE'S BRIDGE!*

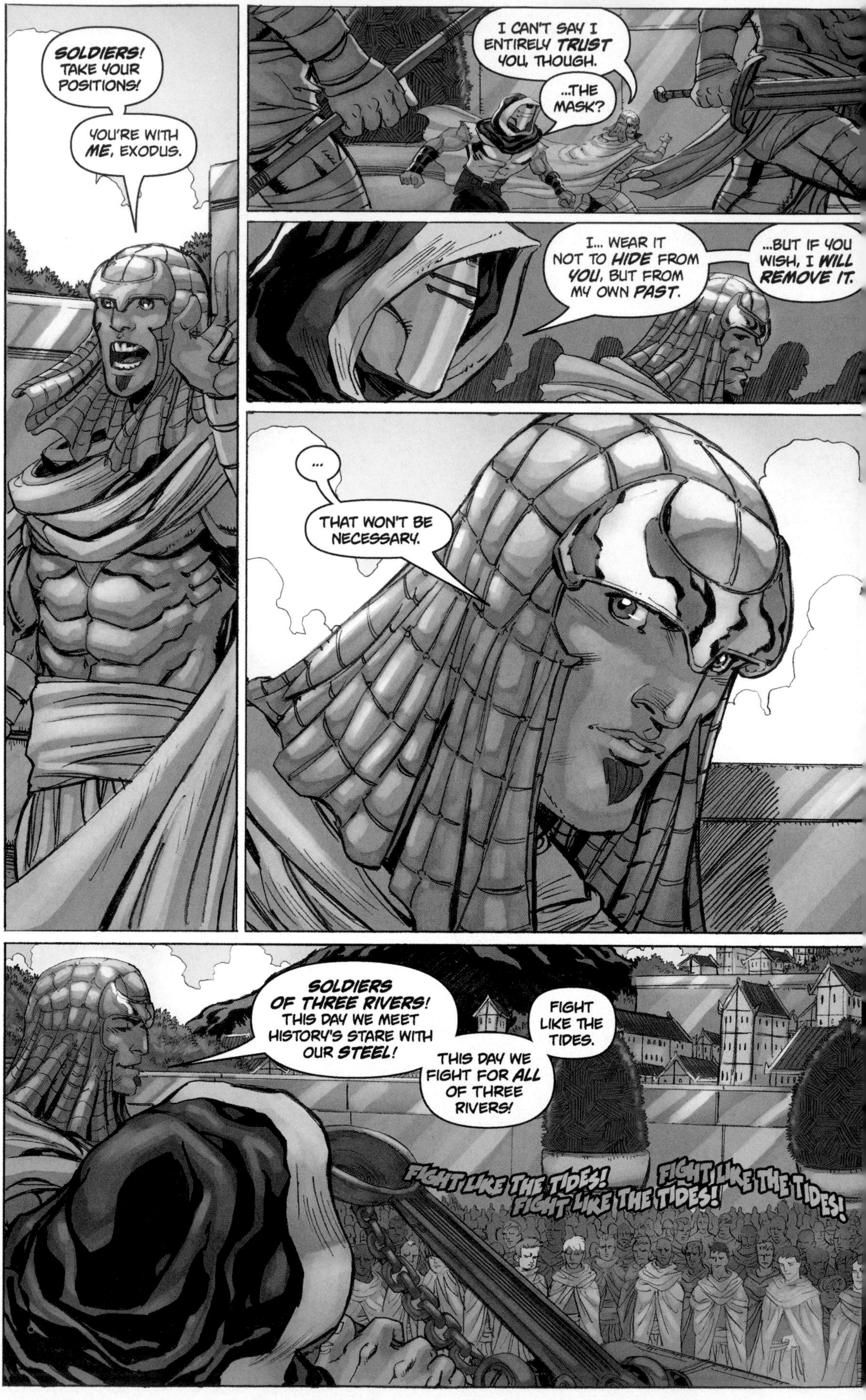
SOLDIERS! TAKE YOUR POSITIONS!
YOU'RE WITH ME, EXODUS.
I CAN'T SAY I ENTIRELY TRUST YOU, THOUGH.
...THE MASK?
I... WEAR IT NOT TO HIDE FROM YOU, BUT FROM MY OWN PAST.
...BUT IF YOU WISH, I WILL REMOVE IT.
...
THAT WON'T BE NECESSARY.
SOLDIERS OF THREE RIVERS! THIS DAY WE MEET HISTORY'S STARE WITH OUR STEEL!
THIS DAY WE FIGHT FOR ALL OF THREE RIVERS!
FIGHT LIKE THE TIDES.
FIGHT LIKE THE TIDES!
FIGHT LIKE THE TIDES!
FIGHT LIKE THE TIDES!

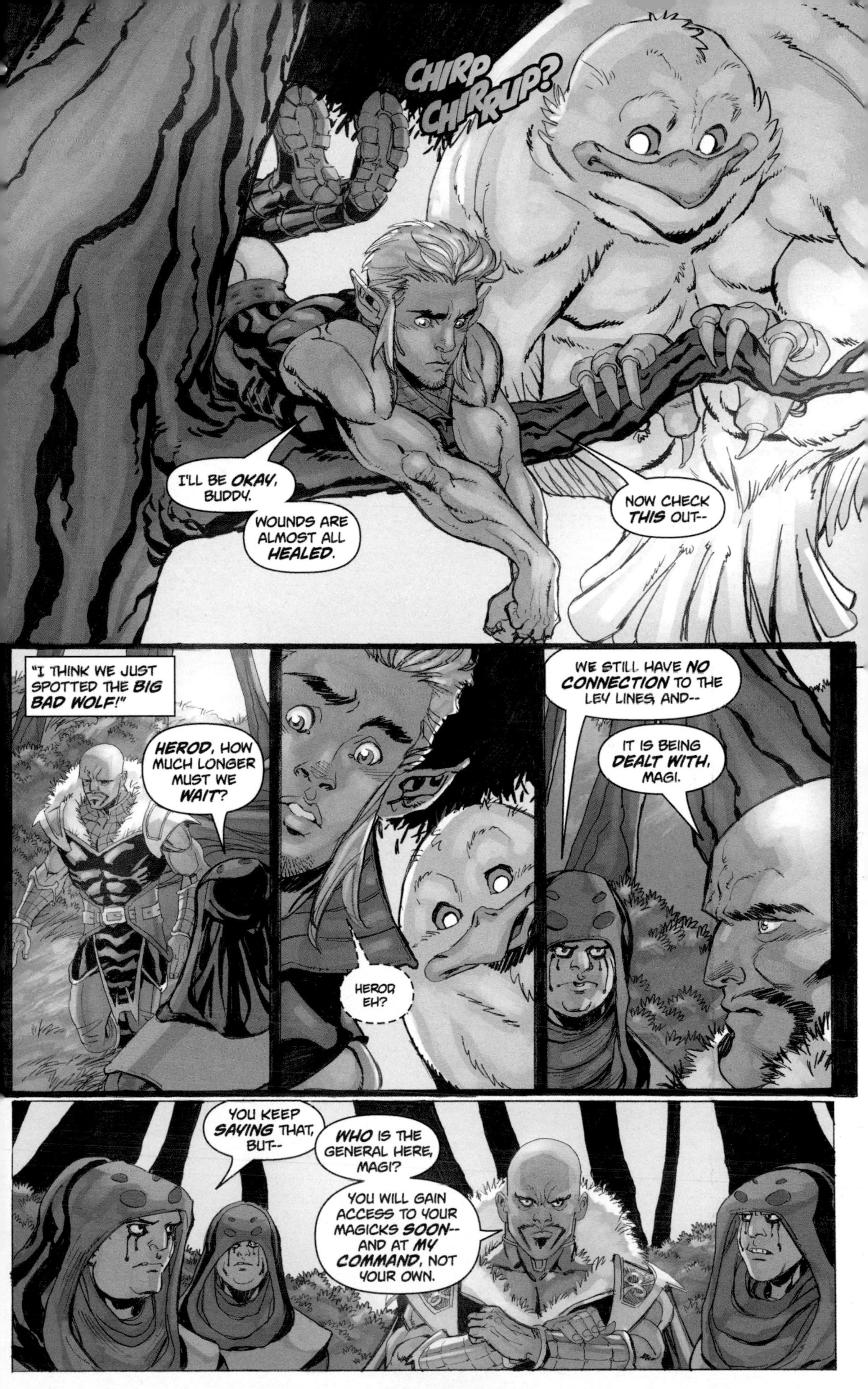
CHIRP CHIRRUP?
I'LL BE OKAY, BUDDY.
WOUNDS ARE ALMOST ALL HEALED.
NOW CHECK THIS OUT--
"I THINK WE JUST SPOTTED THE BIG BAD WOLF!"
HEROD, HOW MUCH LONGER MUST WE WAIT?
HEROD, EH?
WE STILL HAVE NO CONNECTION TO THE LEY LINES, AND--
IT IS BEING DEALT WITH, MAGI.
YOU KEEP SAYING THAT, BUT--
WHO IS THE GENERAL HERE, MAGI?
YOU WILL GAIN ACCESS TO YOUR MAGICKS SOON-- AND AT MY COMMAND, NOT YOUR OWN.

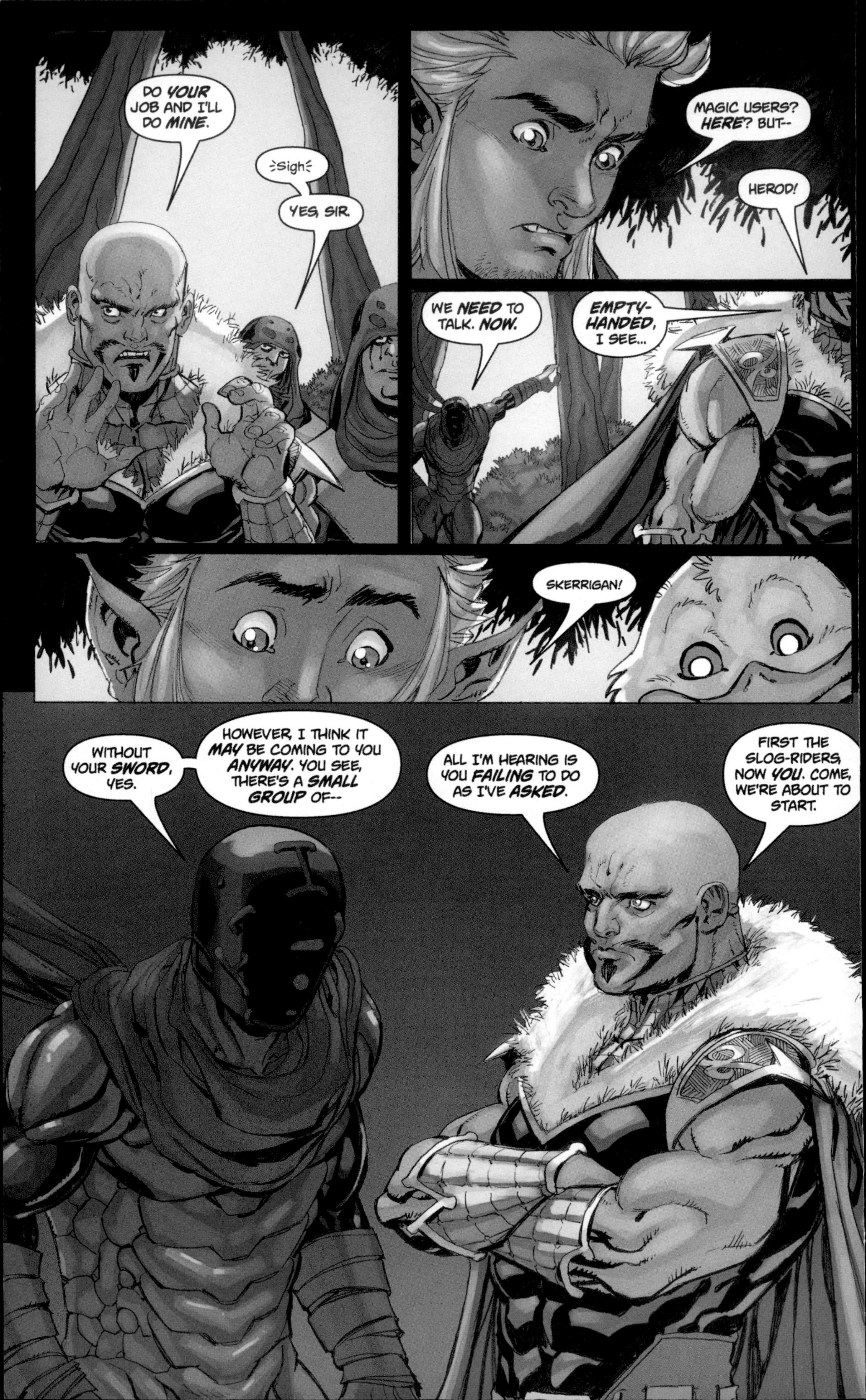
DO YOUR JOB AND I'LL DO MINE.
Sigh
YES, SIR.
MAGIC USERS? HERE? BUT--
HEROD!
WE NEED TO TALK. NOW.
EMPTY-HANDED, I SEE...
SKERRIGAN!
WITHOUT YOUR SWORD, YES.
HOWEVER, I THINK IT MAY BE COMING TO YOU ANYWAY. YOU SEE, THERE'S A SMALL GROUP OF--
ALL I'M HEARING IS YOU FAILING TO DO AS I'VE ASKED.
FIRST THE SLOG-RIDERS, NOW YOU. COME, WE'RE ABOUT TO START.

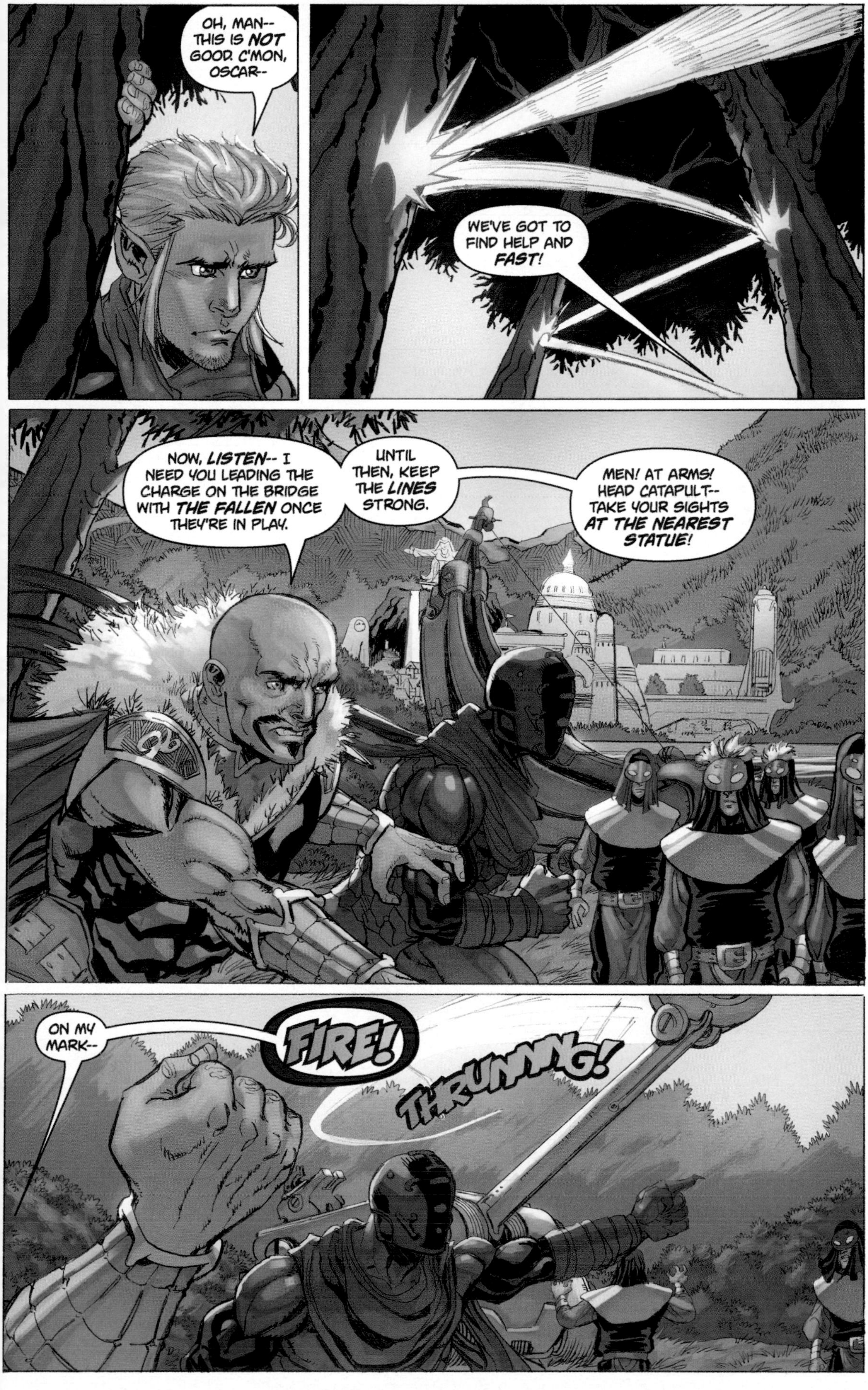
OH, MAN-- THIS IS NOT GOOD. C'MON, OSCAR--
WE'VE GOT TO FIND HELP AND FAST!
NOW, LISTEN-- I NEED YOU LEADING THE CHARGE ON THE BRIDGE WITH THE FALLEN ONCE THEY'RE IN PLAY.
UNTIL THEN, KEEP THE LINES STRONG.
MEN! AT ARMS! HEAD CATAPULT-- TAKE YOUR SIGHTS AT THE NEAREST STATUE!
ON MY MARK--
FIRE!
THRUNNNG!

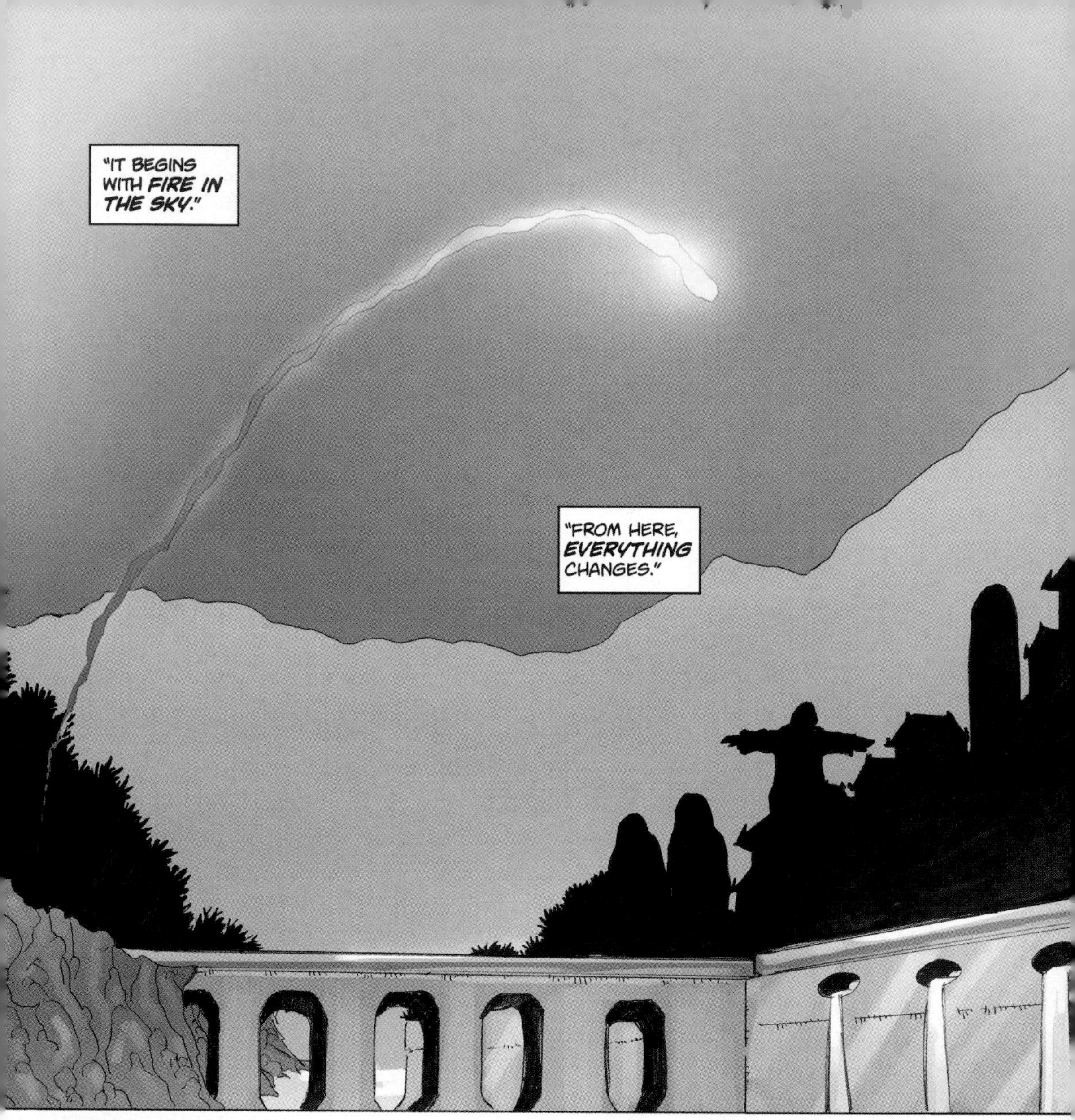
"IT BEGINS WITH FIRE IN THE SKY."
"FROM HERE, EVERYTHING CHANGES."

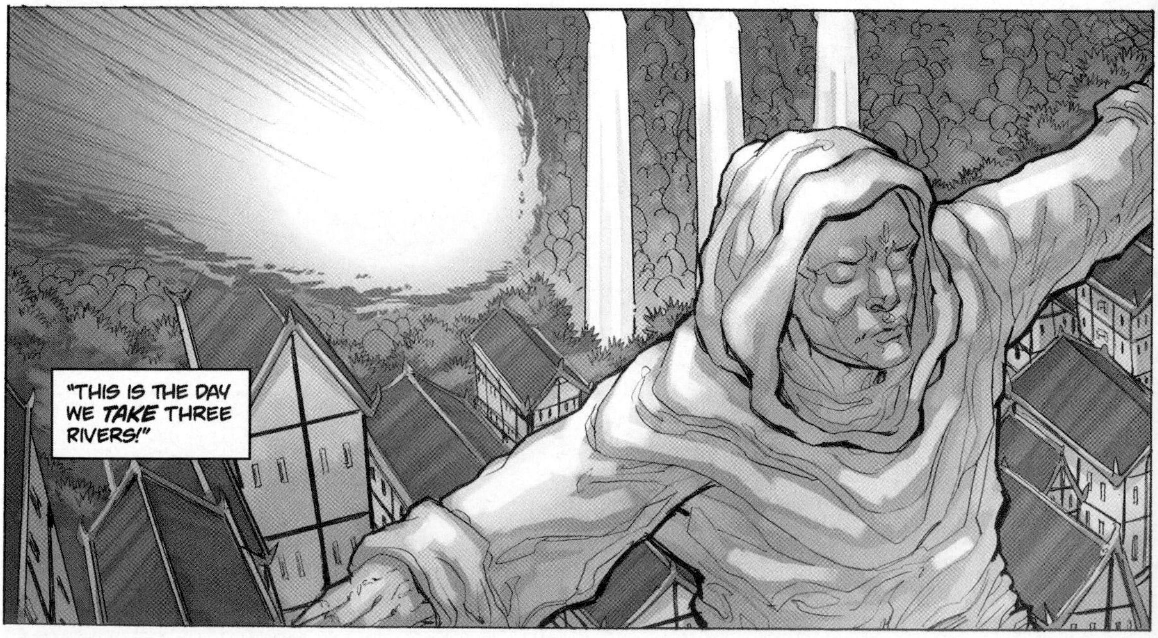
"THIS IS THE DAY WE TAKE THREE RIVERS!"

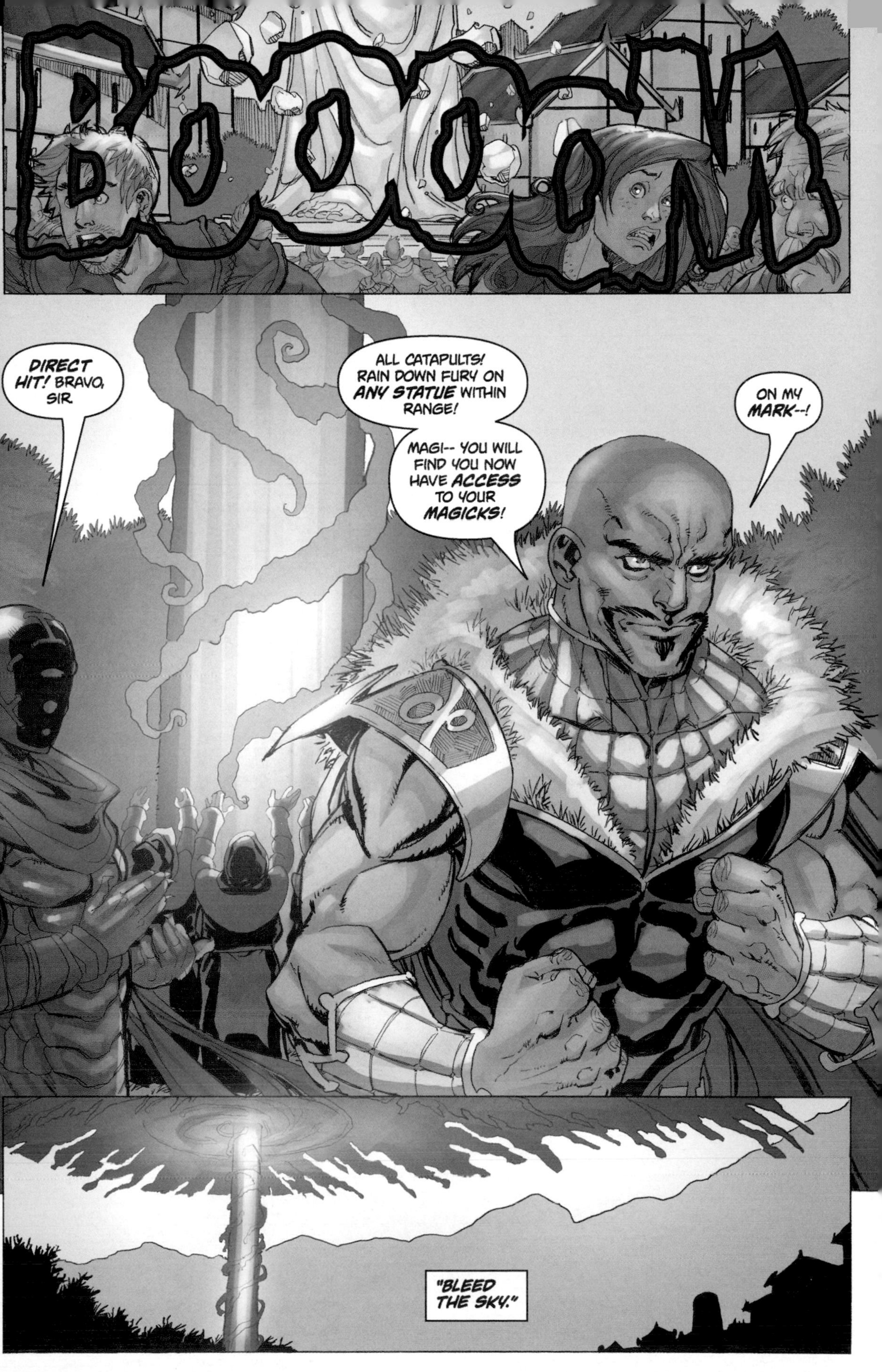
BOOOOM
DIRECT HIT! BRAVO, SIR.
ALL CATAPULTS! RAIN DOWN FURY ON ANY STATUE WITHIN RANGE!
MAGI-- YOU WILL FIND YOU NOW HAVE ACCESS TO YOUR MAGICKS!
ON MY MARK--!
"BLEED THE SKY."

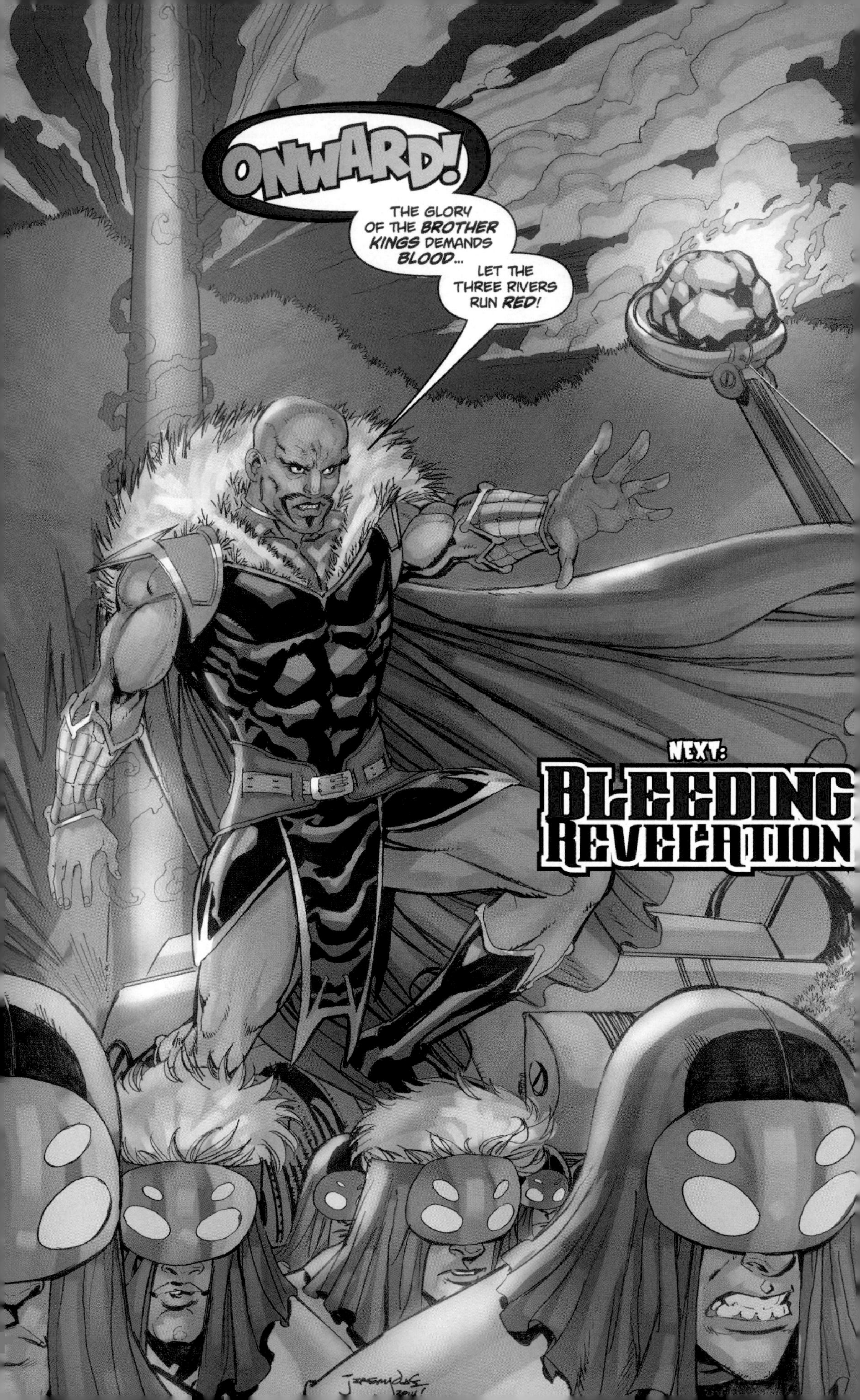

ONWARD!
THE GLORY OF THE BROTHER KINGS DEMANDS BLOOD...
LET THE THREE RIVERS RUN RED!
NEXT:
BLEEDING REVELATION

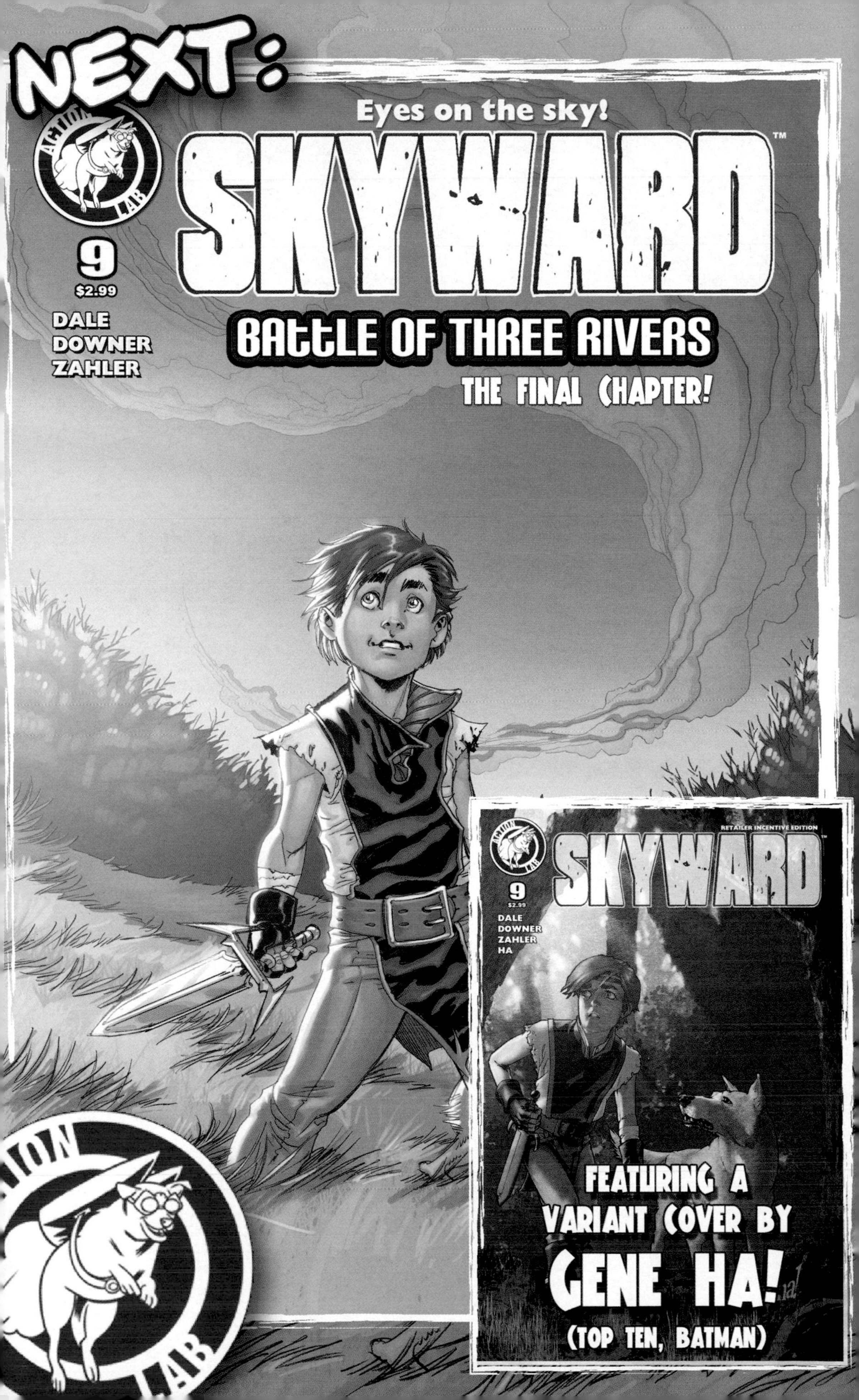
NEXT:
Eyes on the sky!
SKYWARD
9
$2.99
DALE
DOWNER
ZAHLER
BATTLE OF THREE RIVERS
THE FINAL CHAPTER!
RETAILER INCENTIVE EDITION
SKYWARD
9
$2.99
DALE
DOWNER
ZAHLER
HA
FEATURING A
VARIANT COVER BY
GENE HA!
(TOP TEN, BATMAN)

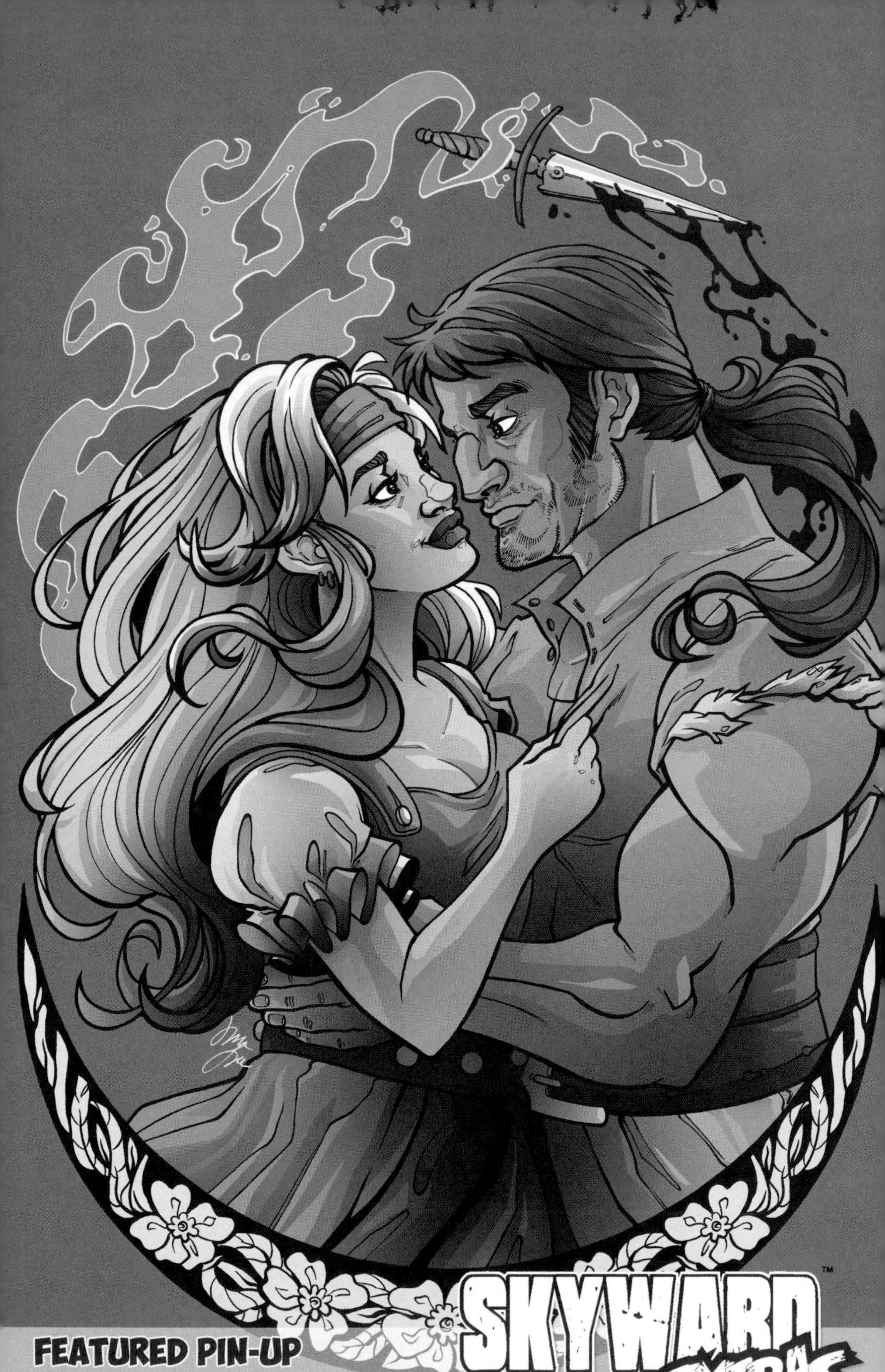

FEATURED PIN-UP
BY **JENN LEE** @y2jenn

SKYWARD™ EXTRAS

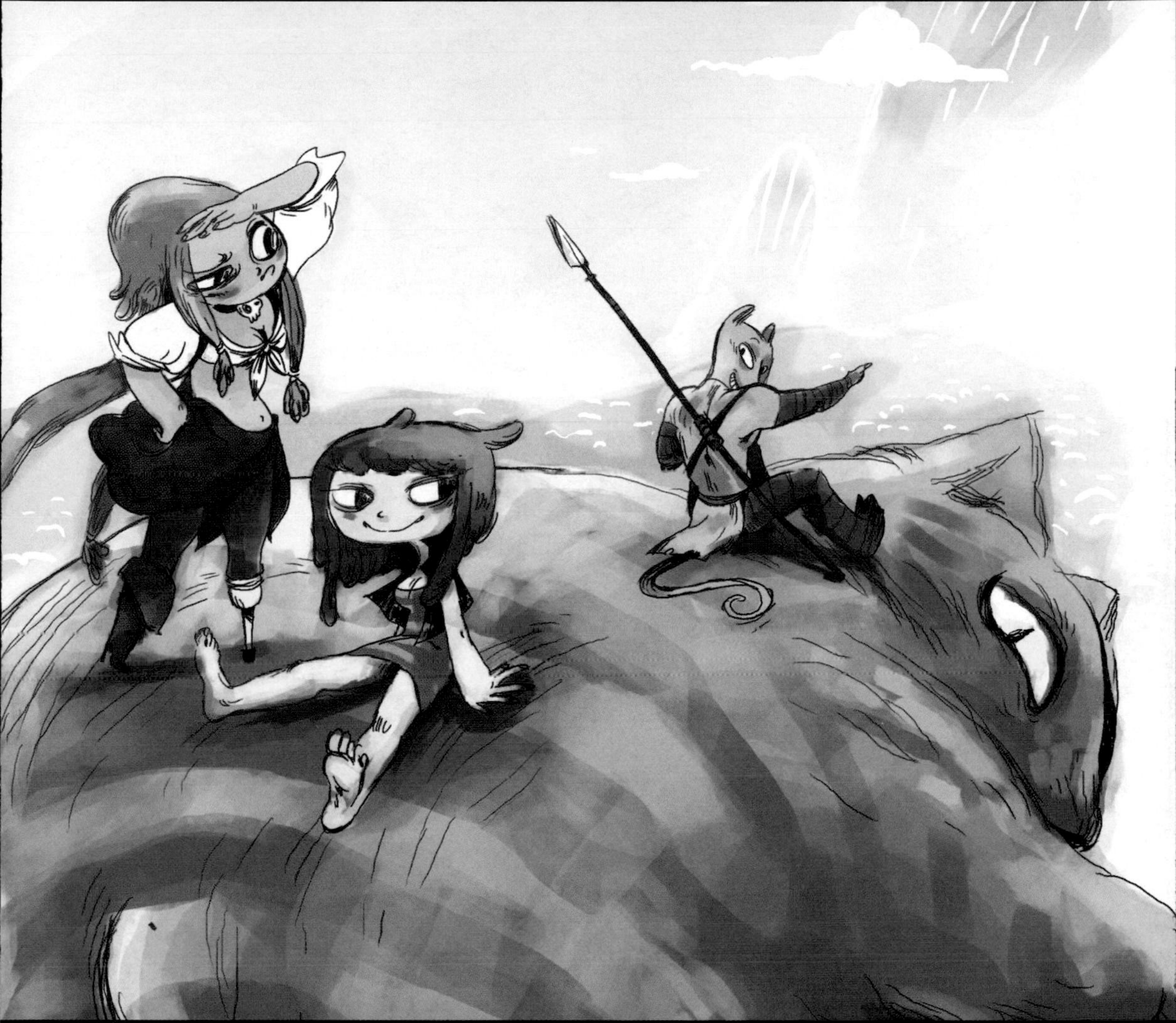

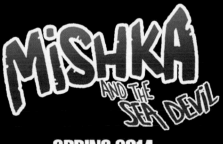

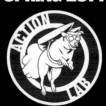

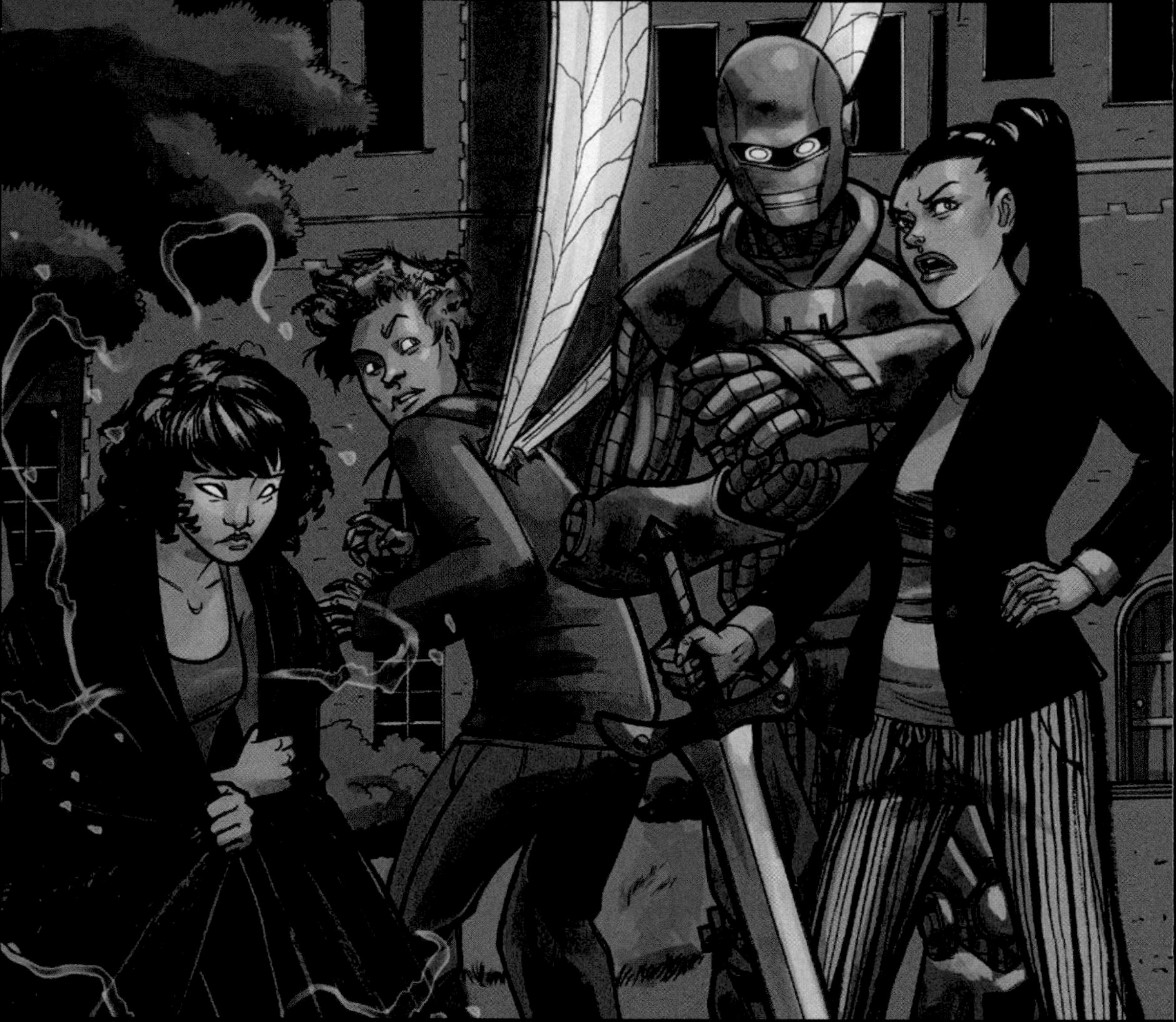

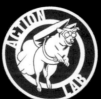

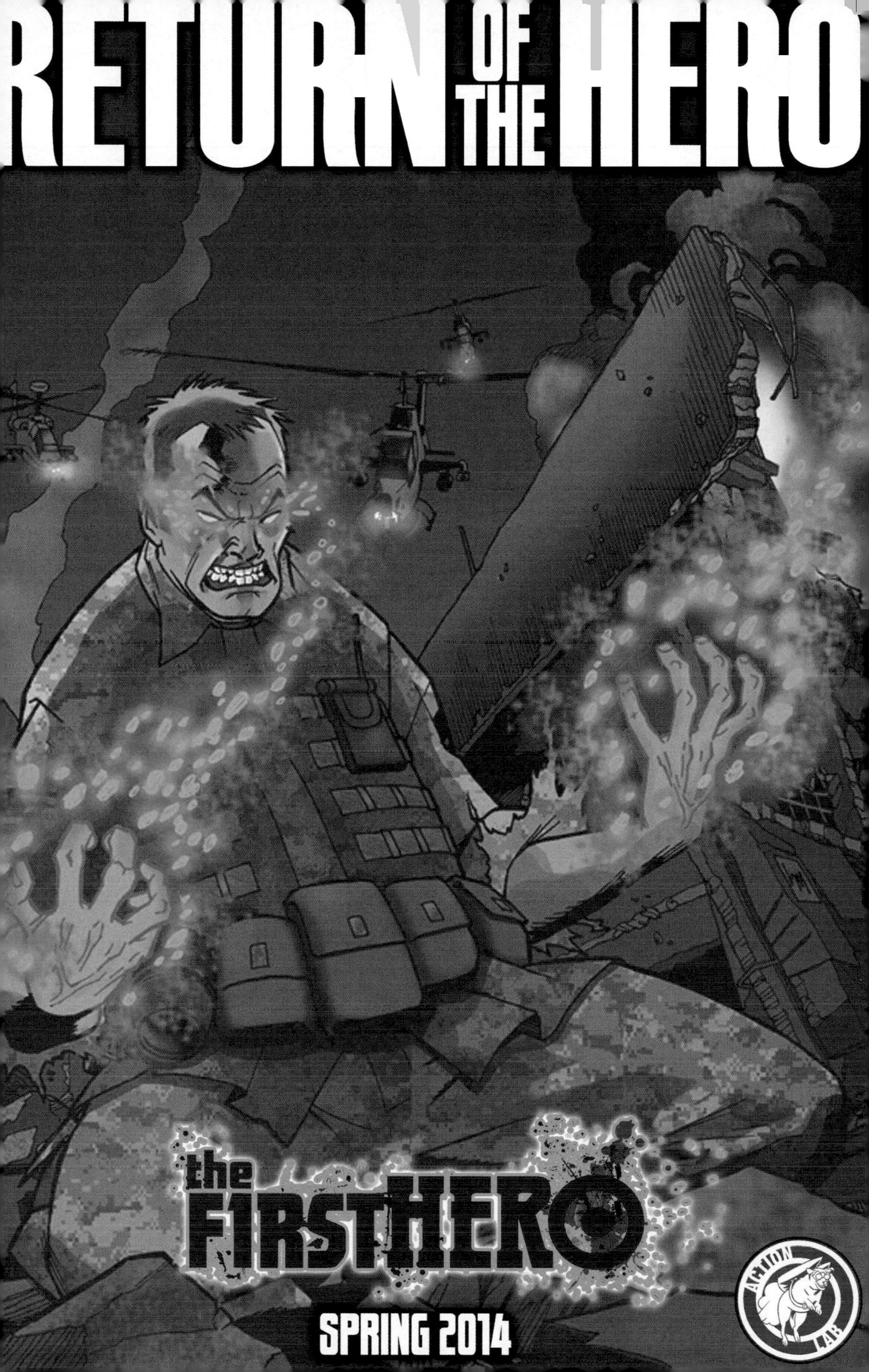
RETURN OF THE HERO
the FIRST HERO
SPRING 2014
ACTION LAB

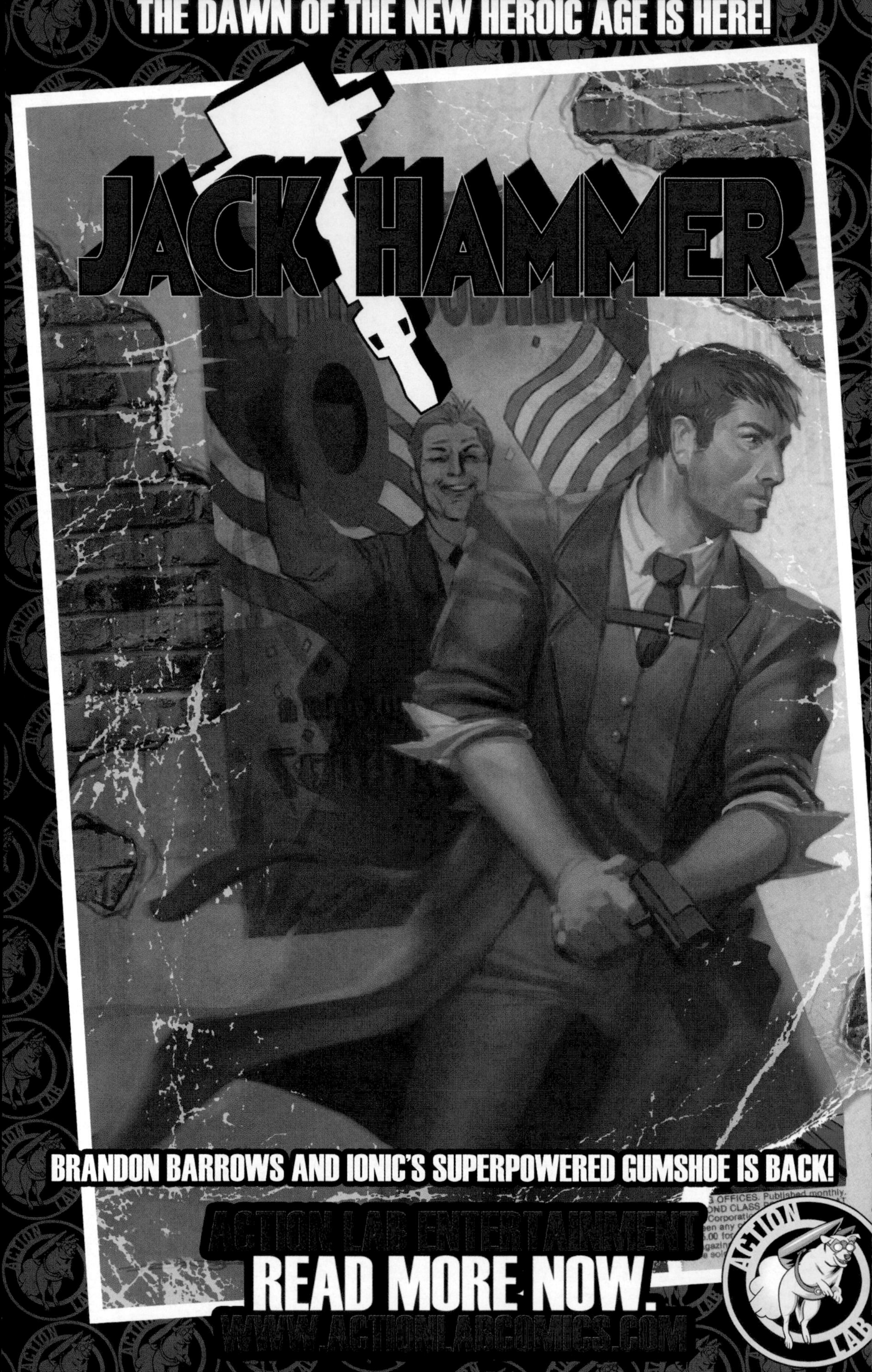
THE DAWN OF THE NEW HEROIC AGE IS HERE!
JACK HAMMER
BRANDON BARROWS AND IONIC'S SUPERPOWERED GUMSHOE IS BACK!
ACTION LAB ENTERTAINMENT
READ MORE NOW.
WWW.ACTIONLABCOMICS.COM

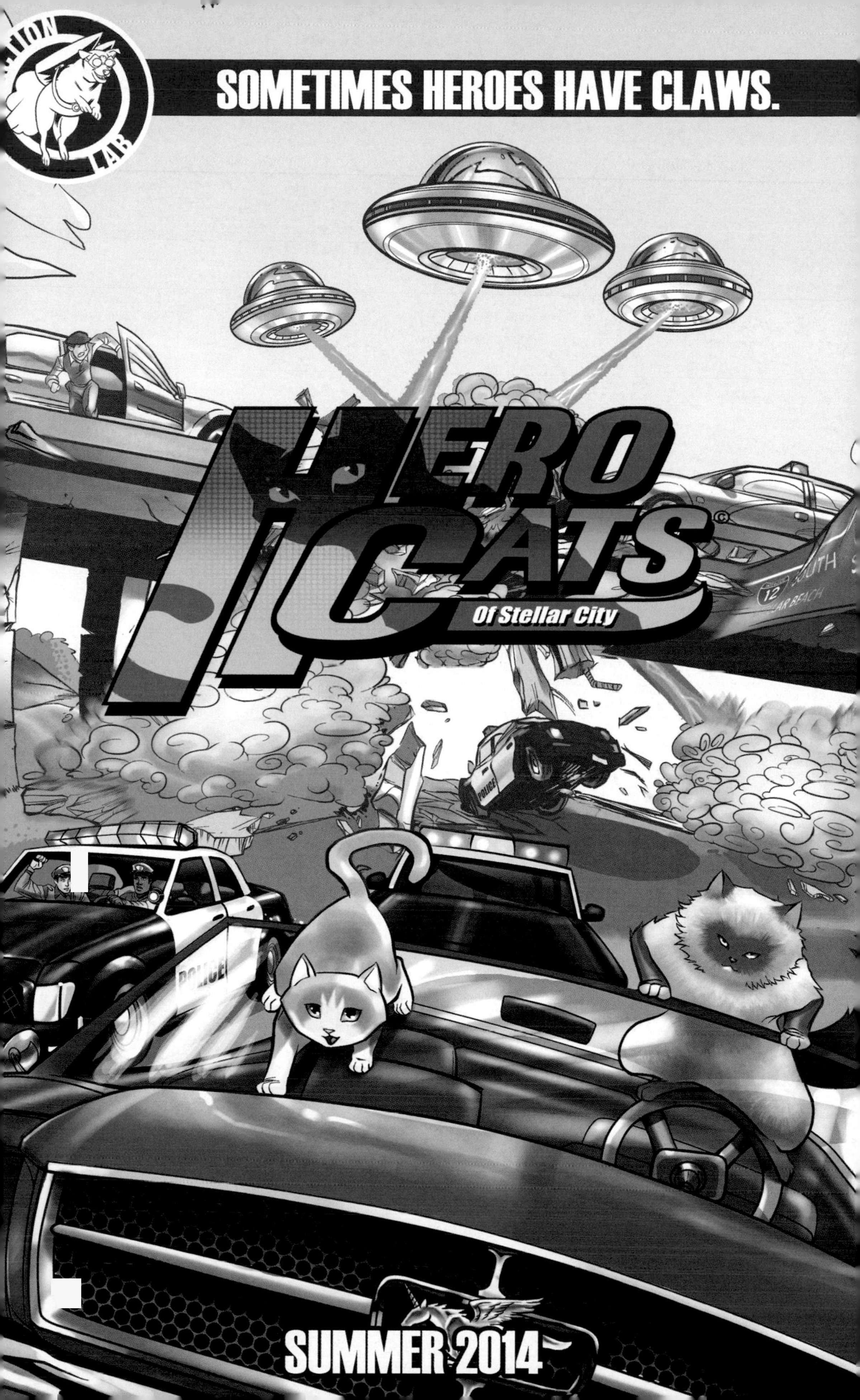
SOMETIMES HEROES HAVE CLAWS.
HERO CATS
Of Stellar City
POLICE
SUMMER 2014

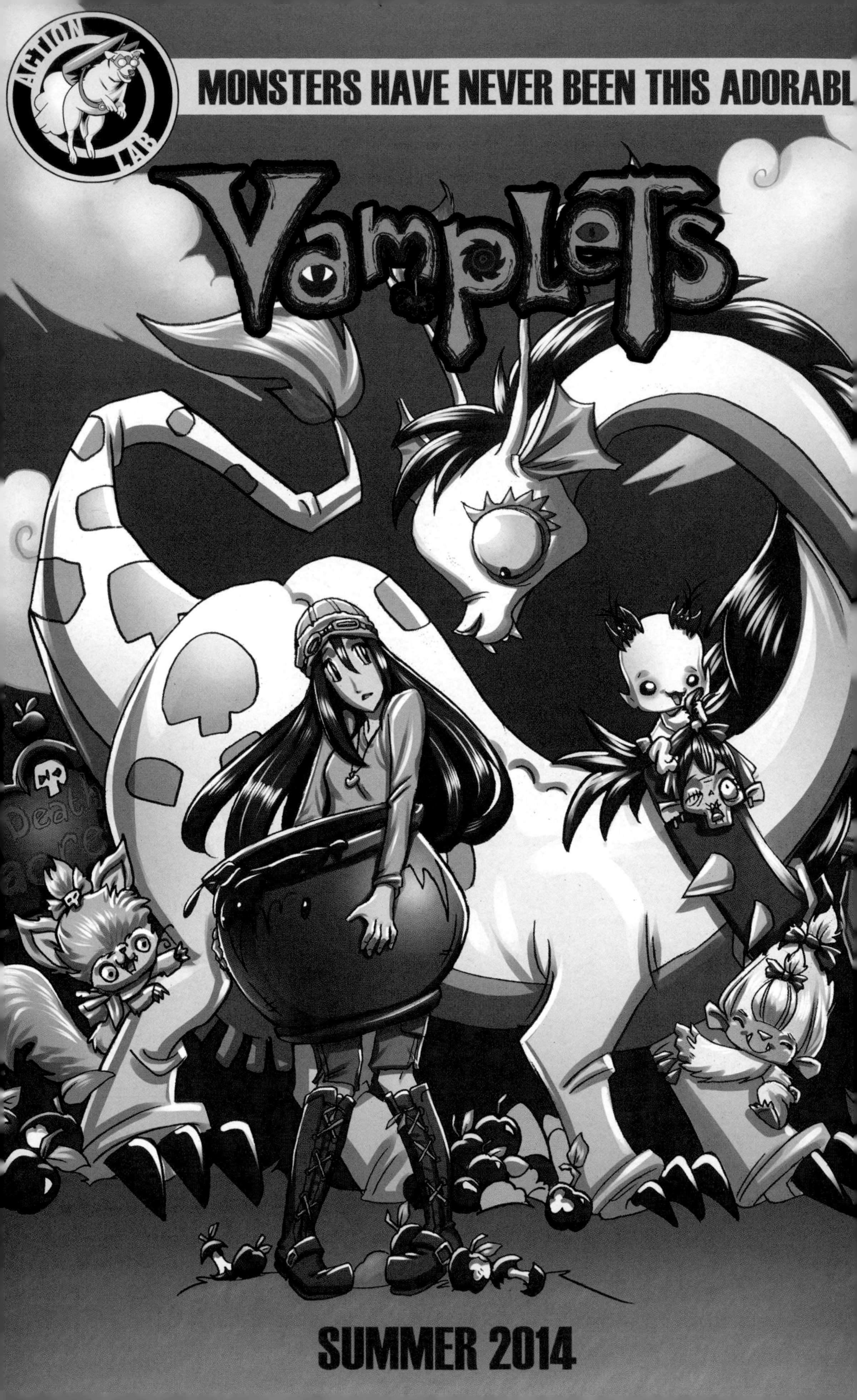
ACTION LAB
MONSTERS HAVE NEVER BEEN THIS ADORABL
Vamplets
SUMMER 2014

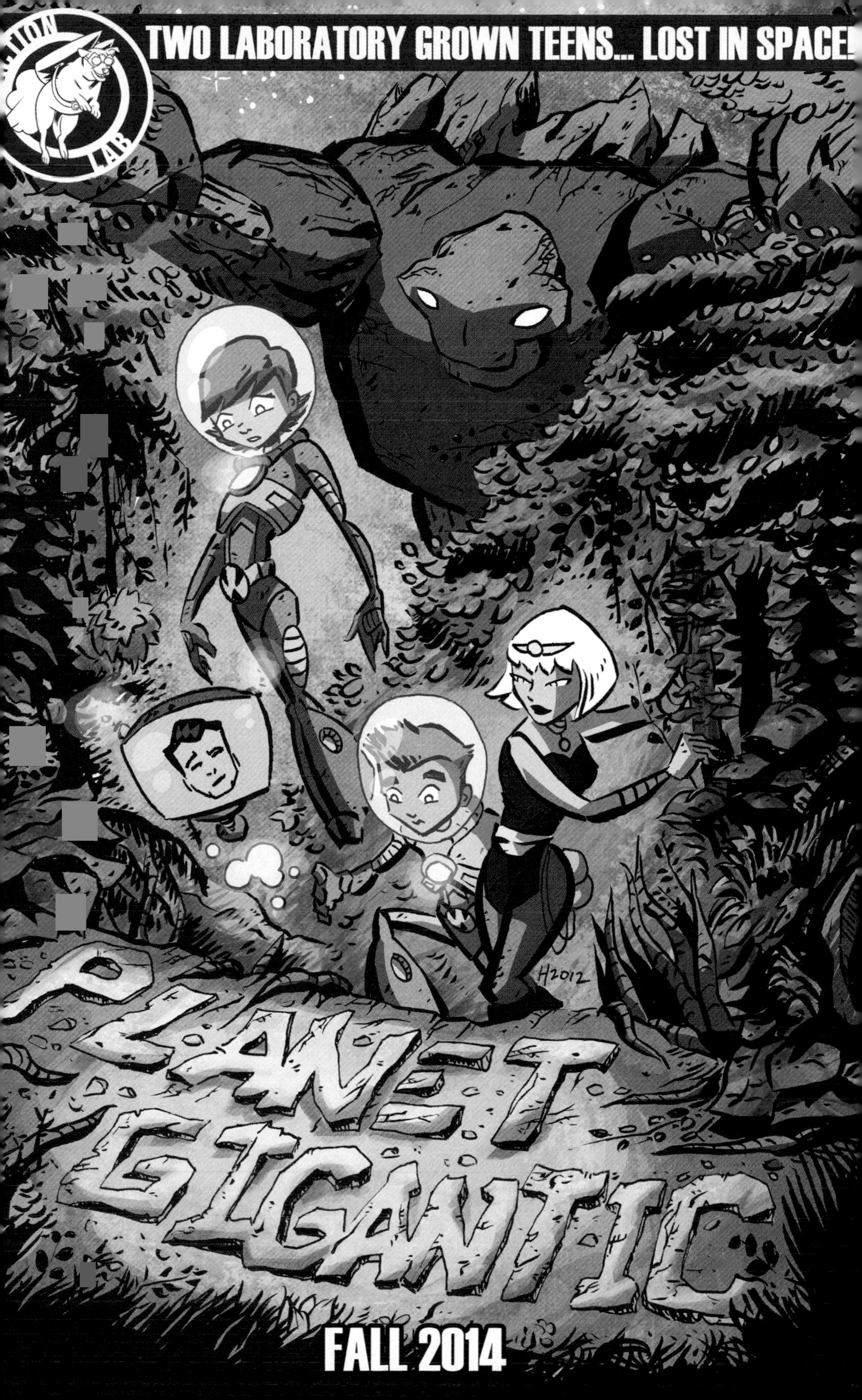

TWO LABORATORY GROWN TEENS... LOST IN SPACE!
H2012
PLANET GIGANTIC
FALL 2014

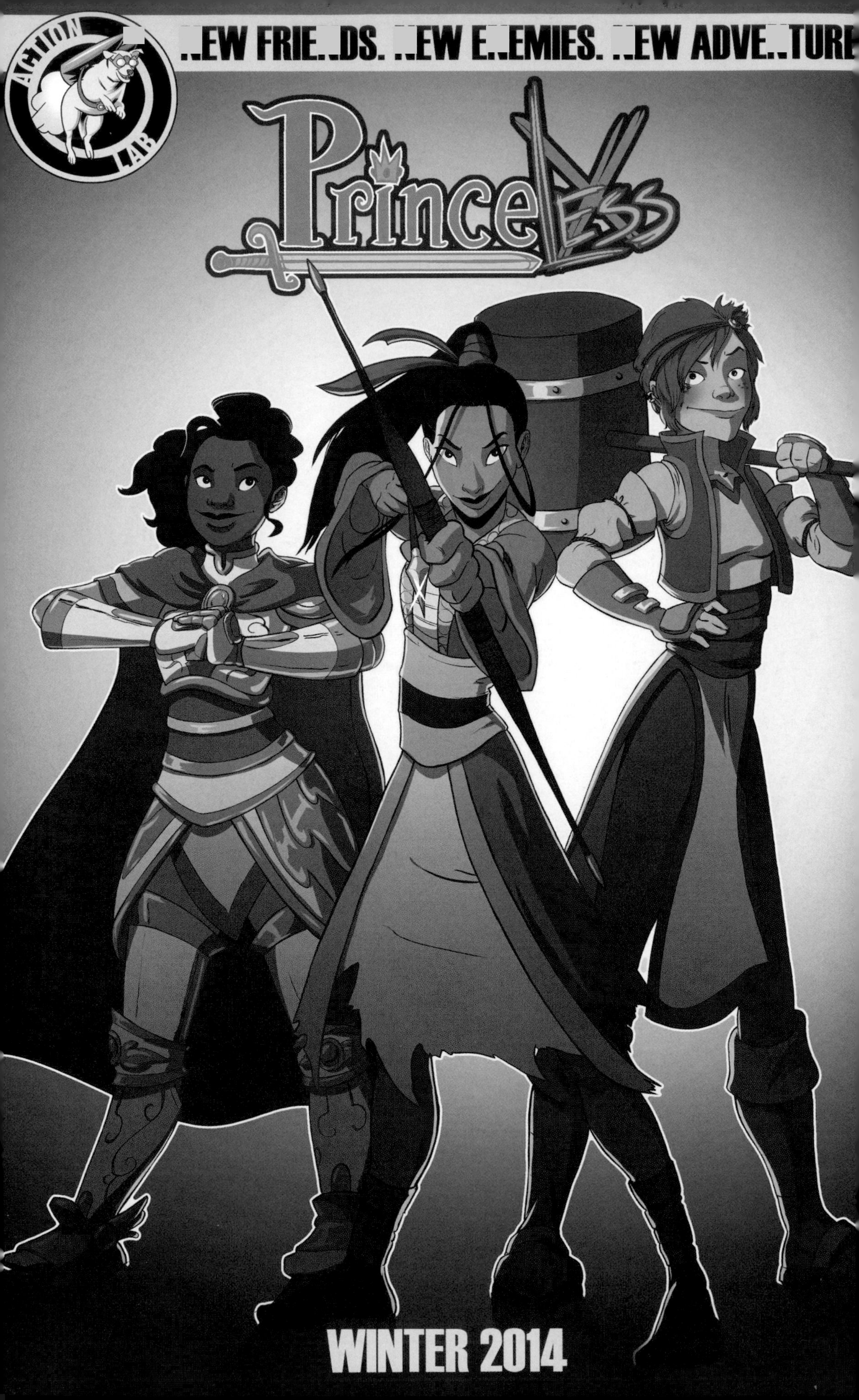
ACTION LAB
NEW FRIENDS. NEW ENEMIES. NEW ADVENTURE
Princeless
WINTER 2014

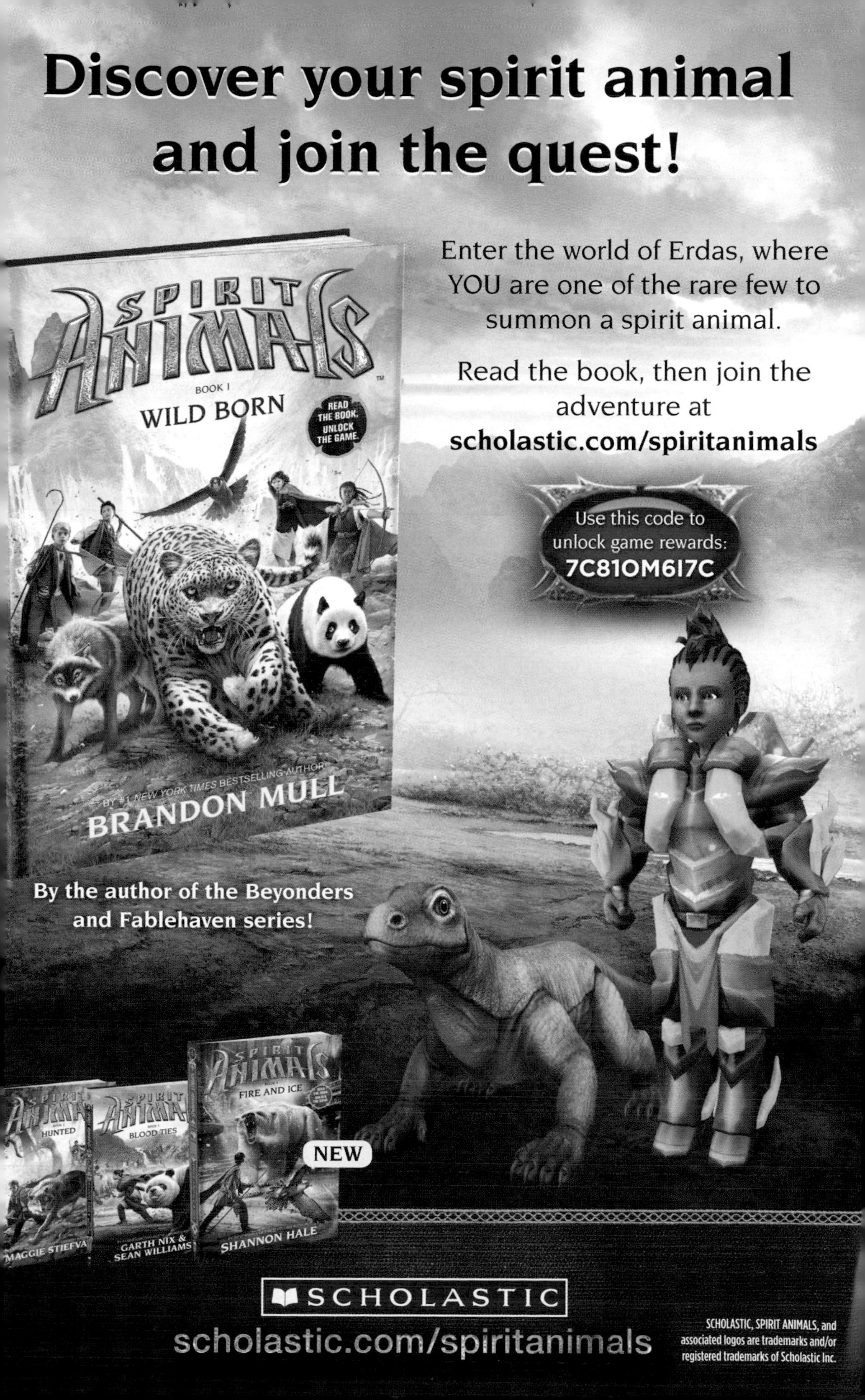

Discover your spirit animal and join the quest!
SPIRIT ANIMALS
BOOK 1
WILD BORN
READ THE BOOK, UNLOCK THE GAME.
BY #1 NEW YORK TIMES BESTSELLING AUTHOR
BRANDON MULL
Enter the world of Erdas, where YOU are one of the rare few to summon a spirit animal.
Read the book, then join the adventure at scholastic.com/spiritanimals
Use this code to unlock game rewards:
7C81OM617C
By the author of the Beyonders and Fablehaven series!
SPIRIT ANIMALS
HUNTED
MAGGIE STIEFVATER
SPIRIT ANIMALS
BLOOD TIES
GARTH NIX & SEAN WILLIAMS
SPIRIT ANIMALS
FIRE AND ICE
SHANNON HALE
NEW
SCHOLASTIC
scholastic.com/spiritanimals
SCHOLASTIC, SPIRIT ANIMALS, and associated logos are trademarks and/or registered trademarks of Scholastic Inc.

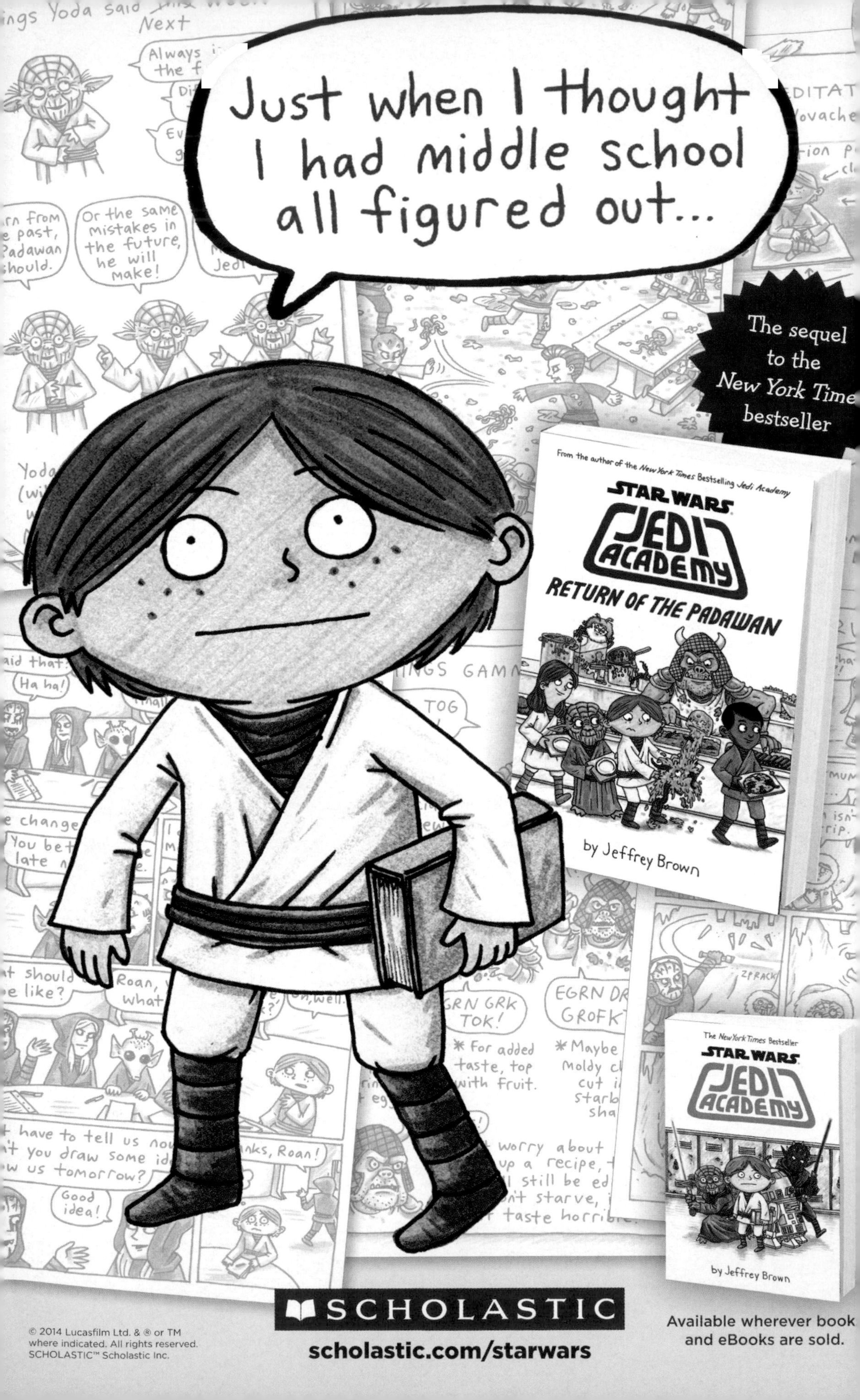

Just when I thought I had middle school all figured out...
The sequel to the New York Times bestseller
From the author of the New York Times Bestselling Jedi Academy
STAR WARS
JEDI ACADEMY
RETURN OF THE PADAWAN
by Jeffrey Brown
The New York Times Bestseller
STAR WARS
JEDI ACADEMY
by Jeffrey Brown
SCHOLASTIC
scholastic.com/starwars
Available wherever books and eBooks are sold.

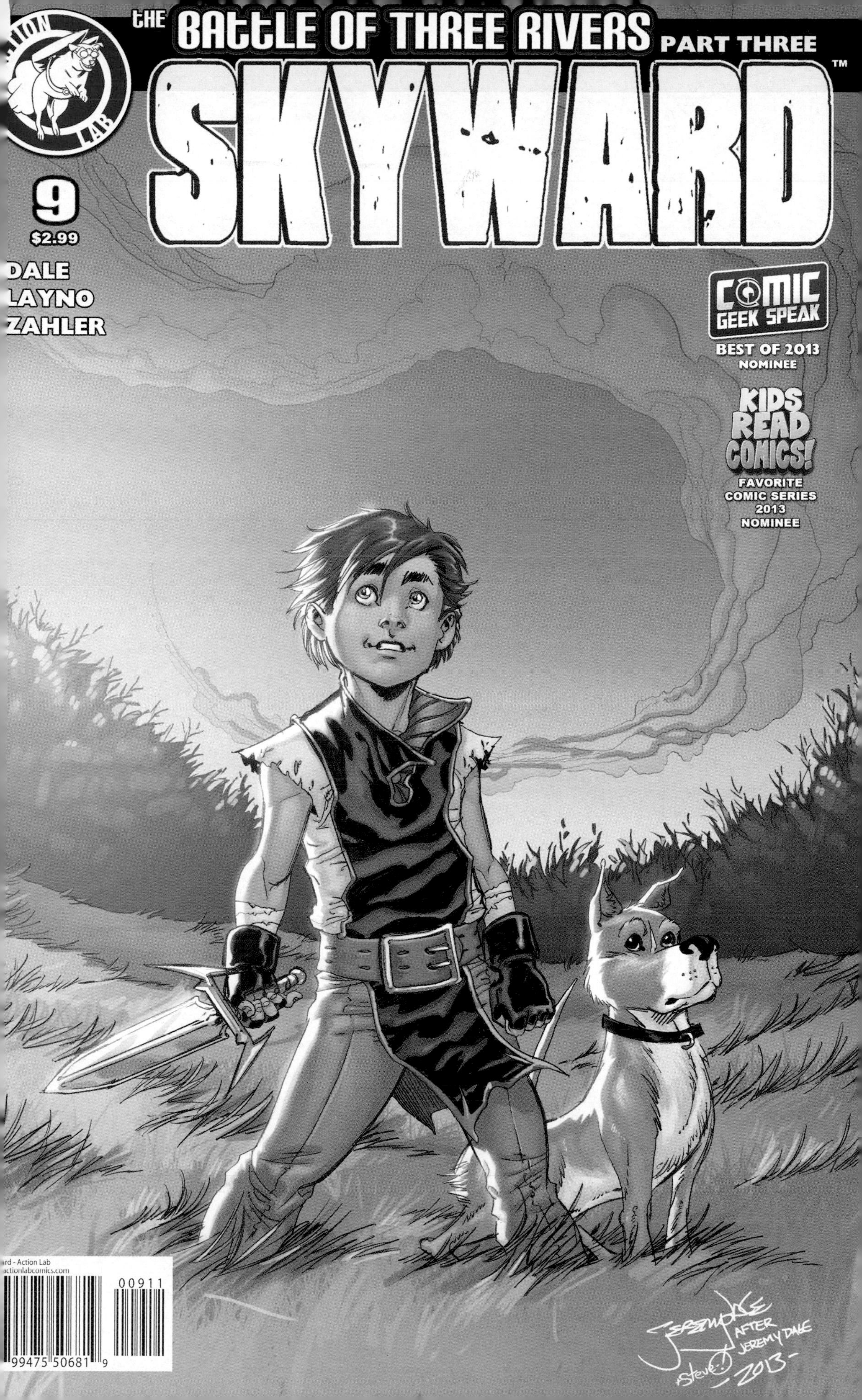
THE BATTLE OF THREE RIVERS PART THREE
SKYWARD™
9
$2.99
DALE
LAYNO
ZAHLER
COMIC GEEK SPEAK
BEST OF 2013 NOMINEE
KIDS READ COMICS!
FAVORITE COMIC SERIES 2013 NOMINEE

SKYWARD

BATTLE OF THREE RIVERS

Jeremy Dale
Creator / Writer / Artist
@jeremydale

Kathryn Layno
Colors
@denimcatfish

Thom Zahler
Letters
@loveandcapes

Hoyt Silva
Color Flats
@hoytsilva

Covers by

Jeremy Dale
@jeremydale

and

Gene Ha
@geneha

For more visit
www.skywardcomic.com

Previously:

This is it-- Herod's armies have begun their siege of Three Rivers! King Edrick has is fending off the invasion as best he can with a new line-up of his elite River Riders at his side.

Meanwhile, Quinn and the Rabites are frantically racing to the scene to do whatever they can to help out against Herod's unholy army.

Luckily, they've stumbled into Prince Dominic and his friend Mia, who have inside information on the town and how it works.

It ends here! Only one side will rise triumphant... and I'm pretty sure Herod has some undead soldiers in his employ...

FOR ACTION LAB ENTERTAINMENT
Kevin Freeman - President
Bryan Seaton - Chief Financial Officer
Shawn Pryor - VP Digital Media
Dave Dwonch - Creative Director
Shawn Gabborin - Editor In Chief
Jason Martin - Editor
Kelly Dale & Jamal Igle - Directors of Marketing
Jim Dietz - Social Media Director
Jeremy Whitley - Education Outreach Director
Chad Cicconi & Colleen Boyd - Associate Editors
WWW.ACTIONLABCOMICS.COM

jeremy-dale.com

JEREMY DALE - the talent

KELLY DALE - project editor

KIRBY THE DOG - canine relations

WWW.JEREMY-DALE.COM

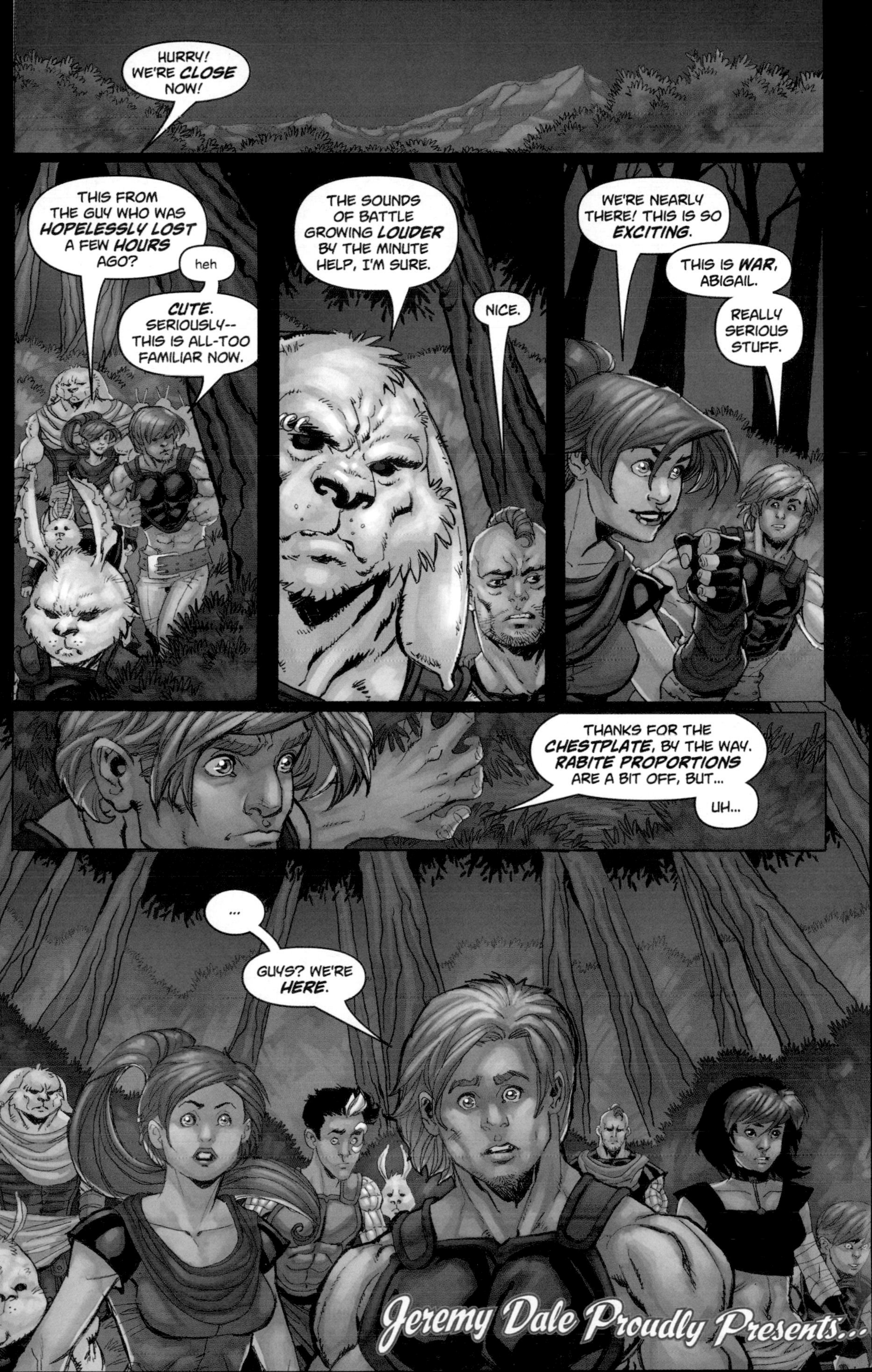
HURRY! WE'RE CLOSE NOW!
THIS FROM THE GUY WHO WAS HOPELESSLY LOST A FEW HOURS AGO?
heh
CUTE. SERIOUSLY-- THIS IS ALL-TOO FAMILIAR NOW.
THE SOUNDS OF BATTLE GROWING LOUDER BY THE MINUTE HELP, I'M SURE.
NICE.
WE'RE NEARLY THERE! THIS IS SO EXCITING.
THIS IS WAR, ABIGAIL.
REALLY SERIOUS STUFF.
THANKS FOR THE CHESTPLATE, BY THE WAY. RABITE PROPORTIONS ARE A BIT OFF, BUT...
UH...
...
GUYS? WE'RE HERE.
Jeremy Dale Proudly Presents...

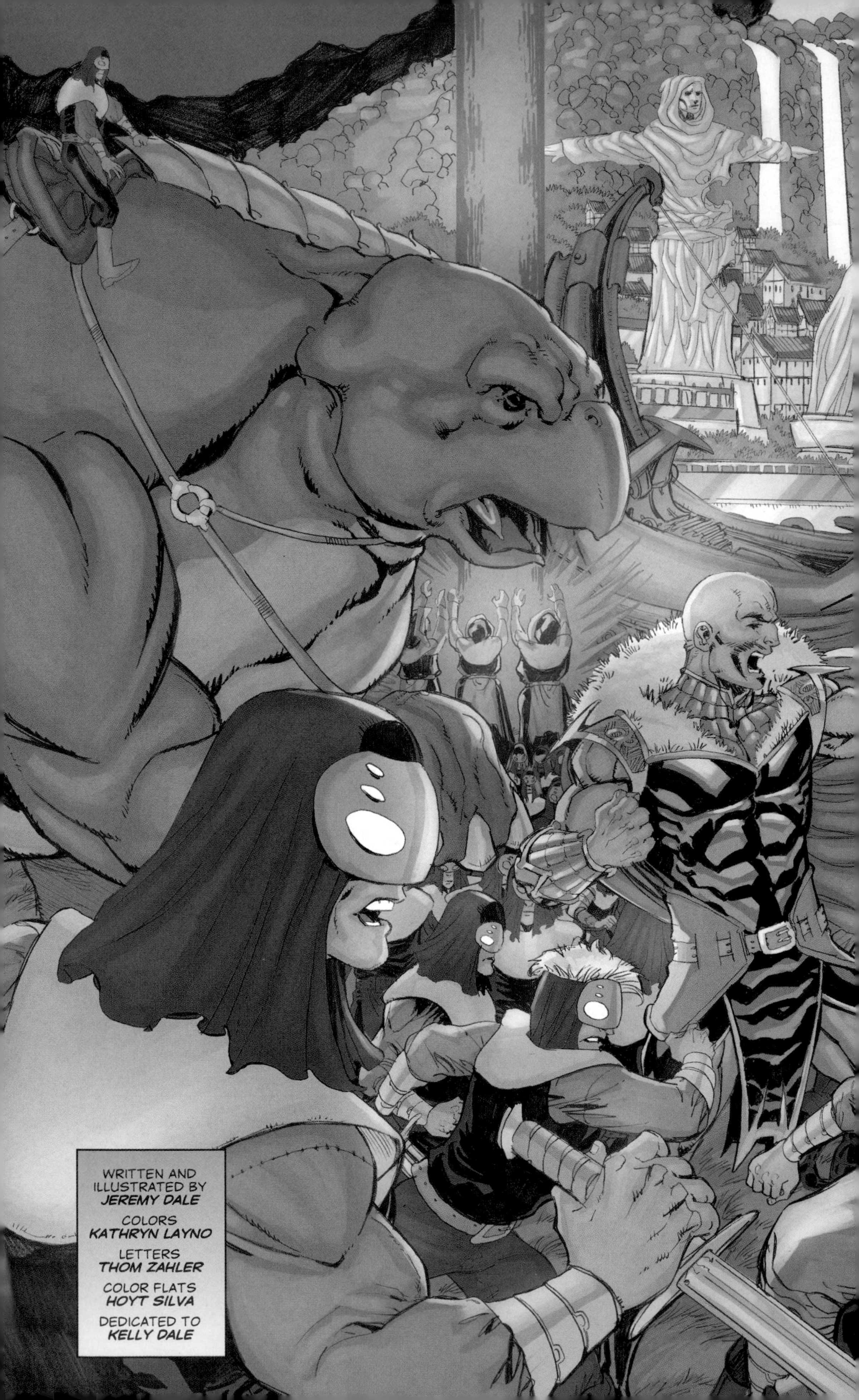
WRITTEN AND
ILLUSTRATED BY
JEREMY DALE
COLORS
KATHRYN LAYNO
LETTERS
THOM ZAHLER
COLOR FLATS
HOYT SILVA
DEDICATED TO
KELLY DALE

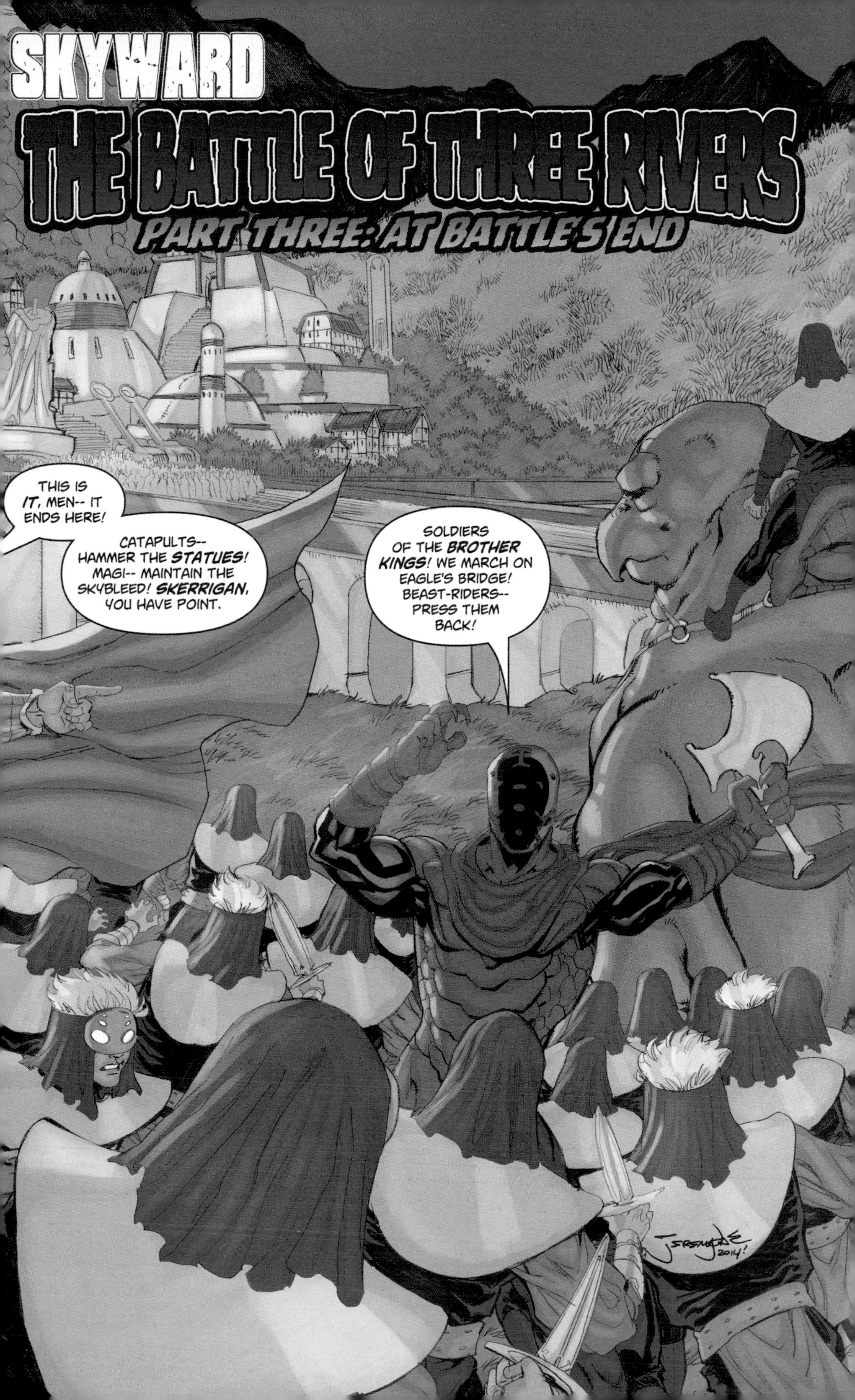
SKYWARD
THE BATTLE OF THREE RIVERS
PART THREE: AT BATTLE'S END
THIS IS IT, MEN-- IT ENDS HERE!
CATAPULTS-- HAMMER THE STATUES! MAGI-- MAINTAIN THE SKYBLEED! SKERRIGAN, YOU HAVE POINT.
SOLDIERS OF THE BROTHER KINGS! WE MARCH ON EAGLE'S BRIDGE! BEAST-RIDERS-- PRESS THEM BACK!

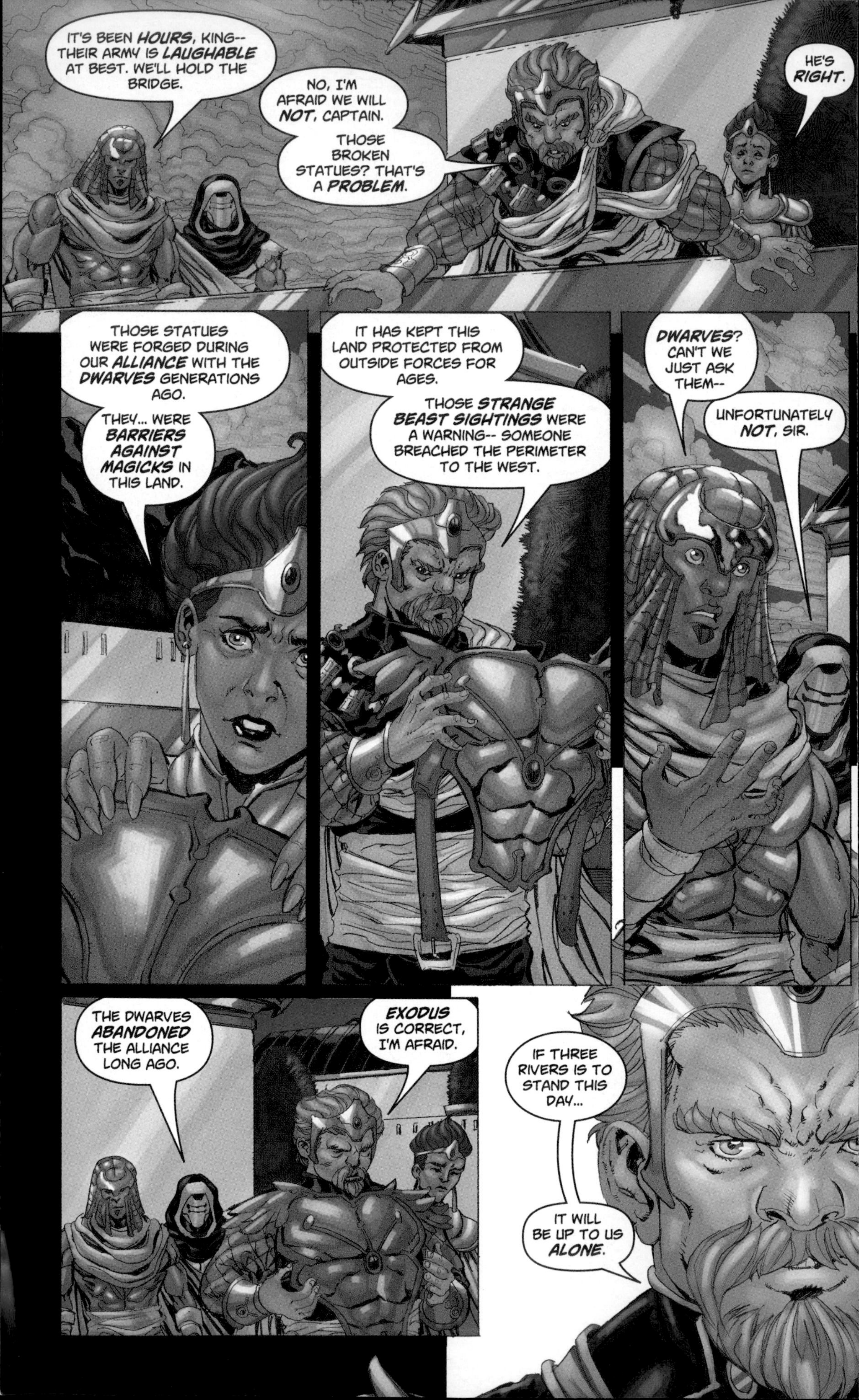
IT'S BEEN HOURS, KING-- THEIR ARMY IS LAUGHABLE AT BEST. WE'LL HOLD THE BRIDGE.
NO, I'M AFRAID WE WILL NOT, CAPTAIN.
THOSE BROKEN STATUES? THAT'S A PROBLEM.
HE'S RIGHT.
THOSE STATUES WERE FORGED DURING OUR ALLIANCE WITH THE DWARVES GENERATIONS AGO.
THEY... WERE BARRIERS AGAINST MAGICKS IN THIS LAND.
IT HAS KEPT THIS LAND PROTECTED FROM OUTSIDE FORCES FOR AGES.
THOSE STRANGE BEAST SIGHTINGS WERE A WARNING-- SOMEONE BREACHED THE PERIMETER TO THE WEST.
DWARVES? CAN'T WE JUST ASK THEM--
UNFORTUNATELY NOT, SIR.
THE DWARVES ABANDONED THE ALLIANCE LONG AGO.
EXODUS IS CORRECT, I'M AFRAID.
IF THREE RIVERS IS TO STAND THIS DAY...
IT WILL BE UP TO US ALONE.

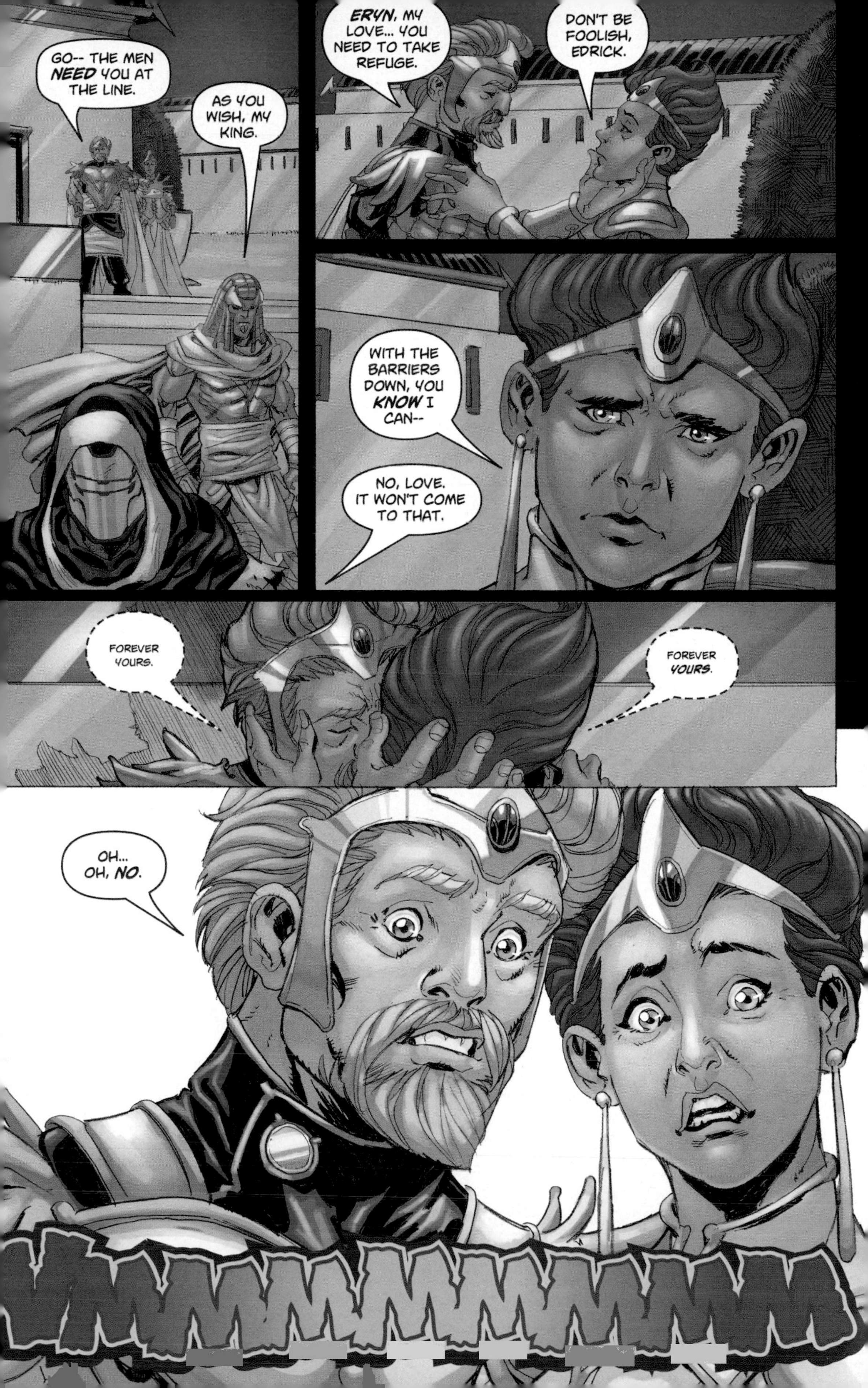
GO-- THE MEN NEED YOU AT THE LINE.
AS YOU WISH, MY KING.
ERYN, MY LOVE... YOU NEED TO TAKE REFUGE.
DON'T BE FOOLISH, EDRICK.
WITH THE BARRIERS DOWN, YOU KNOW I CAN--
NO, LOVE. IT WON'T COME TO THAT.
FOREVER YOURS.
FOREVER YOURS.
OH... OH, NO.

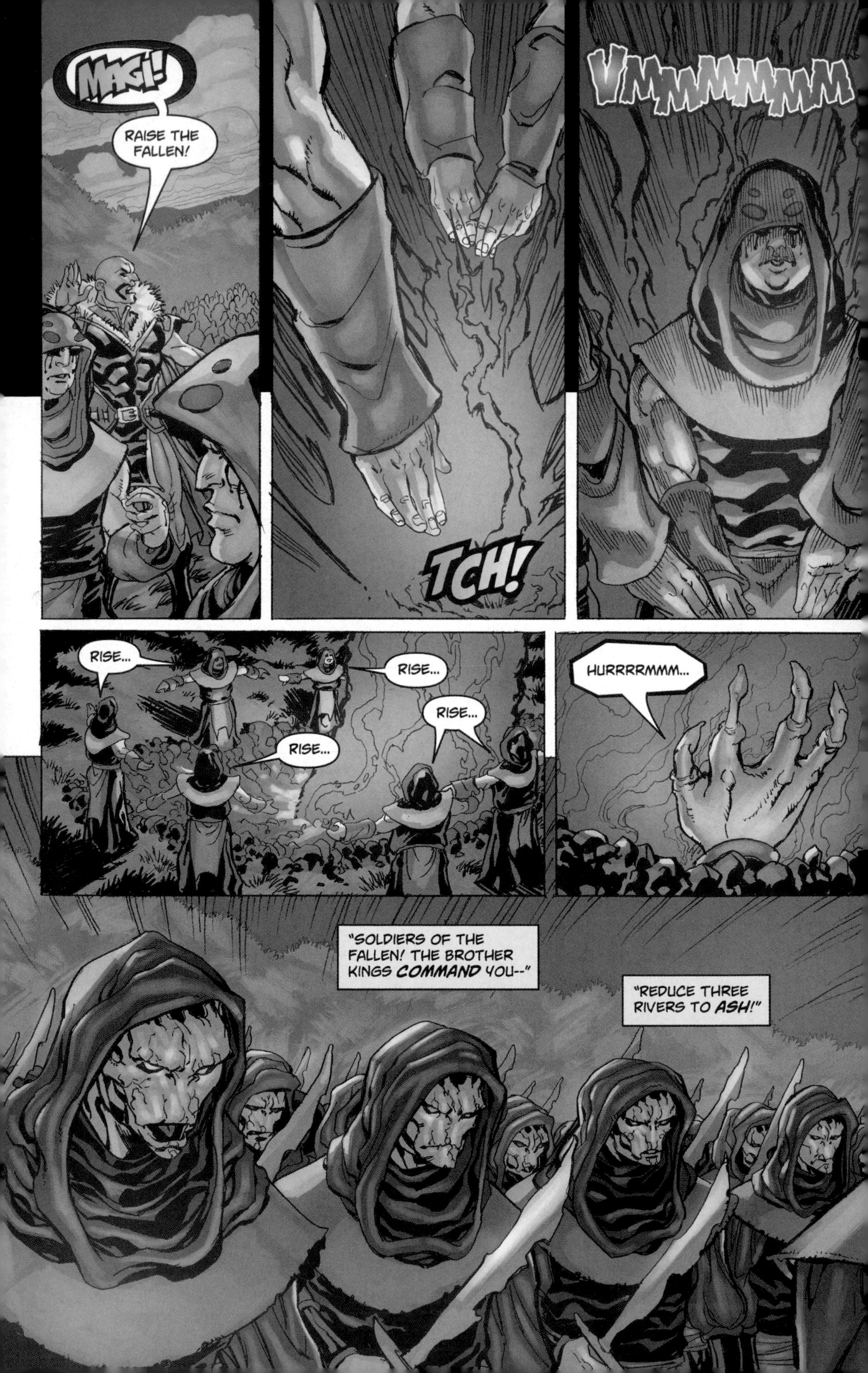
MAGI!
RAISE THE FALLEN!
VMMMMMMM
TCH!
RISE...
RISE...
RISE...
RISE...
HURRRRMMM...
"SOLDIERS OF THE FALLEN! THE BROTHER KINGS COMMAND YOU--"
"REDUCE THREE RIVERS TO ASH!"

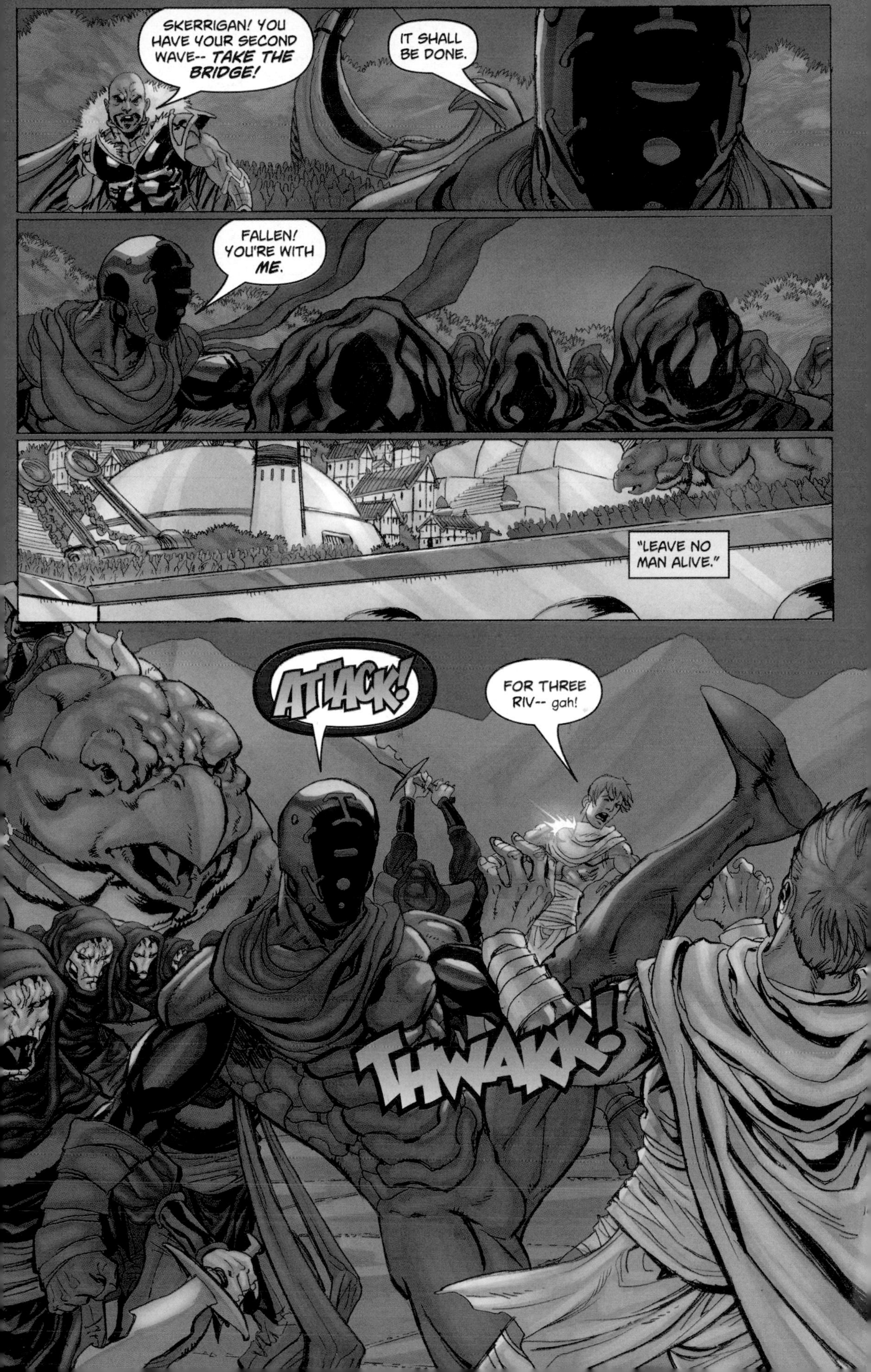
SKERRIGAN! YOU HAVE YOUR SECOND WAVE-- *TAKE THE BRIDGE!*
IT SHALL BE DONE.
FALLEN! YOU'RE WITH *ME*.
"LEAVE NO MAN ALIVE."
ATTACK!
FOR THREE RIV-- gah!
THWAKK!

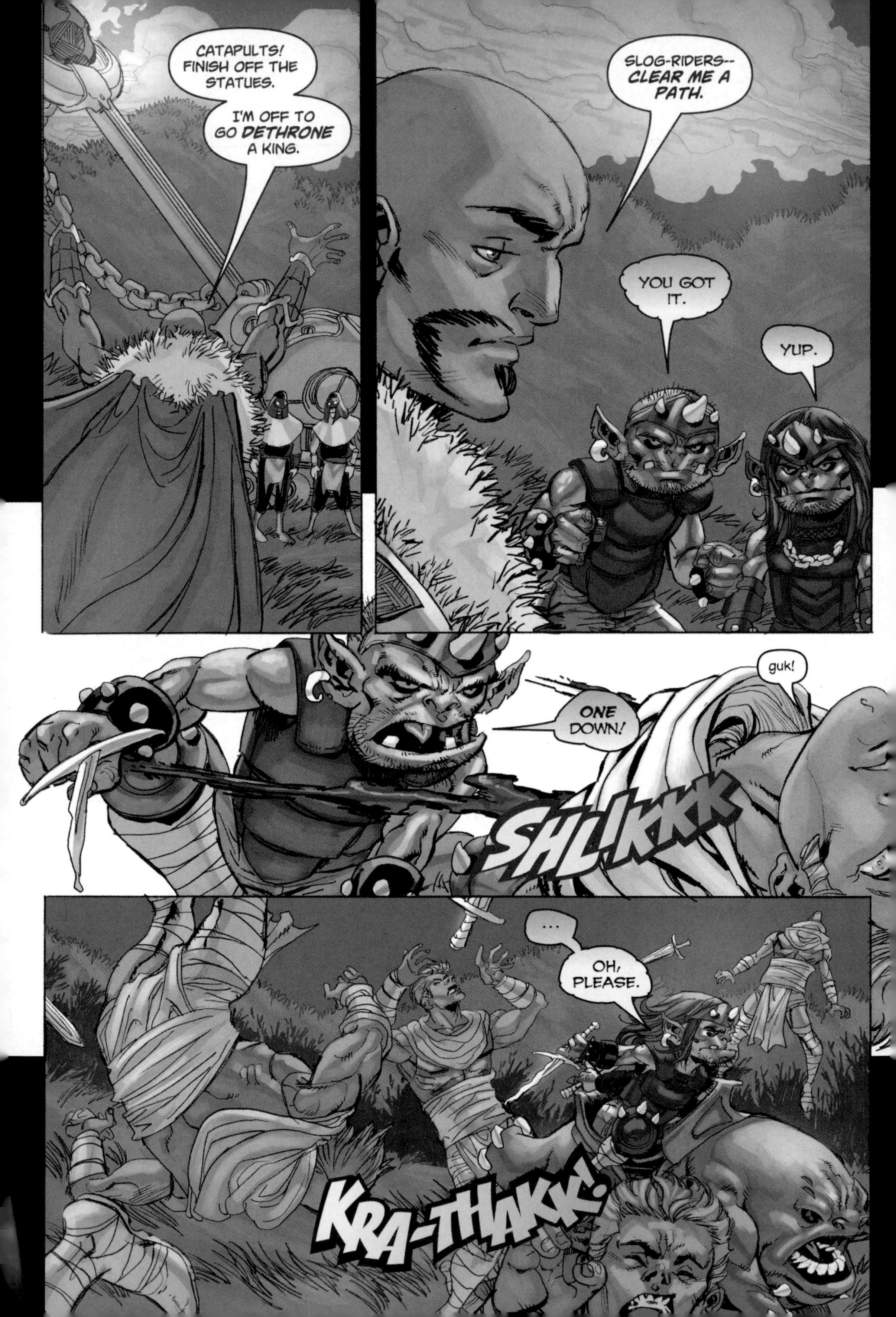
CATAPULTS! FINISH OFF THE STATUES.
I'M OFF TO GO DETHRONE A KING.
SLOG-RIDERS-- CLEAR ME A PATH.
YOU GOT IT.
YUP.
ONE DOWN!
guk!
SHLIKKK
...
OH, PLEASE.
KRA-THAKK!

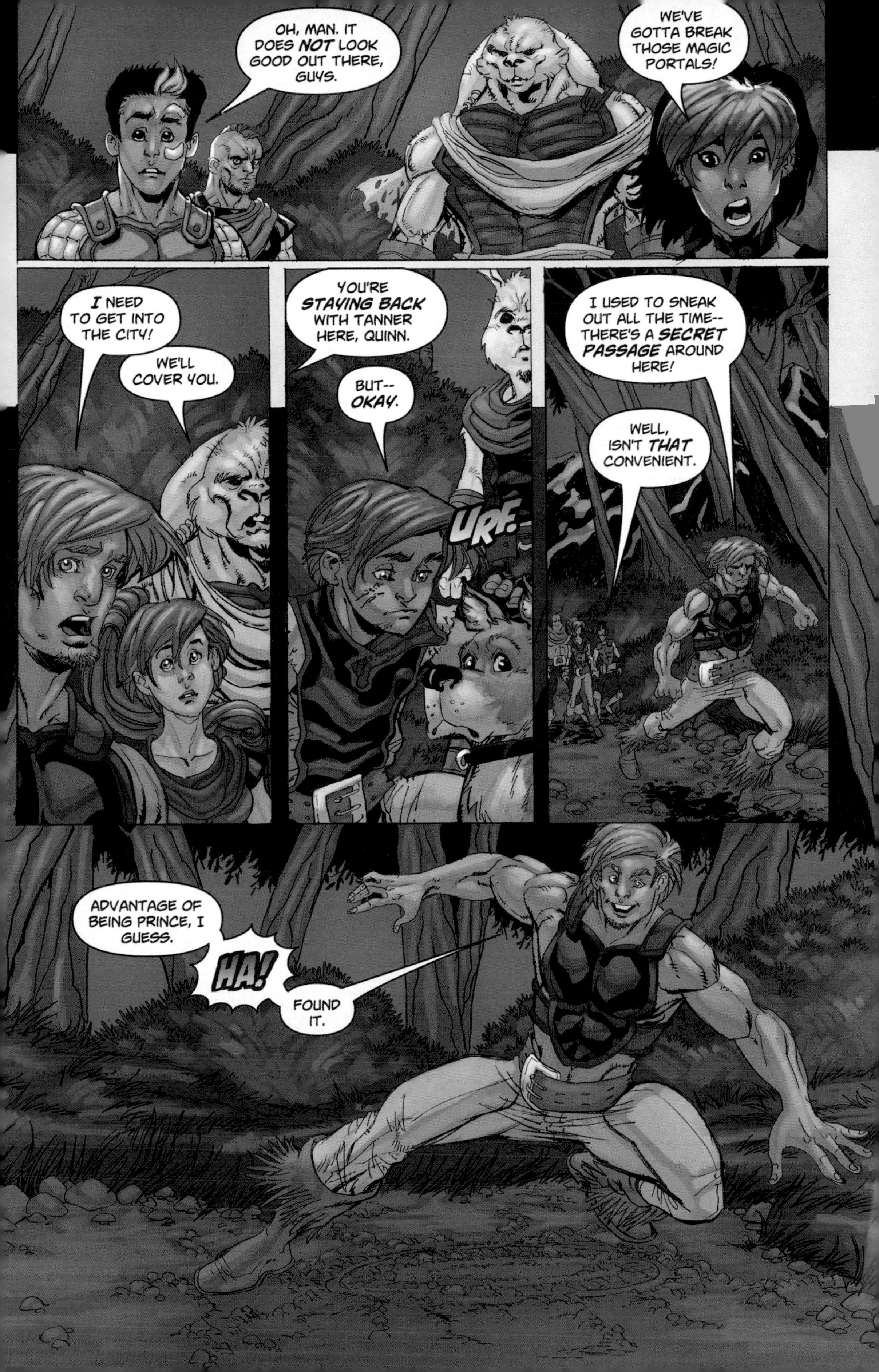
OH, MAN. IT DOES NOT LOOK GOOD OUT THERE, GUYS.
WE'VE GOTTA BREAK THOSE MAGIC PORTALS!
I NEED TO GET INTO THE CITY!
WE'LL COVER YOU.
YOU'RE STAYING BACK WITH TANNER HERE, QUINN.
BUT-- OKAY.
URF.
I USED TO SNEAK OUT ALL THE TIME-- THERE'S A SECRET PASSAGE AROUND HERE!
WELL, ISN'T THAT CONVENIENT.
ADVANTAGE OF BEING PRINCE, I GUESS.
HA!
FOUND IT.

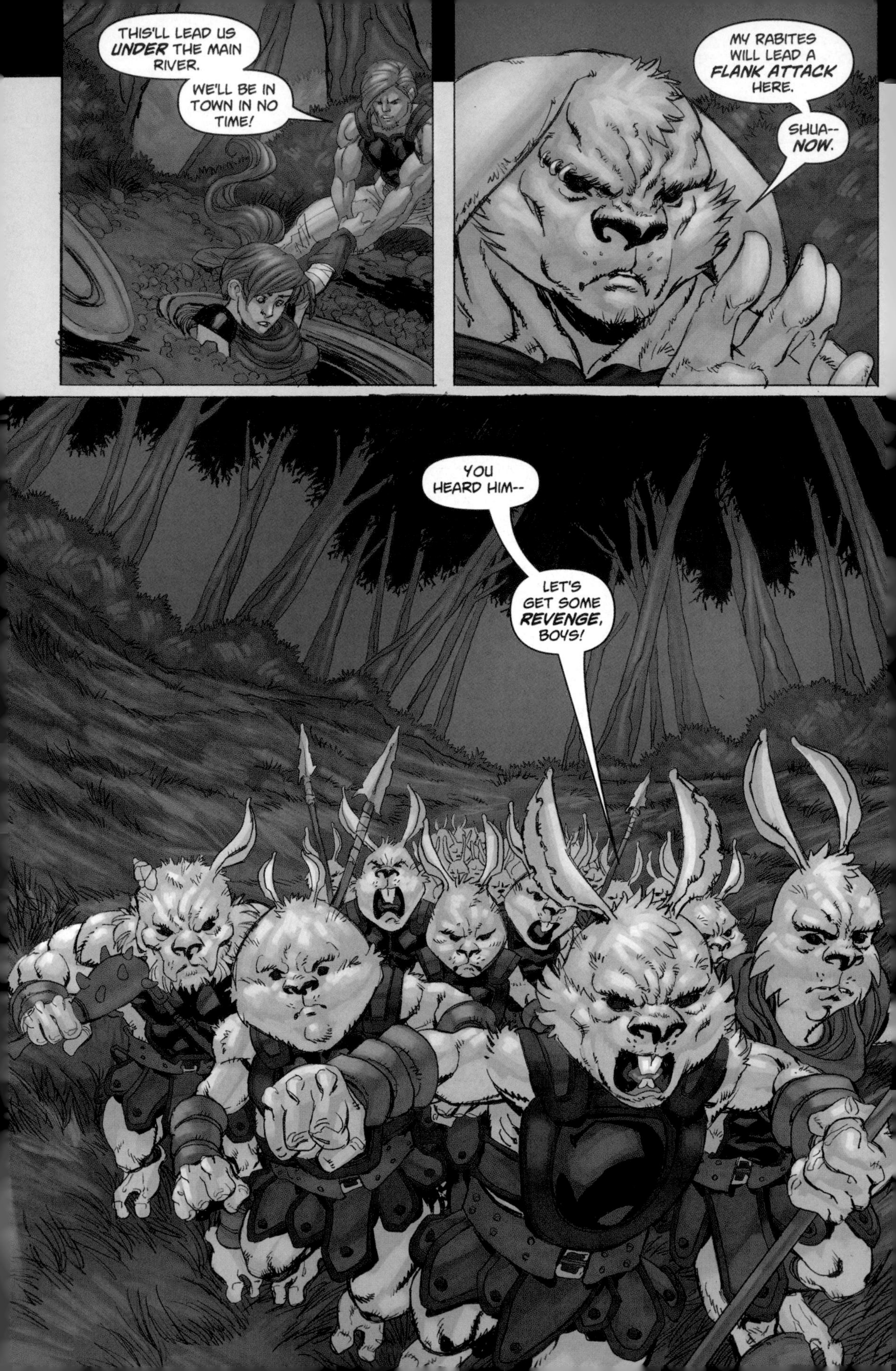
THIS'LL LEAD US UNDER THE MAIN RIVER.
WE'LL BE IN TOWN IN NO TIME!
MY RABITES WILL LEAD A FLANK ATTACK HERE.
SHUA-- NOW.
YOU HEARD HIM--
LET'S GET SOME REVENGE, BOYS!

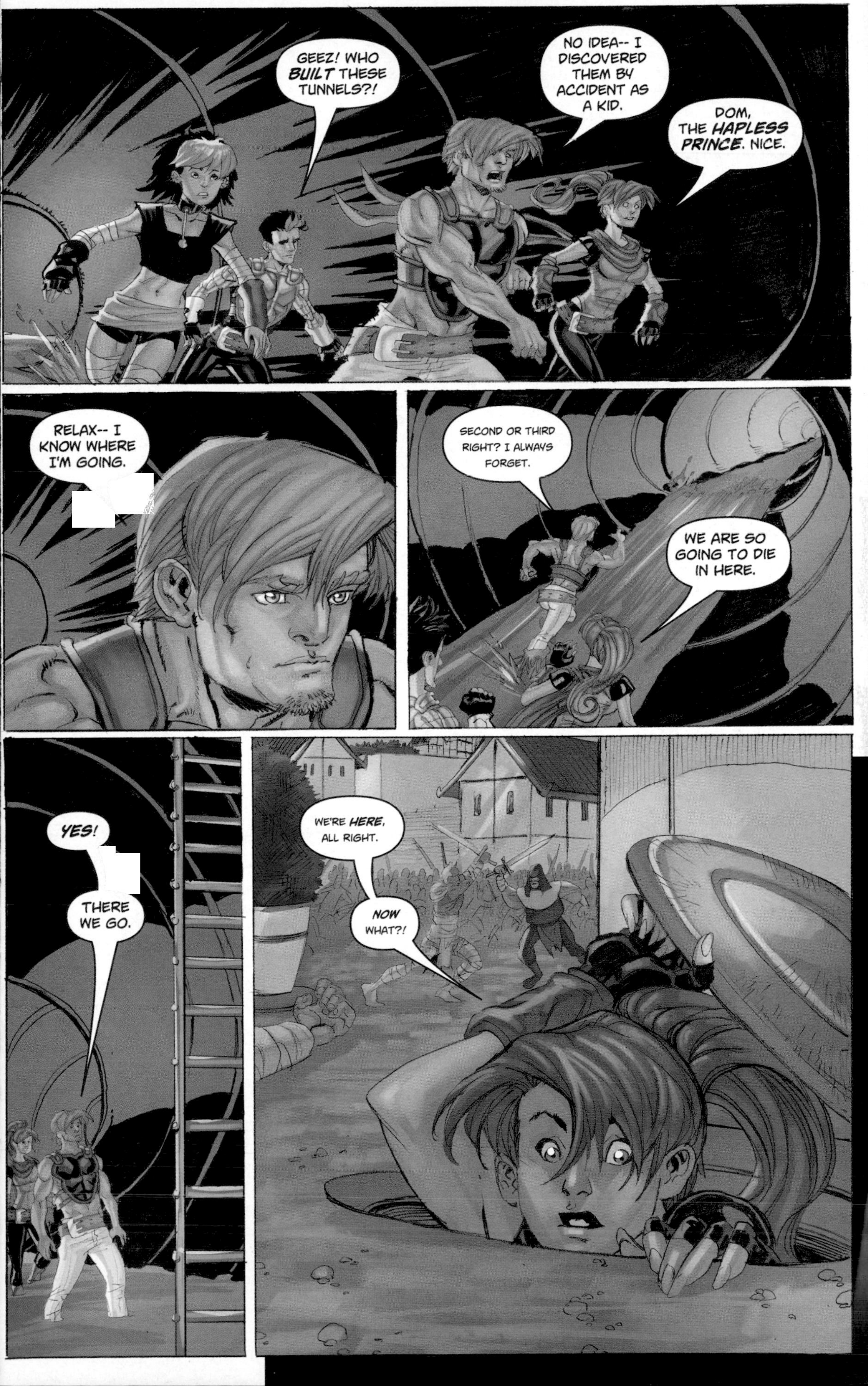
GEEZ! WHO BUILT THESE TUNNELS?!
NO IDEA-- I DISCOVERED THEM BY ACCIDENT AS A KID.
DOM, THE HAPLESS PRINCE. NICE.
RELAX-- I KNOW WHERE I'M GOING.
SECOND OR THIRD RIGHT? I ALWAYS FORGET.
WE ARE SO GOING TO DIE IN HERE.
YES!
THERE WE GO.
WE'RE HERE, ALL RIGHT.
NOW WHAT?!

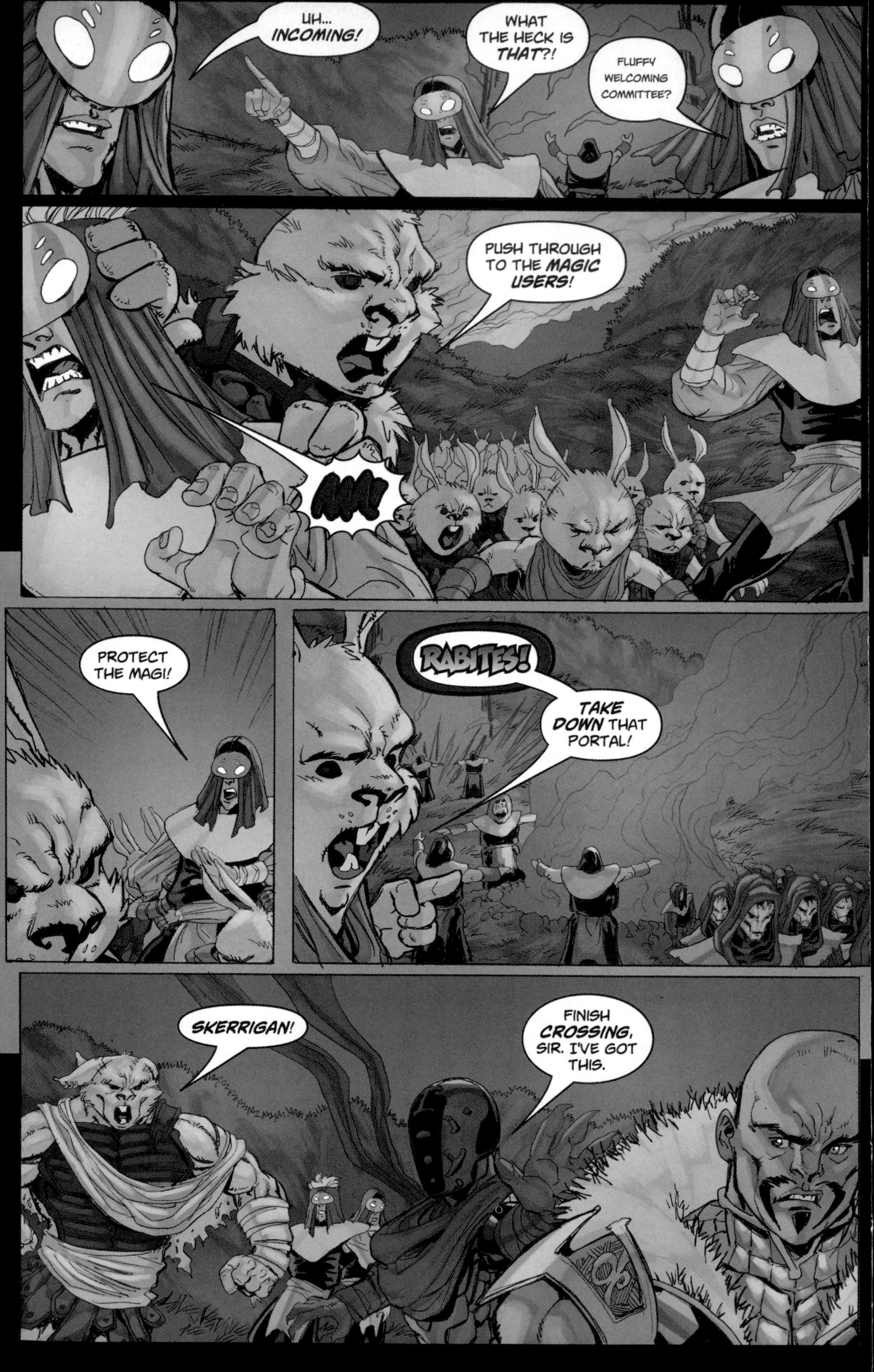
UH... INCOMING!
WHAT THE HECK IS THAT?!
FLUFFY WELCOMING COMMITTEE?
PUSH THROUGH TO THE MAGIC USERS!
HAA!
PROTECT THE MAGI!
RABITES!
TAKE DOWN THAT PORTAL!
SKERRIGAN!
FINISH CROSSING, SIR. I'VE GOT THIS.

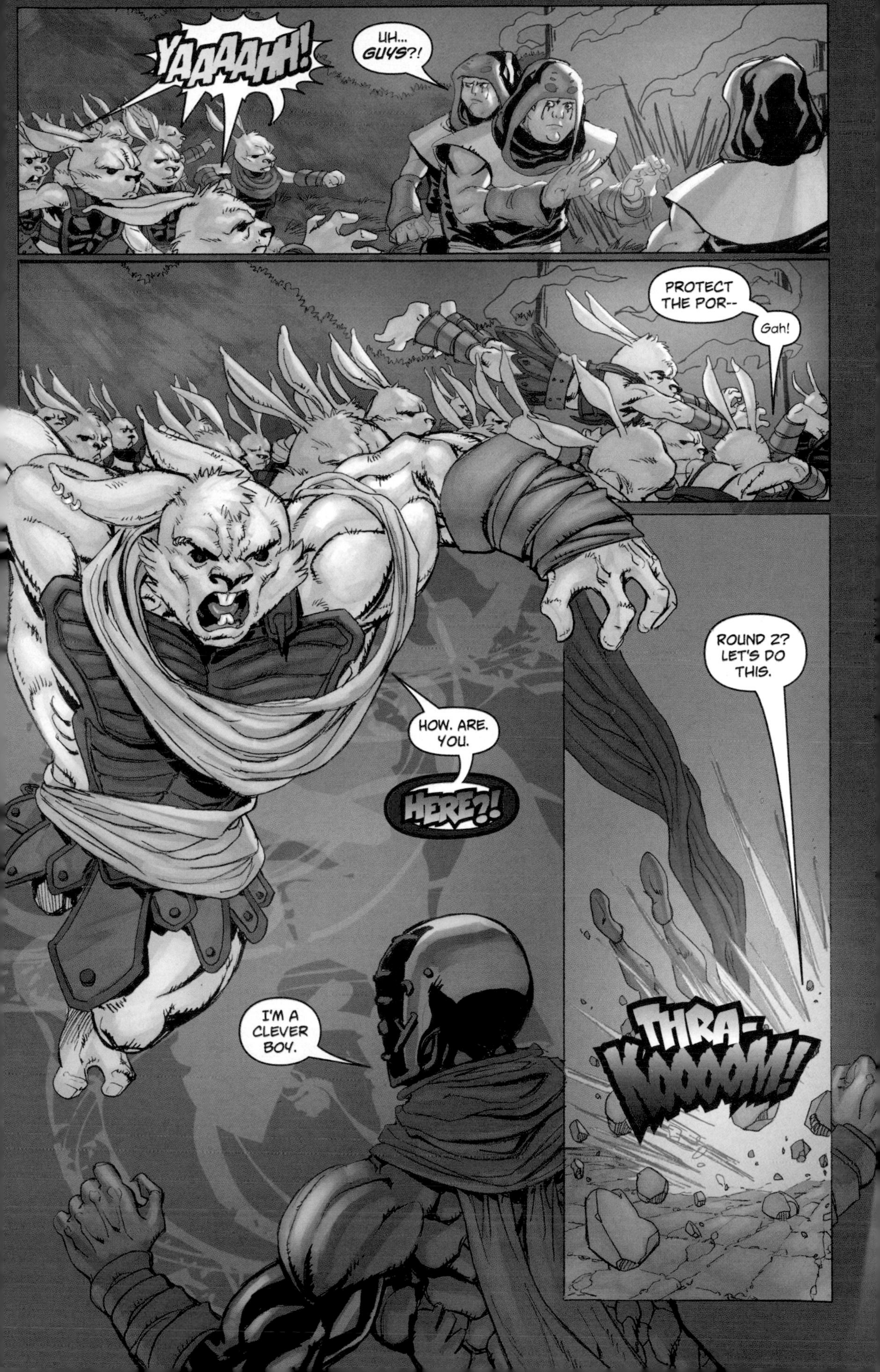
YAAAAHH!
UH... GUYS?!
PROTECT THE POR--
Gah!
HOW. ARE. YOU.
HERE?!
ROUND 2? LET'S DO THIS.
I'M A CLEVER BOY.
THRA-KOOOM!

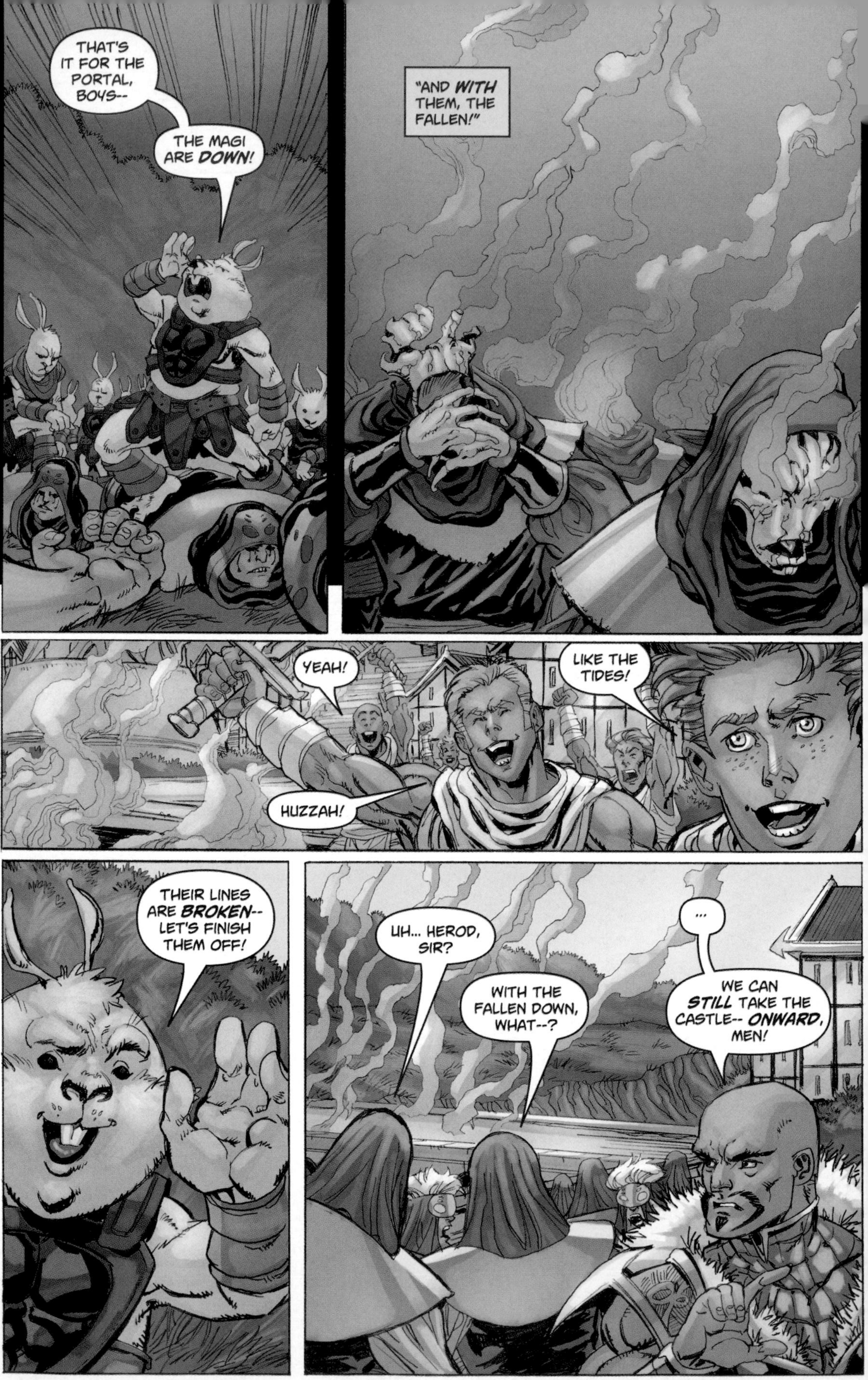
THAT'S IT FOR THE PORTAL, BOYS--
THE MAGI ARE DOWN!
"AND WITH THEM, THE FALLEN!"
YEAH!
LIKE THE TIDES!
HUZZAH!
THEIR LINES ARE BROKEN-- LET'S FINISH THEM OFF!
UH... HEROD, SIR?
...
WITH THE FALLEN DOWN, WHAT--?
WE CAN STILL TAKE THE CASTLE-- ONWARD, MEN!

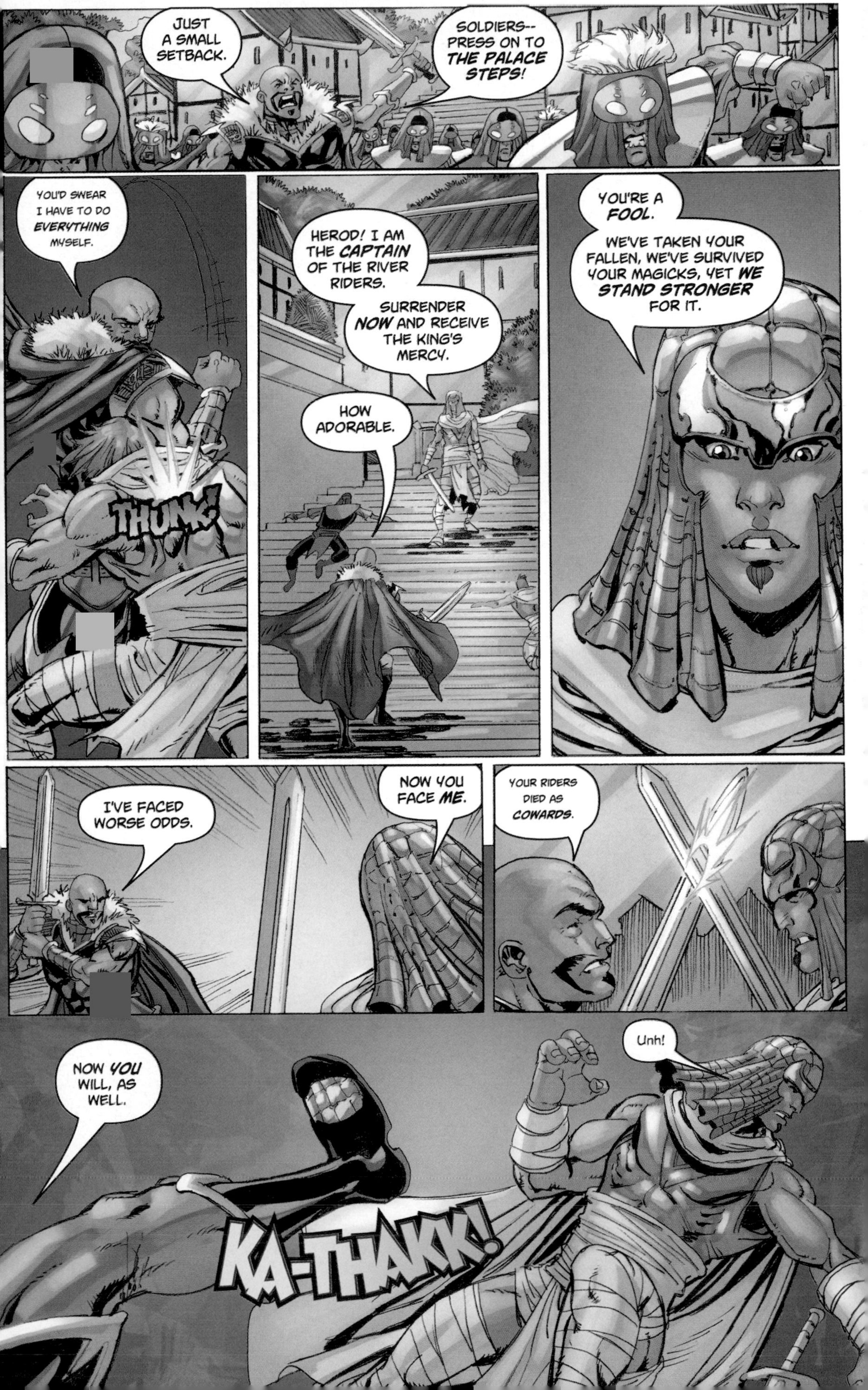
JUST A SMALL SETBACK.
SOLDIERS-- PRESS ON TO THE PALACE STEPS!
YOU'D SWEAR I HAVE TO DO EVERYTHING MYSELF.
THUNK!
HEROD! I AM THE CAPTAIN OF THE RIVER RIDERS.
SURRENDER NOW AND RECEIVE THE KING'S MERCY.
HOW ADORABLE.
YOU'RE A FOOL.
WE'VE TAKEN YOUR FALLEN, WE'VE SURVIVED YOUR MAGICKS, YET WE STAND STRONGER FOR IT.
I'VE FACED WORSE ODDS.
NOW YOU FACE ME.
YOUR RIDERS DIED AS COWARDS.
NOW YOU WILL, AS WELL.
Unh!
KA-THAKK!

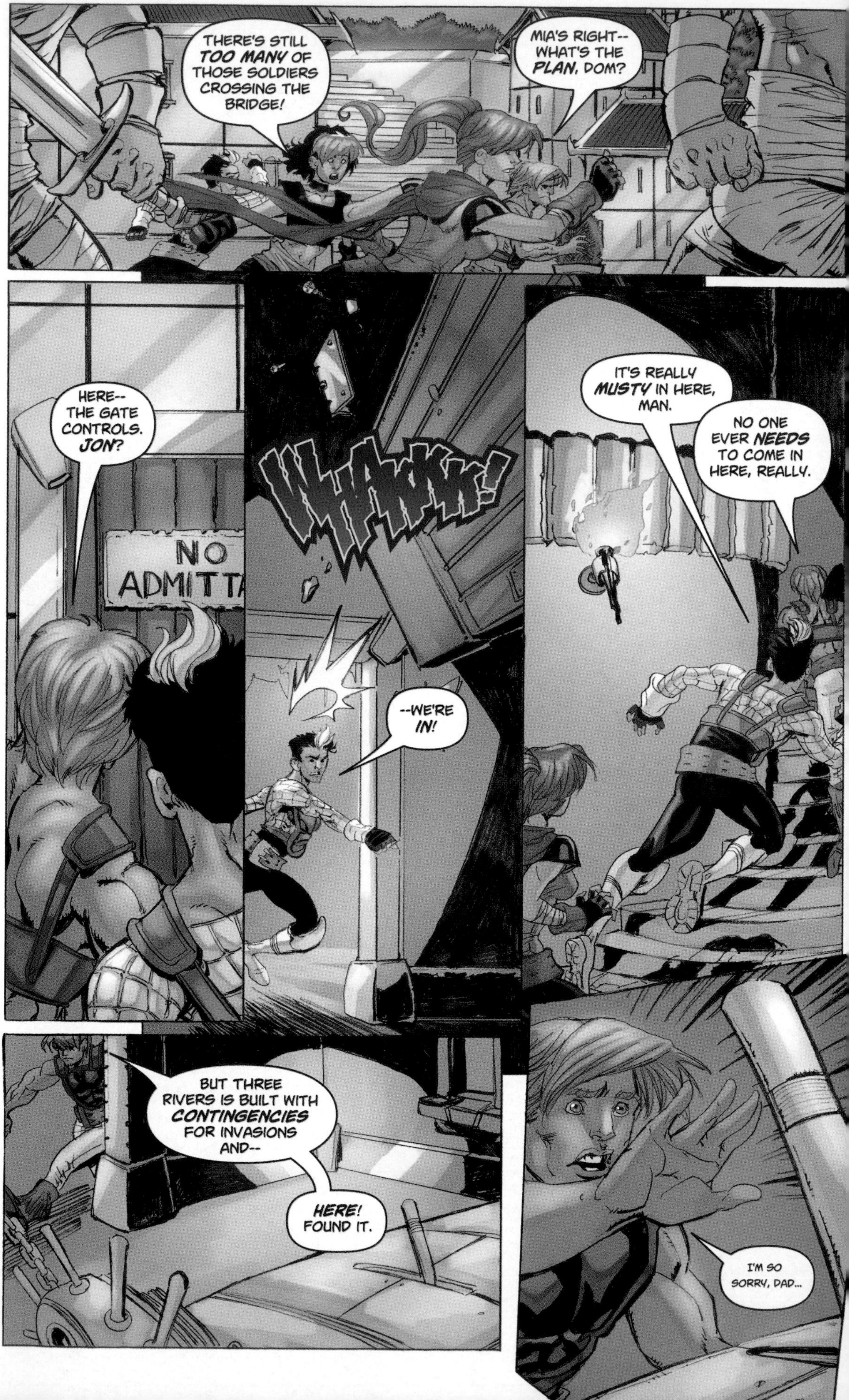
THERE'S STILL TOO MANY OF THOSE SOLDIERS CROSSING THE BRIDGE!
MIA'S RIGHT-- WHAT'S THE PLAN, DOM?
HERE-- THE GATE CONTROLS. JON?
NO ADMITTA
WHAKKK!
--WE'RE IN!
IT'S REALLY MUSTY IN HERE, MAN.
NO ONE EVER NEEDS TO COME IN HERE, REALLY.
BUT THREE RIVERS IS BUILT WITH CONTINGENCIES FOR INVASIONS AND--
HERE! FOUND IT.
I'M SO SORRY, DAD...

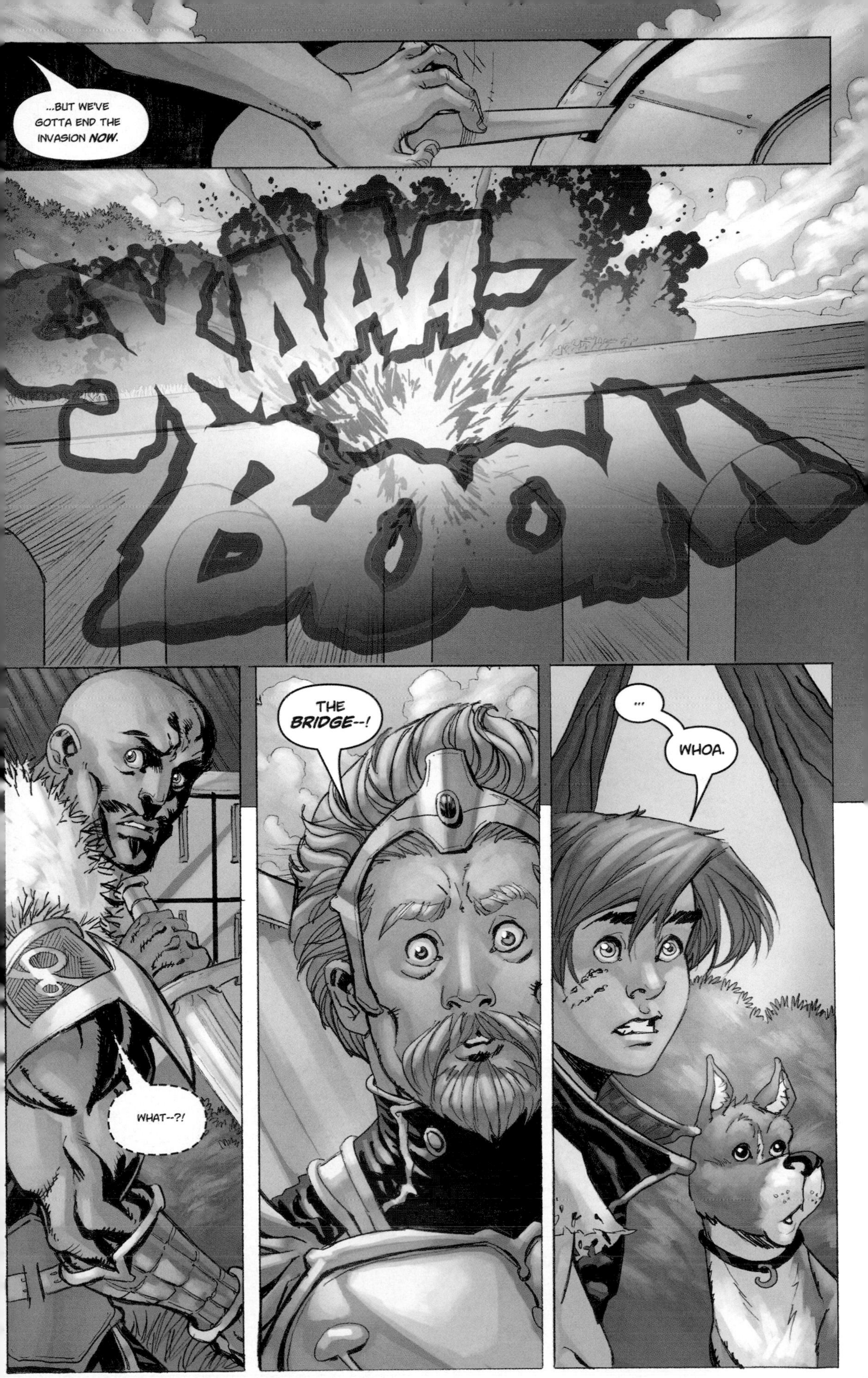
...BUT WE'VE GOTTA END THE INVASION *NOW*.
WHAT--?!
THE *BRIDGE*--!
...
WHOA.

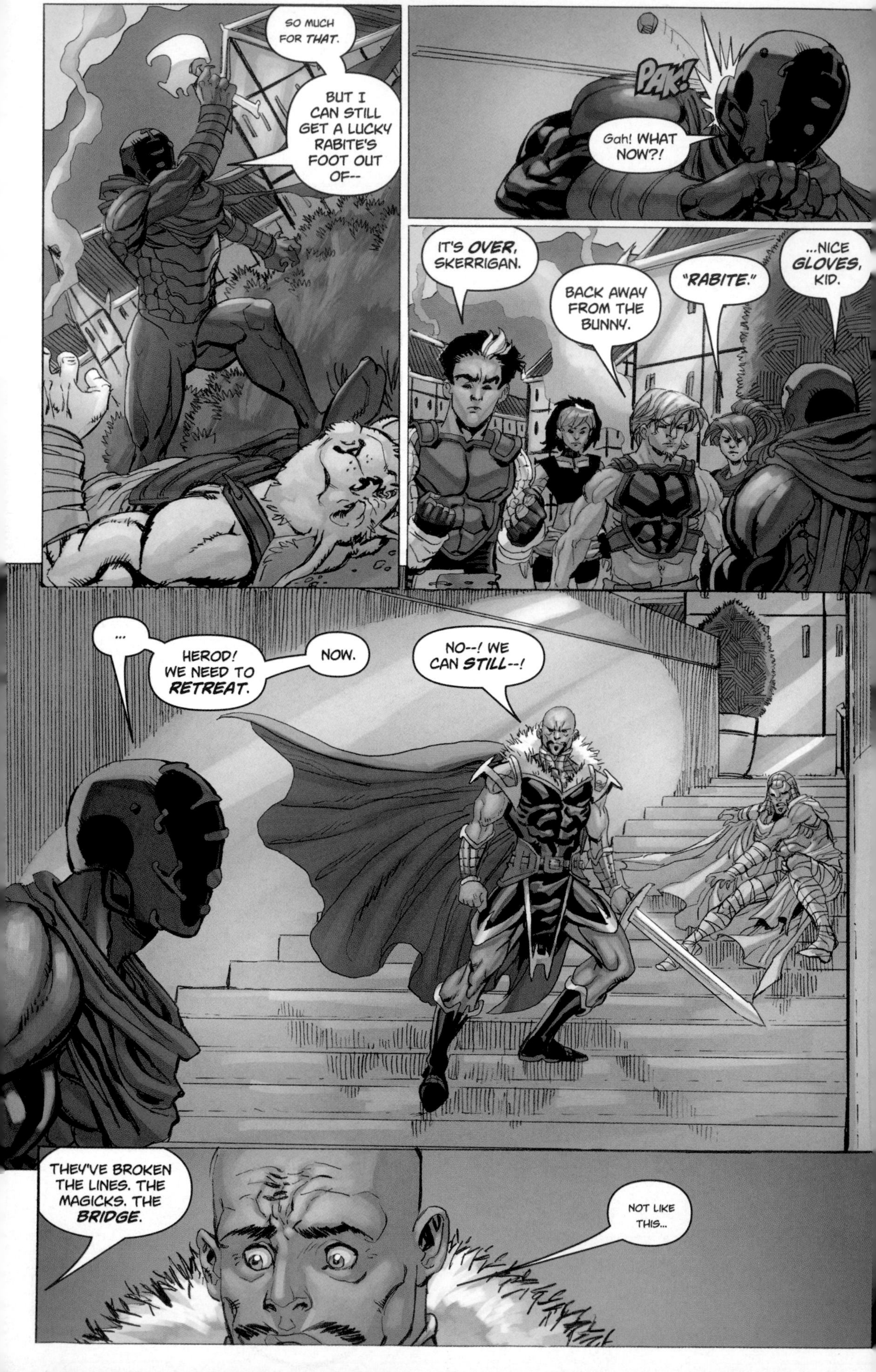
SO MUCH FOR *THAT*.
BUT I CAN STILL GET A LUCKY RABITE'S FOOT OUT OF--
PAK!
Gah! WHAT NOW?!
IT'S *OVER*, SKERRIGAN.
BACK AWAY FROM THE BUNNY.
"*RABITE*."
...NICE *GLOVES*, KID.
...
HEROD! WE NEED TO *RETREAT*.
NOW.
NO--! WE CAN *STILL*--!
THEY'VE BROKEN THE LINES. THE MAGICKS. THE *BRIDGE*.
NOT LIKE THIS...

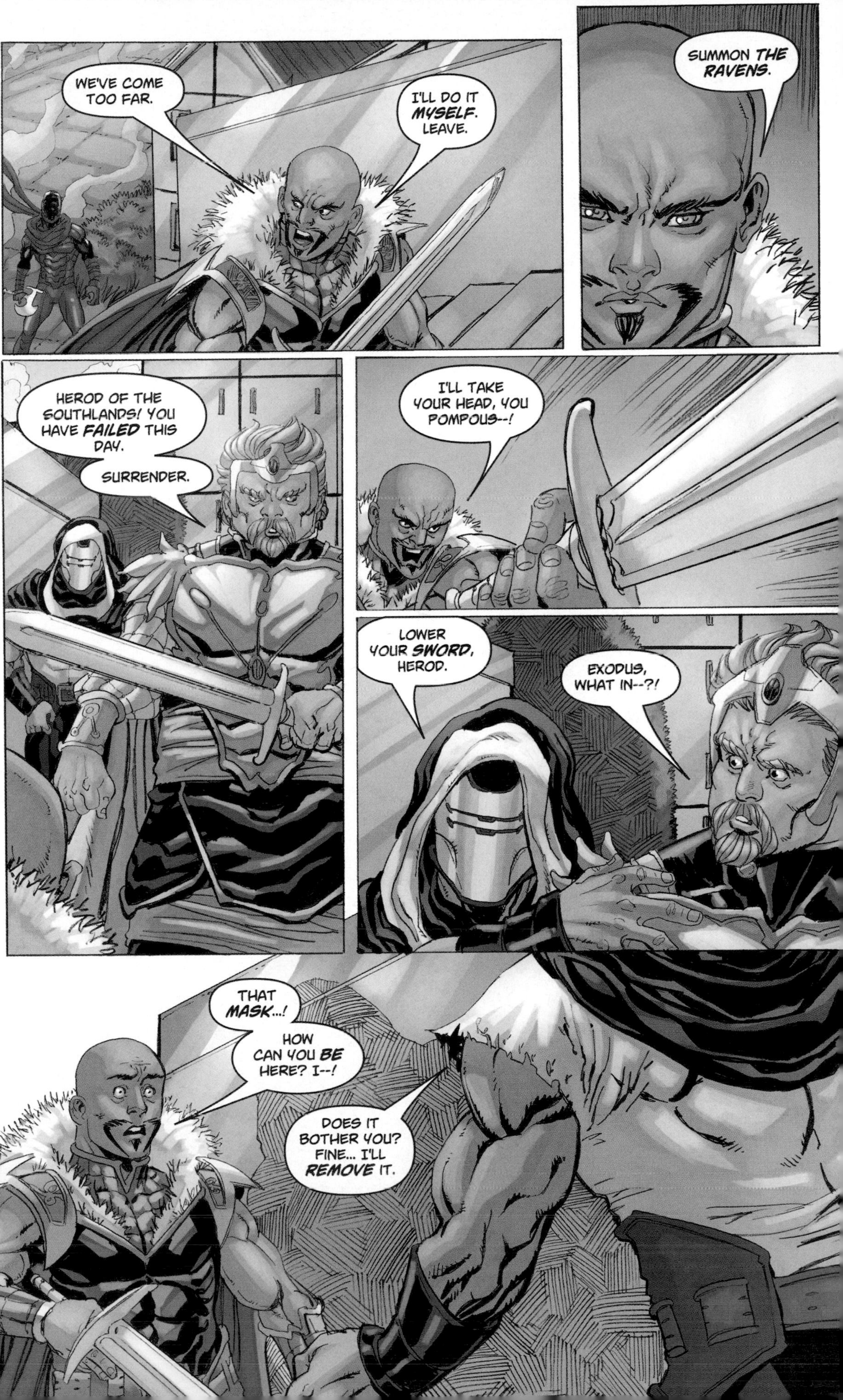
WE'VE COME TOO FAR.
I'LL DO IT MYSELF. LEAVE.
SUMMON THE RAVENS.
HEROD OF THE SOUTHLANDS! YOU HAVE FAILED THIS DAY.
SURRENDER.
I'LL TAKE YOUR HEAD, YOU POMPOUS--!
LOWER YOUR SWORD, HEROD.
EXODUS, WHAT IN--?!
THAT MASK...!
HOW CAN YOU BE HERE? I--!
DOES IT BOTHER YOU? FINE... I'LL REMOVE IT.

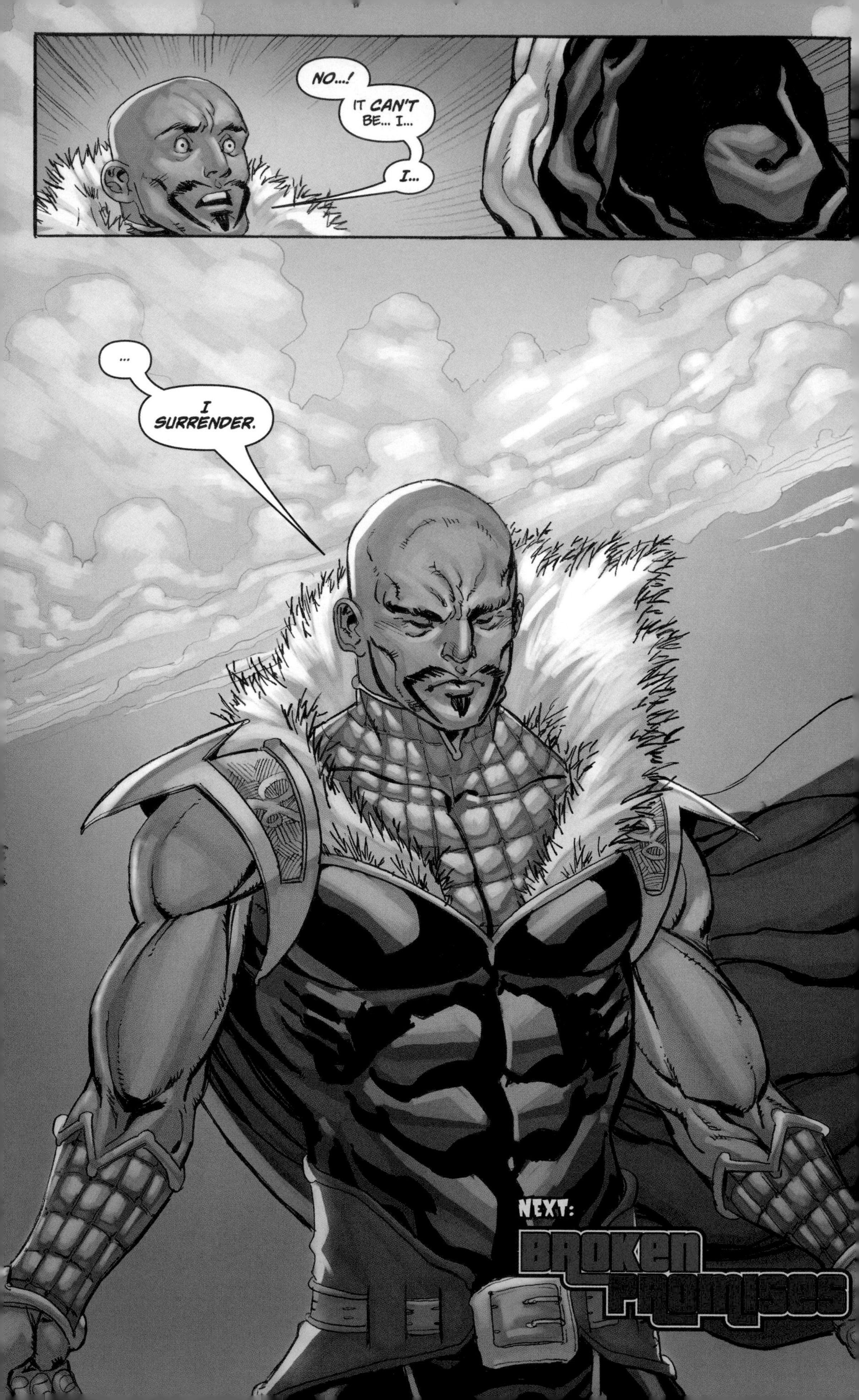
NO...!
IT CAN'T BE... I...
I...
...
I SURRENDER.
NEXT:
BROKEN PROMISES

SKYWORDS

Got thoughts?
Fan art?
Ransom notes?

WRITE US @

skywardfans@gmail.com

What just happened?!

Herod just up and surrendered? Exodus' face must be all craggly and oozy or something-- or worse, he's gorgeous! we'll find out together, I suppose... Jeremy won't tell me yet.

Thanks for hanging in there with us-- spread the word! Just a heads up-- there will be a short delay for issue 10. Between Diamond, health issues, and more, it's been a hard, weird year. We'll still be here!

The letters page returns! See, we promised and you guys kept writing-- we love you guys. Enough rambling!

BRING ON THE LETTERS AND EMAILS!

Skyward Team!

I just wanted to thank you for creating a series that not only can I read and love, my kids love it too. Your characters live and breathe on the page, and we wanted to know when we can expect some Skyward gear? Shirts, stuffed animals, coffee mugs? C'mon, I need my Skyward stuff!

Eric Bennett
email witheld by request

Thanks so much, Eric! We're working overtime on the comics at the moment, but we have been approached with some interesting Skyward licensed ideas-- games, statues, plushies... it's all possibilities. Let us know what you want and we'll make it happen!

Jeremy,

Hey, man! I hope you're doing well. I just got a motivation from DCBS, where I order my comics from, that Skyward 10,11,&12 were cancelled and will be offered later. I'm just curious if you're a little behind and that's why? Regardless, I'm enjoying the book quite a bit. Looking forward to more!

Matthew D. Smith
via Facebook

First off, WE ARE NOT CANCELLED. We've hit delays with Diamond, our publisher, our talent-- hey, everything! But we're still here. Jeremy is 100% committed to this series, and it's very important to him that he gets to tell this story. He's even turned down highly-lucrative gigs to stay on this one. Thanks so much for the enthusiasm!

Dear Mr. Dale,

Hi! I am Max Steele and I met you in Acme Comics in Greensboro. I bought your comic book and you signed it for me. Thank you again. I really liked it and hope to read more soon. It was very sad because Quinn's mom and dad died.
Bye, from Max

Max, we loved meeting you at Acme-- they're great guys over there in Comic Book City, USA! It was very sad, yes-- and it looks like it hit Quinn very hard. He's trying to figure out his place in the new world around him. Keep reading-- we have some amazing things to share very, very soon. :)

Hi Jeremy,

Can we see a crossover with Skullkickers or Tellos anytime soon? I need that in my life.

Arclite
via deviantArt

Well, that would be a lot of fun, but not anytime soon-- but hey, drop the idea in Jim and Todd's ears, you never know what could happen. ;)

***NEXT: DO NOT MISS ISSUE TEN.** You've been here since issue one, right? Issue ten has a reveal so amazing, your BRAIN WILL EXPLODE. I showed the drawn pages to a fan at SDCC and he couldn't stop screaming and cheering.*

BE THERE. Skyward #10: ***THE BIGGEST SHOCK EVER.***

- kelly (and jeremy, too)

FANART OF THE MONTH

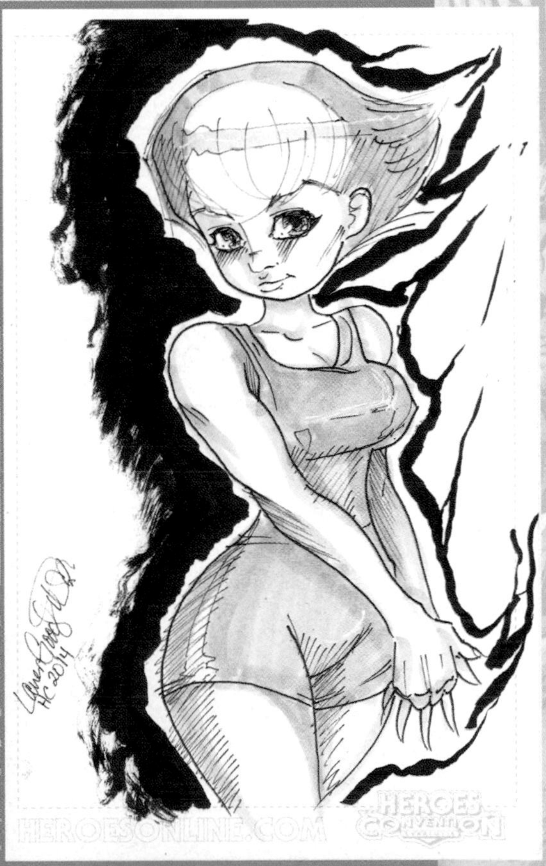

Lauren Goodnight HC 2014
HEROESONLINE.COM
HEROES CONVENTION

THIS ISSUE'S FANART OF THE MONTH of Mia comes courtesy of voice actress LAUREN GOODNIGHT!
Thanks for the amazing art! See more her work at:
http://www.imdb.com/name/nm1454552/

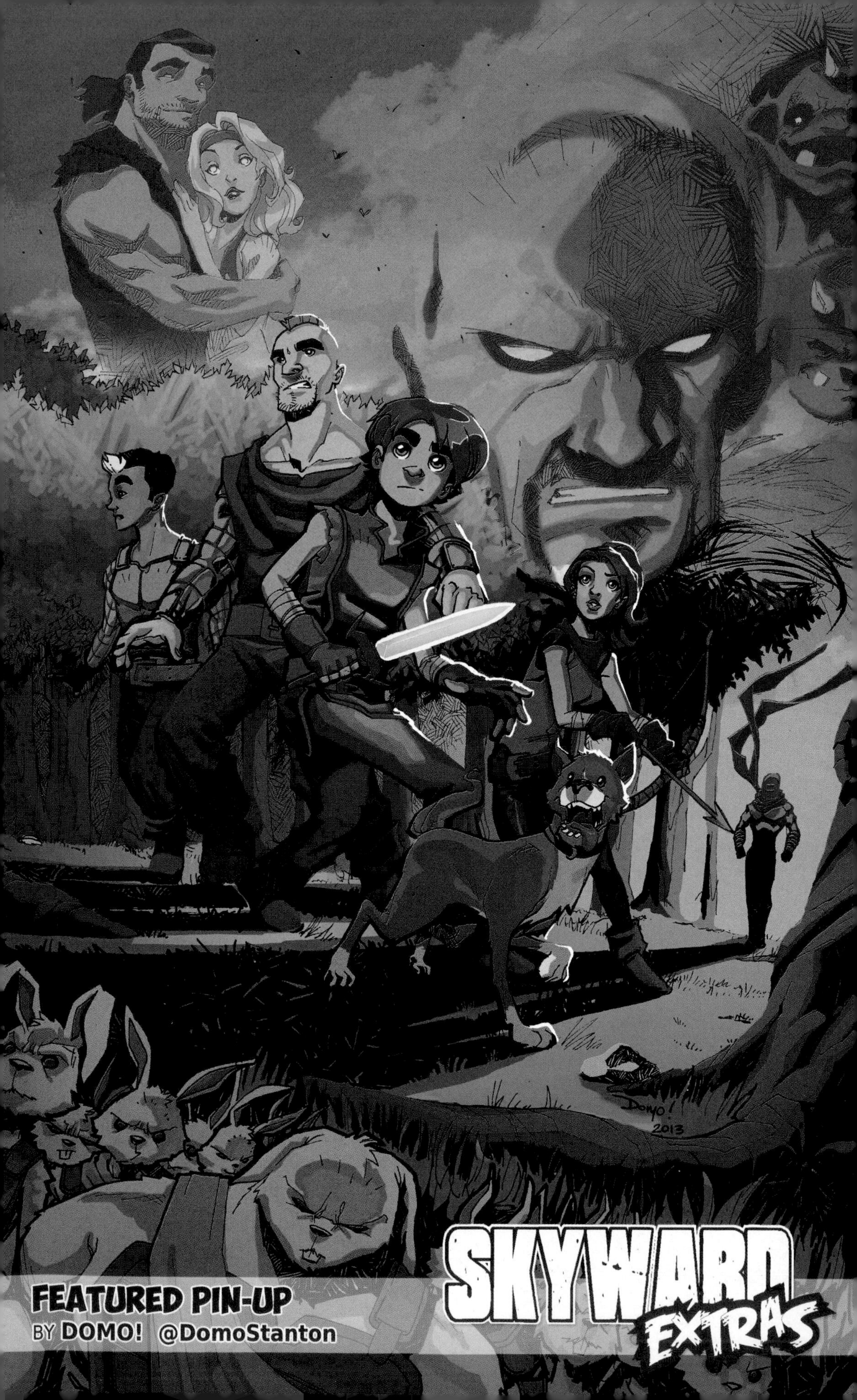
DOMO! 2013

FEATURED PIN-UP
BY DOMO! @DomoStanton

SKYWARD EXTRAS

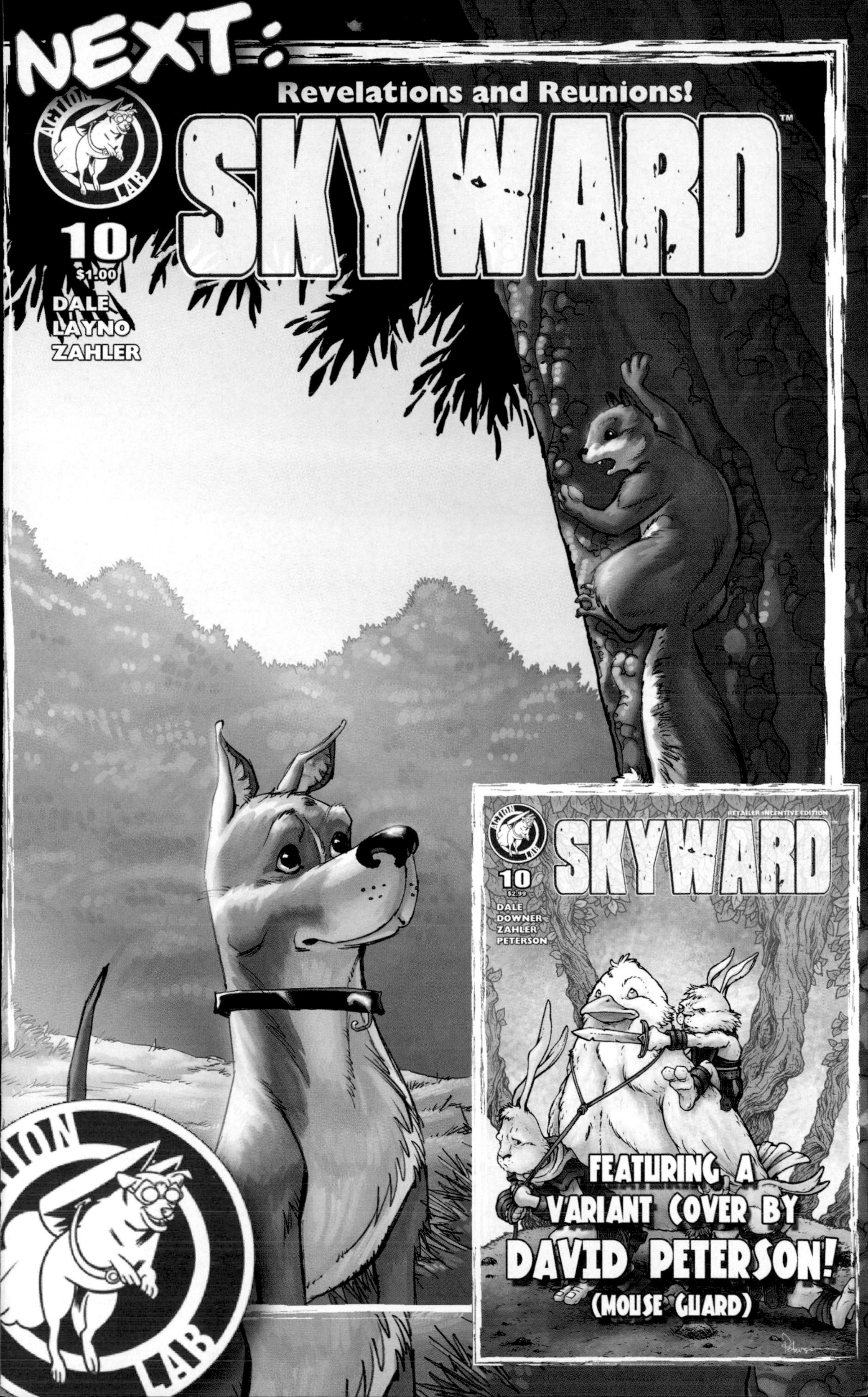
NEXT:
Revelations and Reunions!
SKYWARD™
10
$1.00
DALE
LAYNO
ZAHLER
RETAILER INCENTIVE EDITION
SKYWARD
10
$2.99
DALE
DOWNER
ZAHLER
PETERSON
FEATURING A VARIANT COVER BY DAVID PETERSON!
(MOUSE GUARD)

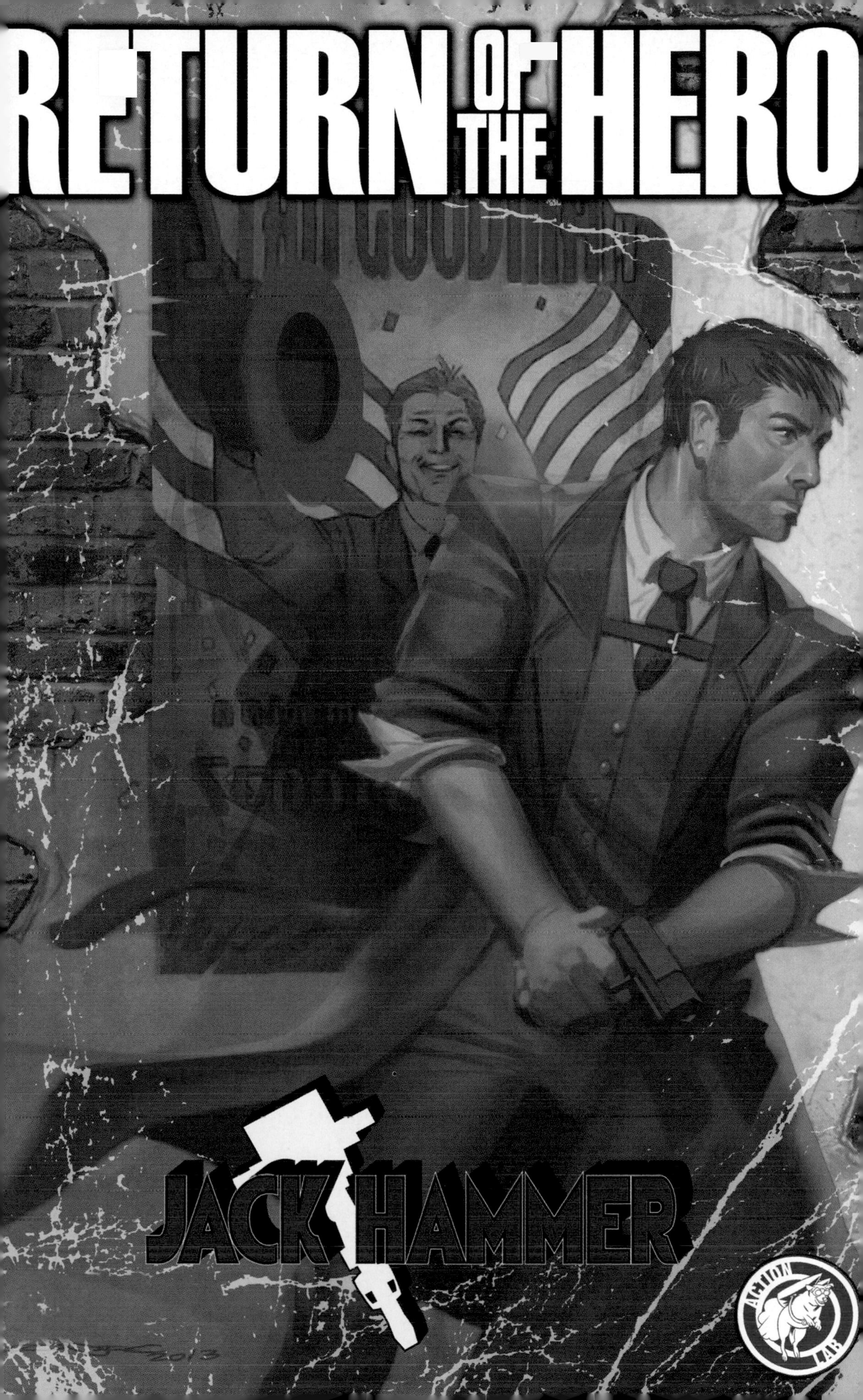
RETURN OF THE HERO
JACK HAMMER
ACTION LAB

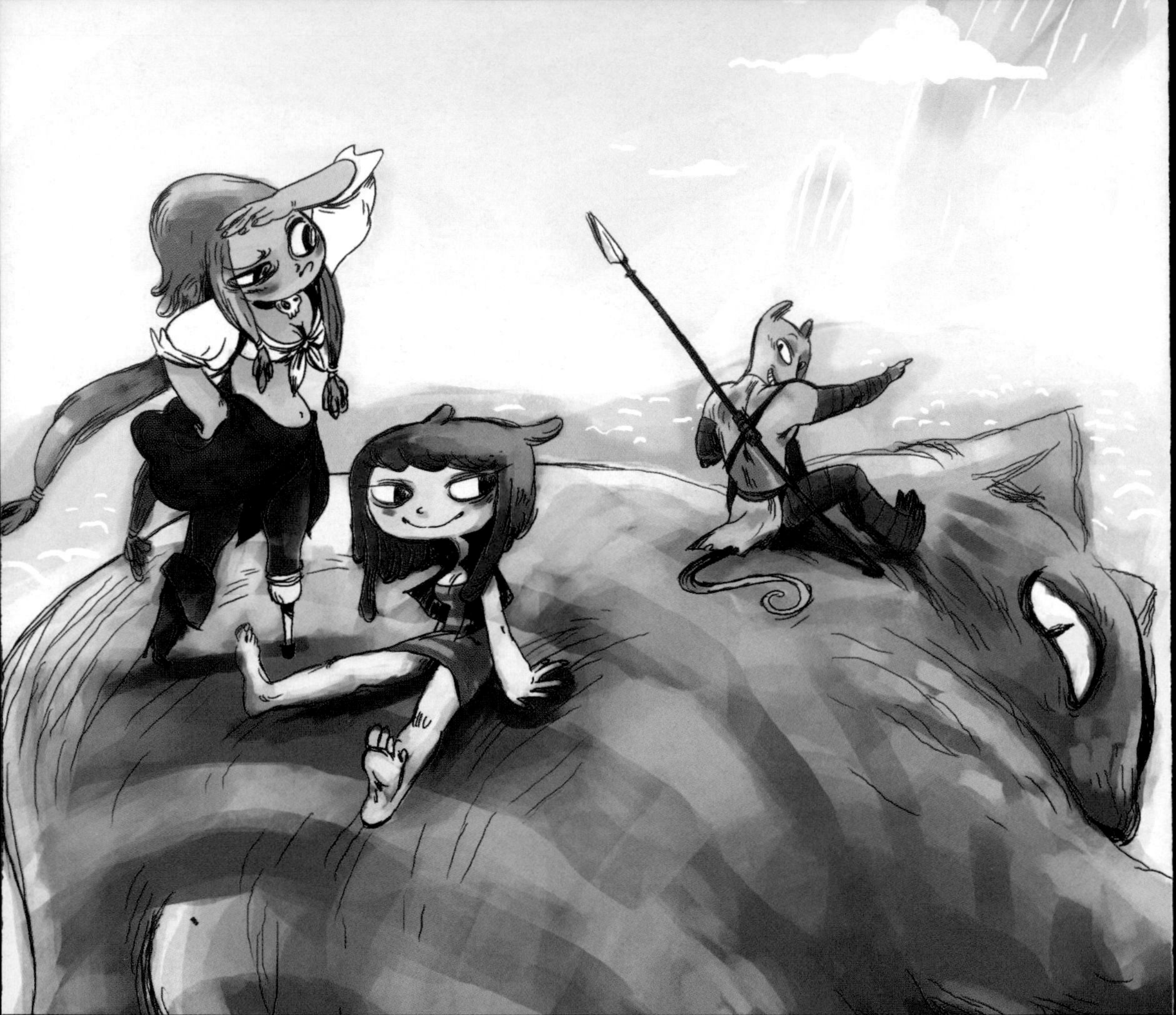

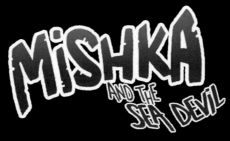

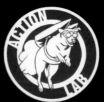

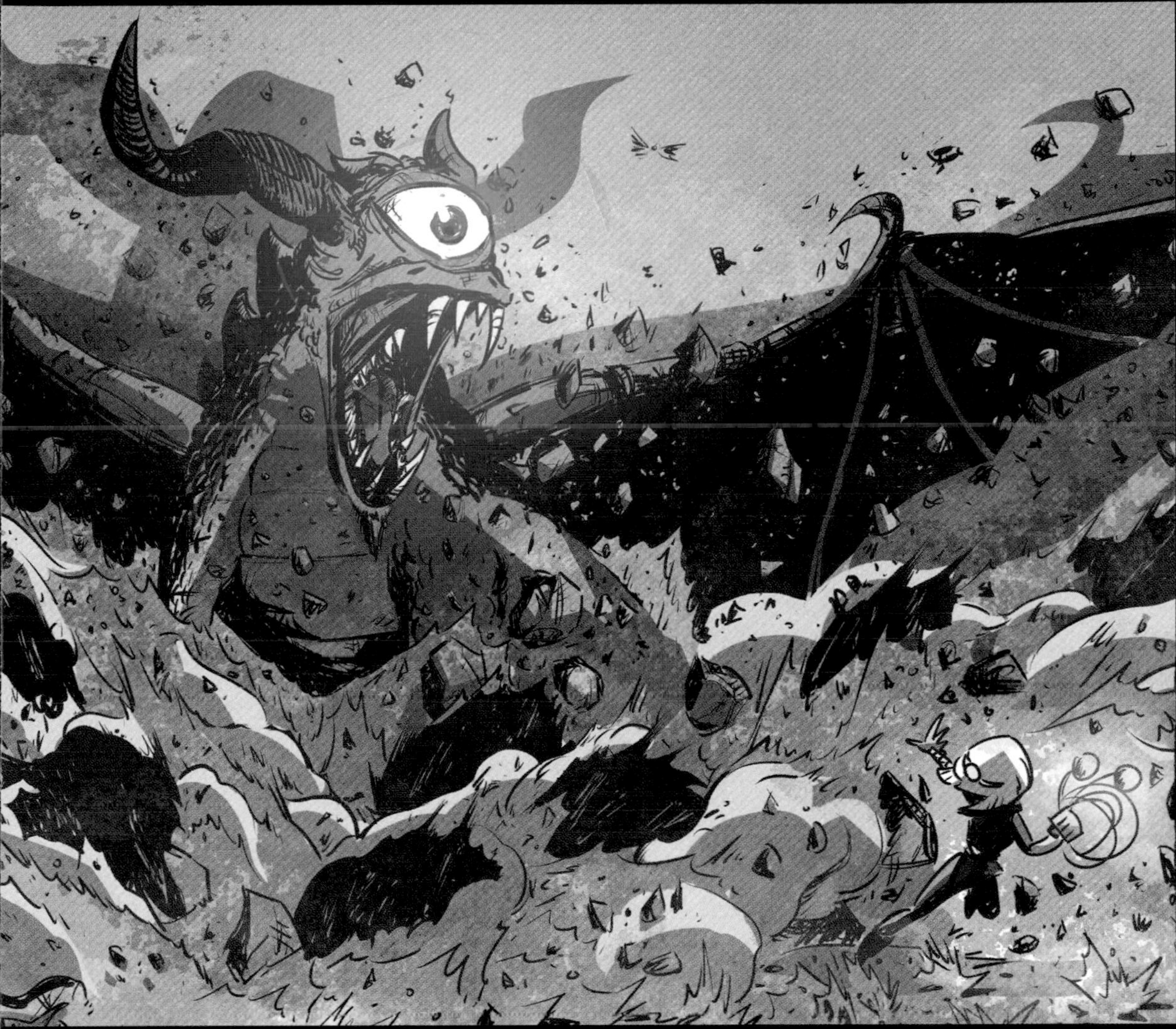

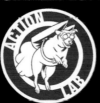

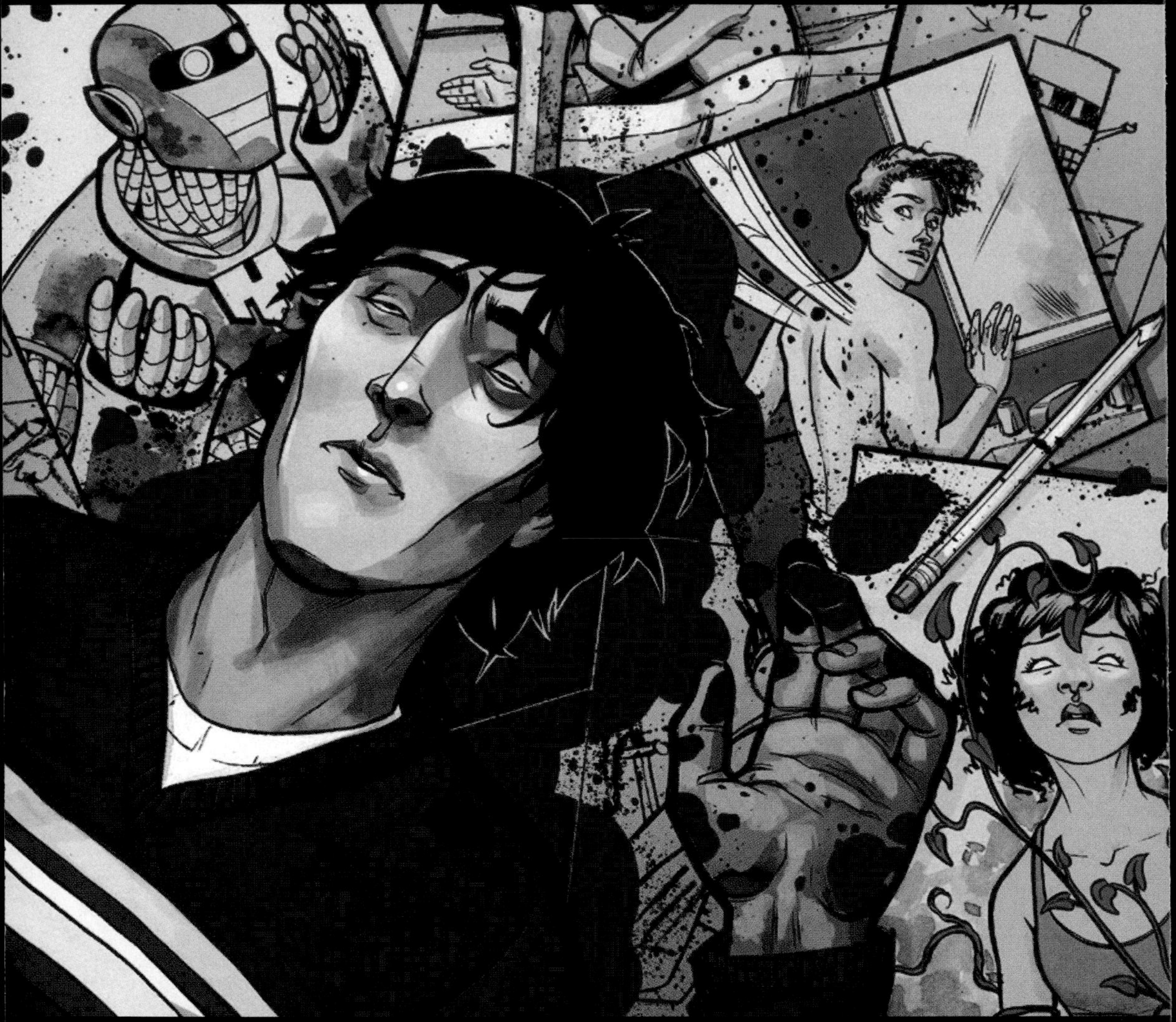

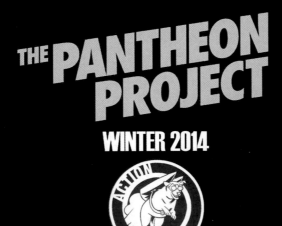

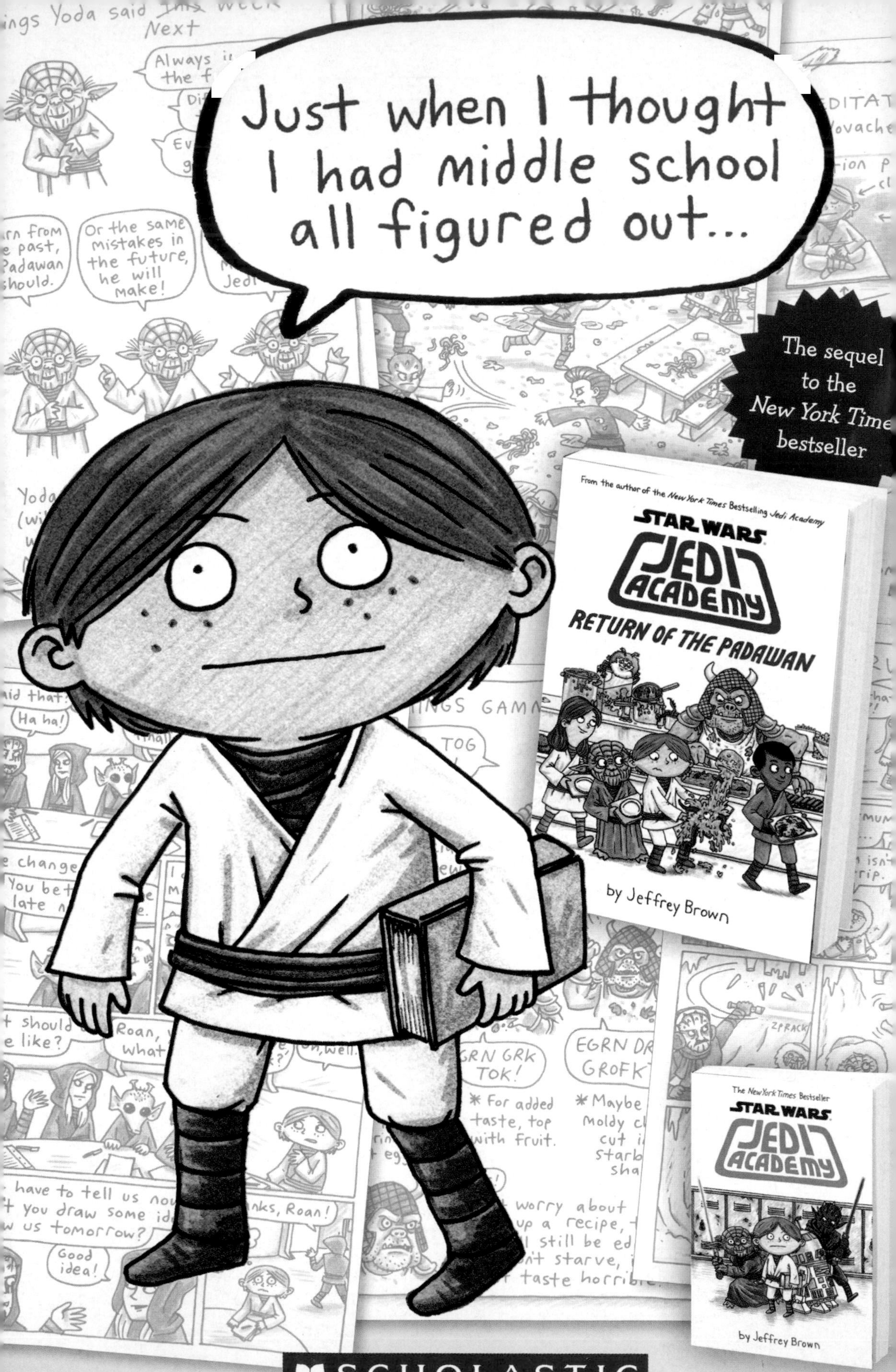
Just when I thought I had middle school all figured out...
The sequel to the New York Times bestseller
From the author of the New York Times Bestselling Jedi Academy
STAR WARS
JEDI ACADEMY
RETURN OF THE PADAWAN
by Jeffrey Brown
The New York Times Bestseller
STAR WARS
JEDI ACADEMY
by Jeffrey Brown